George Foster
and the 1977 Reds

ALSO BY MIKE SHANNON
AND FROM MCFARLAND

Baseball Books: A Collector's Guide (2008)

*Coming Back to Baseball: The Cincinnati Astros
and the Joys of Over-30 Play* (2005)

*Everything Happens in Chillicothe: A Summer in the Frontier League
with Max McLeary, the One-Eyed Umpire* (2004)

*Diamond Classics: Essays on 100 of the Best Baseball Books
Ever Published* (1989; paperback 2004)

WRITTEN BY MIKE SHANNON
ILLUSTRATED BY SCOTT HANNIG

*Hutch: Baseball's Fred Hutchinson
and a Legacy of Courage* (McFarland, 2011)

George Foster and the 1977 Reds
The Rise of a Slugger and the End of an Era

MIKE SHANNON

McFarland & Company, Inc., Publishers
Jefferson, North Carolina

ISBN (print) 978-0-7864-6451-7
ISBN (ebook) 978-1-4766-3664-1

LIBRARY OF CONGRESS CATALOGUING DATA ARE AVAILABLE

BRITISH LIBRARY CATALOGUING DATA ARE AVAILABLE

© 2019 Mike Shannon. All rights reserved

No part of this book may be reproduced or transmitted in any form or by any means, electronic or mechanical, including photocopying or recording, or by any information storage and retrieval system, without permission in writing from the publisher.

Front cover: Cincinnati Reds left fielder George Foster at bat (photograph by Clifton Boutelle)

Printed in the United States of America

McFarland & Company, Inc., Publishers
Box 611, Jefferson, North Carolina 28640
www.mcfarlandpub.com

For John Mansfield Shannon and Janice Veronneau Shannon, my beloved brother and sister-in-law who score extremely high in the categories which really count: courage, selflessness and love.

Table of Contents

Acknowledgments	ix
Introduction	1
1. The 1976 World Series: A Subdued Celebration	7
2. Spring Training 1977: Human Nature and Hubris	14
3. April 1977: A Pair of Slow Starts	27
4. May 1977: Getting Untracked	47
5. June 1977: Gaining Momentum	74
6. July 1977: Spreading the Souvenirs Around	105
7. August 1977: "Doctor Foster's no imposter"	127
8. September–October 1977: Getting Over the Hump	149
9. Fall 1977 and Beyond: The Rest of the Story	171
Appendix A. Log of George Foster's 52-Home Run Season in 1977	189
Appendix B. Statistical Breakdown of the 52 Home Runs Hit by George Foster in 1977	192
Appendix C. George Foster's Career Home Runs in Perspective	194
Appendix D. Single-Season Home Run Leaders for Every Major League Franchise	196
Bibliography	199
Index	201

The Making of a Foster Homer

The amazing thing is not
What he did with Welch's fastball
(Naked at the waist on three and oh)
But what he did to get it:
Pressing down with bat and hand
The paths of chin high screamers past
As if to say with blatant dare:
"Get that down, and you'll be sorry."

[*The Mantle-Mays Controversy Solved.*
Catcher Press, 1982.]

Acknowledgments

As always, a lot of people helped me with this book, and I must thank them here. Jerry Dowling, Chris Eckes, John Erardi, Greg Gajus, Scott Hannig, and Kostya Kennedy all supplied some fascinating information about George Foster or Reds baseball, and their contributions will be apparent to the reader. I spent ten years working on the book, and one reason it took so long was that I had to keep publishing *Spitball: The Literary Baseball Magazine*. Without the help of the following people, that task would have been even more time consuming and a lot less fun that it was: fiction editor Mark Schraf, artist and graphic designer Donnie Pollard, book review editor Tom Eckel, illustrator Richard Tomasic, CASEY Award Committee members Jack Greiner and Doug King, BALLZAK the Magnificent (aka Steve Blessinger), and the manager of the website www.spitballmag.com Zach Sanzone. I must also thank a group of people who helped just by being great friends: Bob Carson, Jim Crowley, Reid Duffy, Chris Felix, Deron Grothaus, Jerry Hazelbaker, Anne Jewell, Michael Leahy, Jon Libbert, Charles Mandel, Brian Mueller, Greg Rhodes, Billy Roebel, Scott Schmidt, Jeff Singleton, John Skurkay, Charlie Spears, Al Turnbull, Fred Zigler, and Joe Zureick. Also, Mark Fletcher went out of his way to provide the great photo of Foster in a White Sox uniform.

I have a large and wonderful family who is always tolerant of my passion for baseball and supportive of my writing, and it would be the height of ingratitude not to mention them here. So I thank Laura and Jeff Smiley, Susie and Lyle Klemmt, John and Janice Shannon, and Tim and Carla Shannon. I could not be prouder of my children, all of whom are smarter and more talented than I: Meg, Casey, Mick, Babe, and Nolan Ryan; and I tip my cap to their wonderful spouses or "significant others" who've joined the Shannon clan: Chris Kaholz, Keith Schneider, Mel Shannon (nee Sell), and Hassan Al Atat. And those marvelous grandkids! Maeve, McKenna, Aidan, Evie Quinn, Ronan, Finleigh, and Fiona. Most of all, I must thank my beautiful wife and "soul mate," Kathy Dermody Shannon. As I tell her all the time, "she made my life," and all my dreams have come true under her watch.

Acknowledgments

From a professional standpoint, I am indebted to three people without whom the book would never have been written. It's almost inconceivable that a baseball book can be written today without the author continually consulting the greatest and most useful baseball website in existence, Baseball Reference, and as it was of immense help to me in the writing of this book, I thank its founder, Sean Forman.

Ten years is a long time for a publisher to wait on a book, and I am grateful that McFarland was willing to wait that long for this one. But I wasn't really surprised that they did, for I have known for a long time that the people who work at McFarland are publishing major leaguers, one and all. In particular, I must thank Amy Donley for checking up on me and vice president and editorial director Steve Wilson for his patience and encouragement. A few kind words help tremendously when the end of a book writing project seems far off, and Steve sent me more than a few such words.

And, finally, I must thank Bob Hertzel, the *Cincinnati Enquirer* Reds beat man, who was there every day of the 1977 baseball season with pen and notebook in hand. Hertzel did a first-class job covering the team, and this book could not have been written without the record he left behind in the pages of the *Enquirer*. Thanks, Bob. I hope you, of all people, enjoy this trip back to 1977.

Introduction

Passion for any field of human endeavor can blind those under its spell to the fact that others do not share (and are furthermore completely under no obligation to share) that same consuming interest; meaning that the uninitiated also lack the knowledge of that field which naturally accrues to the devoted. In this matter, baseball is no different from any other subject. What most brought this tenet clearly home to me was the Johnny Bench exhibition staged a few years ago at the Cincinnati Reds Hall of Fame and Museum. Bench is almost universally acknowledged to have been the best all-around catcher in baseball history; he is also alive and well, enjoying retirement and making numerous public appearances. Nevertheless, when asked about the educational value of dedicating so much space and effort to such a well-known, perhaps even over-exposed, practically contemporary player, museum director of guest services Chris Eckes begged to differ. "Oh, no," he said, "it's not a waste of time to publicize his career. Half of the school kids who are visiting the exhibit have never heard of Johnny Bench before."

Thus, to lament ignorance of Bench's greatness on the part of anyone, even those who are born and go on to live in the spacious reaches of terra firma appropriated by the Cincinnati ballclub, is to decry the human condition itself, a fruitless exercise; for long before Shelley penned *Ozymandias*, the poets have reminded us of the vanity and impermanence of both power and fame.

What then of George Foster, the regular left fielder of Cincinnati's redoubtable "Big Red Machine" once it really got into gear starting in the middle of the 1970s? Is it reasonable to expect his to be a household name any more than that of Paul Householder, the speedy switch-hitter who succeeded Foster in the left field garden of Riverfront Stadium and then quickly played the public's memory of him into near-oblivion?

The question boils down to the obvious truth that Foster falls between Householder and Bench in the continuum of achievement on the major league level with correspondingly similar positions as regards their fame and the respect accorded them by the baseball cognoscente. Less obvious to the latter and not at all understood by the ordinary citizen and casual baseball fan is how much closer Foster is to baseball royalty (represented by Johnny Bench) than to its serfs; i.e., players of Householder's caliber. In sports parlance, and as Reds fans discovered too late, Householder "couldn't carry Foster's jock." He couldn't tote Foster's black bat either (but few players could during George's prime). On the other hand, Foster was a great hitter, a record-setting player, and, like teammates Bench, Pete Rose, and Joe Morgan, a winner of a National League Most Valuable Player Award. In 1978 Foster became only the fourth player in baseball history (along with Ty Cobb, Babe Ruth, and Joe Medwick) to unilaterally lead his league in RBI three seasons in a row (Honus Wagner lead the NL in RBI in 1921 and 1922 but tied George Kelly for the most RBI in 1920). Foster led the National League in home runs three consecutive years (1976–78); and he entered the 1982 season having led both leagues for the previous six seasons in RBI with 671 and having hit more home runs (198) than any other player except Mike Schmidt (221). This is the kind of hitting dominance that requires national sports magazines to put a photo of such a player on their covers and engenders discussion about that player eventually becoming an elected resident of Baseball's Valhalla in Cooperstown, New York. In fact, Foster did grace the cover of *Sports Illustrated*'s baseball issue for 1978, along with Rod Carew of the Minnesota Twins; and in that issue writer Jim Kaplan declared: "Carew is assured of a place in the Hall of Fame, even if he never gets another hit; if Foster has a couple more seasons like '77, he'll join him in Cooperstown." (Kaplan's hesitancy in regard to Foster was mirrored by that *Sports Illustrated* cover, which centered Carew, sitting on a stool, but staged Foster standing behind and peeking around him.)

The feat Kaplan was referring to, of course, was the 52 home run/149 RBI work sheet which Foster turned in for the 1977 National League campaign; and it turned out to be, despite Kaplan's subjunctive reference to the possibility of more of the same, Foster's only such effort. It was Foster's career year and such a monster performance that few other players have created with their peak season as great a differential between their typical and career-best years. To appreciate what Foster did in 1977 we need merely consider the fact that only four other National League sluggers had previously hit 50 or more home runs in a season (Hack Wilson; Johnny Mize; Ralph Kiner, twice; and Willie Mays, twice), with the latest 50-home run season having come in 1965, compliments of the incomparable Mr. Mays. In addition, Foster missed joining another exclusive NL club by a single RBI. Prior to 1977 only Rogers Hornsby, Hack Wilson, Mel Ott, Joe Medwick, and Tommy Davis had ever driven in 150 or more runs in a season, and Davis was the most recent of the bunch to do so, in 1962 (Hack Wilson was the only one of all these players to combine 50-home run and 150-RBI seasons in the same year, 1930).

Clearly, the batting barrage unleashed by George Foster in 1977 was a rare feat not only for him personally but for the era of major league baseball itself during which he played. It made Johnny Bench feel, in his own words, "inadequate," and prompted the gutter-tongued Pete Rose to exclaim, "George is fucking awesome!" Foster was rewarded with the NL MVP Award and plenty of other media recognition, yet the spotlight on him faded faster than a burst of fireworks against a night sky in July. Why? He was simply overshadowed by the superstars with super egos all around him: Rose, Bench, Morgan, and, until he was traded to Montreal, Tony Perez. In Cincinnati even the Reds' silver-haired, grandfatherly manager, Sparky Anderson, was considered to be more of a baseball celebrity than Foster; and with all these media darlings constantly sucking the very air out of the locker room with their endless banter, bragging, needling, cajoling, predictions, and (from Anderson) quasi–Stengelese ramblings, Foster was able to take only a few shallow breaths of the heady Mt. Olympus atmosphere that sustained his more extroverted, attention-greedy colleagues.

It is also certainly true that Foster, by nature, was averse to self-promotion and the self-indulgent lifestyle that so many successful pro athletes adopt as an entitlement.

Foster was born into a rural Southern matriarchal religious household, and even though his mother moved the family from Alabama to California when he was ten years old, his personality and values—solid as a Louisville Slugger—had already been formed by his early environment. Shy, humble, and introspective, Foster as a young professional ballplayer preferred a quiet evening of Bible reading and perhaps exercising (or the reading of a self-help book) to a night of drinking and carousing. Conspicuous for virtues rather than vices, he stuck out like a pair of bright red plaid bellbottoms. Foster's Boy Scout mentality—it was not a pose—amused and astonished teammates, especially the fun-loving ones like Pete Rose who incredulously told a reporter, "You want to know who he [George] took to Hawaii for that Superstar TV show? His mother!"

Despite walking such a straight line, Foster suffered from doubts that never seem to afflict the typically cocky, self-absorbed major leaguer. He got help with this problem during a demotion to the minor leagues in Indianapolis when he consulted with a psychologist who taught him to practice techniques of positive visualization, but a residual lack of self-confidence on some level made him years later a poor candidate to don the mantle of franchise savior of the New York Mets, who played after all in the media capitol of the world.

Whether from a lack of ability, a lack of confidence, a stubborn adherence to his own understanding of what his role on the ballclub should be, or some combination of these factors, Foster remained pretty much a one-dimensional player. He was a high-average slugger and RBI machine ... not a hot shot base-stealer or fancy glove man; although he made more than a couple of outstanding plays (catches and throws) in left field over the years. Risking injury by aggressively sliding into bases or crashing into outfield walls made no sense to Foster since an injury was likely to take his big bat out of the lineup, yet such sensible caution did not play well with blue-collar Reds fans used to the kamikaze ways of Rose who wouldn't think twice about running over a good friend blocking home plate in order to win a ball game (as he ran over Ray Fosse to win the 1970 All-Star Game for the National League). Never mind the fact that Foster won the 1978 All-Star Game with his bat, Reds fans seemed to punish him more for what he wasn't good at than to give him credit for what he excelled at. Things got so bad that prior to the 1980 season Foster hired a public-relations agency to improve his image and to help him "gain the recognition for the things I've done." Judging by the "good riddance" attitude of many Reds fans to the trade of Foster to the Mets, the agency's campaign met with little success.

Hitting 52 home runs in one season in 1977 was a big deal. It put Foster in the company of Babe Ruth, Jimmie Foxx, Hank Greenberg, Mickey Mantle, and Roger Maris, in addition to that of their eminent National League counterparts; and the feat would not be repeated by a hitter in either league until 1991, when the Yankees' Cecil Fielder smashed 51 homers to join the still-at-that-time exclusive club. No player in the National League reached the 50-homer summit until 1998 when Mark McGwire shattered the single-season home run record by blasting a tainted total of 70 home runs. This means, in other words, that George Foster was the only player in either league to hit 50 or more home runs in a single season for a period of two decades: the entire 1970s and 1980s. Foster never received proper credit for his gargantuan season for the reasons outlined above, and his achievement is even less valued today in the aftermath of the steroids or PED (perform enhancing drug) era. During that disgusting period, ten additional batters hit 50 or more homers in a single year and long-standing, honestly-set, revered records were technically bested. But at least half of those new members of the club cheated to gain admittance—Ken Griffey, Jr., and Jim Thome have never been suspected of cheating—and would not have been a good bet to hit 50 homers in a season without the aid of PEDs; excepting Mark McGwire and Alex Rodriquez, who might have reached 50 on their natural talent and strength.

Legitimately speaking, then, George Foster remained the last player to hit 50 or more home runs in a National League season until 2017 when Giancarlo Stanton hit 59 for the Florida Marlins. Some observers suspect that Stanton's barrage of homers, as well as that of the New York Yankees' Aaron Judge who hit 52 in 2017, his rookie season, was made possible in part by a juiced-up baseball. Whether that is the case or not is beyond the scope of this discussion; and it suffices to point out that the subject of this book, George Foster, remains the single-season home run champion of the Cincinnati Reds ballclub; for his 52-home run season of 1977 withstood even the challenges of the players who suited up for the Reds during the steroids era. And while Reds teams of recent vintage have featured some pretty fair country hitters on the roster in players such as Adam Dunn, Jay Bruce, Joey Votto, and Adam Duvall, Foster's home run total of 1977 must look as reachable to them as one of the lakes on the moon. As for McGwire, Sammy Sosa, Barry Bonds, and the rest of their interloping ilk, they owe apologies to Foster, to Fielder, and to their brethren, who conquered one of baseball's most challenging peaks the honest, old-fashioned way. Since no apology will be forthcoming from the cheaters, I am happy, with this book, to celebrate Foster's 1977 season and to give him what he worked so hard to earn, the long-overdue recognition inherent in the title: George Foster: Cincinnati Reds Home Run King.

It goes without saying that the story of George Foster's great year in 1977 is also a Cincinnati Reds story. The two are intertwined and inseparable. Foster was integral to the team's rise and maturation, at last, after a half decade of frustration, into back-to-back World Champions. He was key to a very good team's transformation into a dynastic powerhouse, known forever after as the Big Red Machine. The irony for Foster is that he blossomed into a great player when the Big Red Machine stumbled and faltered. He became a superstar as the team's core of other stars, who had always out shone him, dimmed a bit. Thus, while 1977 was Foster's triumphant, transcendent season, it was a disaster for the Cincinnati Reds and a huge disappointment for their fans. This dichotomy has also worked against Foster and the regard in which his spectacular season has been held. The 1977 season was a bad time in Cincinnati. It was the summer of disillusionment when the Big Red Machine's aura of invincibility slowly faded. It was most unfortunate, but it was that painful unraveling which served as backdrop for the most accomplished season ever turned in by a Cincinnati Reds hitter.

1

The 1976 World Series
A Subdued Celebration

On the cold and damp night of October 21, 1976, a home-made banner hanging from a railing in the upper deck of New York's refurbished Yankee Stadium read "YOU CAN'T LOVE A MACHINE." As Cincinnati Reds reliever Will McEnaney began to throw his warm-up pitches before the start of the bottom half of the ninth inning, George Foster who stood in left field, his mind racing and his heart bursting, would have disagreed. Minutes before, Foster's teammates had sealed the fate of the Yankees, putting a gigantic "4" on the scoreboard and widening the Reds lead to 7–2 in this fourth game of the 1976 World Series. The crusher had been a one-out three-run home run, yanked into the left field seats by Johnny Bench just over the glove of the Yankees' leaping left fielder Roy White. Bench had connected against Dick Tidrow, who'd come on in relief of starter Ed Figueroa; after Figueroa had walked Tony Perez and designated hitter Dan Driessen. Tidrow had retired Foster on a fly ball to center—George had just gotten under it—but he didn't fool Bench. No, Bench had put a good swing on an outside fastball and he'd made the Yankees pay dearly.

As regulars for the past two years on a team that was poised to pull off a four-game sweep and be crowned back-to-back World Champions, Foster and Bench now enjoyed a certain equality of status that had been a long time in coming for George, but Foster was still awed by Bench's performance. Who wouldn't have been? The three-run homer in the top of the ninth was Bench's second of the game. He'd hit a two-run shot in the fourth inning, so that together the two homers accounted for five of the Reds' seven runs. Foster had contributed too, as his fourth-inning single immediately prior to Bench's first homer had driven home Joe Morgan and tied the game at one apiece, and Foster could still feel a glow at the thought of that solid rap to left. But this was Johnny's night and Johnny's World Series too. Bench had not had a typically great "Johnny Bench year," true, but like most great players he'd turned it on when it counted the most. He had to be batting over .500 for the Series, and the writers would surely name him the MVP. He deserved it, and Foster looked forward to being one of Bench's first teammates to congratulate him.

After McEnaney delivered his final warm-up and the Reds infield tossed the ball around on its way back to the mound, Foster reminded himself to get off the field quickly after the final out. The Yankees were participants in the World Series for the first time since 1964, and their rabid fans who'd become spoiled by the franchise's historical dominance would not be satisfied with the moral victory of the team having reached the Series. Anything less than another World Championship, the birthright of Yankee fans, would be regarded as an ignominious failure. Yankees fans were as capable of boorish behavior as Yankees manager Billy Martin was capable of picking a fight. Their behavior in the rubber game (Game 5) of the American League Championship Series against the Kansas City Royals had been disgraceful. They'd thrown bottles and all sorts of debris out of the stands and onto the field all game, even pelting Kansas City manager Whitey Herzog with a rotten tomato during the pre-game introductions. And then, after the Yankees had won the excruciatingly tense, exciting game and the series on a Chris Chambliss home run in the bottom of the ninth, they'd poured out of the grandstands like a swarm of souvenir-seeking, hero-lusting locusts. Chambliss had had to literally fight people off to get around the bases, and as he'd run the gauntlet of frenzied fans trying to rip the shirt off his back, other fans had ripped into the playing surface, uprooting home plate, stealing bases, and scooping up hunks of sod and handfuls of clay. In the following days it had taken hundreds of man hours and approximately $100,000 to get the diamond into playable condition for Game 3 of the World Series. In view of that riotous performance, Reds players had been warned to get off the diamond immediately after the final pitch of Game 4 should it conclude the Series.

Despite the Yankees' desperate position, a sellout crowd of 56,700 had shown up for Game 4, hoping to witness the beginning of a miracle Bronx Bombers comeback. Bench's home run in the top of the inning had sent thousands of them heading for the exits and darkened the mood of those determined to stay to the bitter end. Back-up catcher Otto Velez, pinch-hitting for good field-no hit shortstop Jim Mason, was going to lead off the ninth inning for New York. Foster glanced to his left to see how deep Cesar Geronimo, the Reds' center fielder, was going to play Velez. Center field. That's the position the great Willie Mays had played; the same Willie Mays who'd been George's boyhood hero.

1. The 1976 World Series

Getting signed in 1968 by the San Francisco Giants out of El Camino Junior College had been a dream come true for Foster, just because the Giants were Mays' team. And then, just a year later, when Foster found himself for the first time playing in the same outfield next to Mays … well, it had been akin to what a surrealistic LSD trip must be like; although Foster neither drank nor smoked nor chewed, much less used illegal drugs of any kind. Looking back towards the plate and noticing camera crew members beating a hasty retreat, probably towards the Reds' clubhouse, Foster probably wondered if Willie was watching the game on television somewhere. Whenever Foster thought about Mays he was reminded of another Giants outfielder he'd played with, Bobby Bonds. Foster had roomed with Bonds, and it was Bonds even more than Mays who'd gone out of his way to draw the super-shy, diffident Foster out of his shell. Bonds would drag the green Foster along to sports banquets and rubber-chicken dinners and even gradually pushed the young player into standing up once in a while and saying a few words. Foster always remembered his friends with genuine affection, and it was having to leave them that had caused him to feel so devastated in 1971 when he'd learned that he'd been traded to the Reds. He would have laughed if someone had asked him now how in the world had he thought getting traded to the Cincinnati Reds was the worst thing that could ever have happened to him.

Foster had cups of coffee in 1969 and '70 with the San Francisco Giants, the major league team he originally signed with. He was thrilled to be on the same team as Willie Mays, his childhood hero. After appearing in 36 games with the Giants in 1971, he was traded for shortstop Frank Duffy to the Cincinnati Reds. At first upset by the trade, he later realized what a tremendous blessing it was. In a total of 54 games with the Giants he batted .279 with four home runs.

Foster tried to get his mind back on the game as Velez eagerly dug in to face McEnaney. The left-handed McEnaney had come on for the Reds with two outs in the seventh inning, in relief of starter Gary Nolan. Unlike the fidgety Nolan who constantly tried to loosen his chronically injured shoulder between pitches, McEnaney was a fast worker with a smooth, compact delivery. He got the sign, wound up, and fired away. He struck out Velez on four pitches, strike three coming on a swing and a miss at a curveball over the heart of the plate. Two outs to go! If Foster had looked past Geronimo to right field, he would have seen his roommate Ken Griffey stationed there; trying, as George was trying, to keep his excitement under control until the final out. George had never met a finer person than Griffey, and he felt truly honored to call Kenny a close personal friend. The bonds between Foster and Griffey had been formed in Indianapolis during the summer of 1973 when the two players had first started rooming together. Having been assigned to the Triple A Indians out of Reds spring training that year, after he'd already played some in the big leagues since 1969, seemed like a demotion; and the demoralized Foster had almost quit the game. A "We'll have no quitting in this family" pep talk from his mother, sessions with a psychologist in Indy designed to boost his confidence, and the friendship of Griffey had saved Foster and his career. What a friend George had in Griffey, and what a ballplayer Griffey was! The left-handed hitting Griffey was a tough out, a perennial .300 hitter. He could run like a deer and he fielded his position expertly. Griffey, who never seemed to make a mistake, simply did not get the credit he deserved. The public may not have appreciated him, but his teammates certainly did, especially Foster. Driving in runs was Foster's main job on the Reds, and it seemed to George that every other time he came to bat, there was his roomie on base, waiting for George to knock him in.

George moved a few steps closer to the infield because a left-handed batter was stepping into the batter's box: New York's center fielder and leadoff hitter, Mickey Rivers. Foster was on his toes because Rivers, hitting to the opposite field, had already flied out to him twice in the game. Mickey was the quintessential table setter and a fast runner who loved to bunt for a base hit, so his speed had to be respected. Before the Series had begun Reds manager Sparky Anderson had decided to ask third baseman Pete Rose to cheat in a few steps whenever Rivers came to bat to discourage him from even attempting to bunt. Rose had done more than that; for four games he had moved in so close to home plate every time Rivers approached the plate that he was, in ballplayer jargon, practically living inside Rivers' jock strap. And he'd often done so with that big stupid "I dare you" grin on his face. That Rose … he was crazy! But the tactic had worked splendidly, limiting Rivers to three hits in 17 at bats and one run scored. George couldn't help but smile as he watched the cocky Rose settle into his tiger-like crouch, only yards away from the skin area around home plate, and while he didn't feel sorry for the Yankees, he was glad that a competitor as consistently gung-ho as Rose was on his side. Foster was not especially close to Rose, but he felt indebted to him nevertheless. Not for that goofy nickname "Yahtzee" (whatever that meant) that Rose had bestowed on him when he'd first joined the Reds back in 1971, but for making room for him in the starting lineup. In the first couple of weeks of the 1975 season the Reds had been getting no offense from the third base position, while Foster full of untapped potential was languishing on the bench half the time as a platoon player. Sparky had had the brainstorm of moving Rose from left field to third and giving Foster the chance to prove himself as the regular left fielder. Rose's response to the suggestion was, "When do you want me to start?" Rose had taken a million ground balls and become more than a decent third baseman, as Mickey Rivers realized all too well. Taking aim at the drawn-in Rose, Rivers swung at the first pitch and lined it foul down the third base line. Rose didn't even flinch. McEnaney threw another fastball and Rivers also hit this one hard and fair, but straight to Rose, who snatched it out of the air as if it were a $100 bill. Rose fired the ball across the diamond to second baseman Joe Morgan and after it came back to him, Rose didn't even deign to touch it with his bare hand. To give it back to McEnaney he flipped the ball to him straight out of his glove.

The Yankees were down to their last out, and if they were going to keep the game going it would be up to left fielder Roy White; 0–4 on the night with the four at bats all having come against Nolan. As the switch-hitting White approached the plate, Yankees catcher Thurman Munson stepped into the on-deck circle. If anybody was hotter than Bench it was his counterpart Munson, who was 4–4 in the game and six for his last six at bats. While the Reds felt they had the best catcher in baseball on their team, they respected Munson. He was old school tough, a street fighter, and had suffered through the lean years in the Bronx as the Yankees had slowly built the team back into a pennant winner. The five-run lead felt pretty safe, but everybody in gray and red uniforms felt that they'd just as soon not see Munson come to bat again. In baseball you never knew. Munson couldn't tie the game, even with a home run, but it was always best not to let the other guys start thinking they might be able to beat you.

Munson never got another chance. Batting right-handed, White took a low fastball for ball one and a high outside fastball for ball two. McEnaney fired another low fastball, and White swung at it, lifting it into left-center field. Drifting about 20 feet to his left, Foster settled under the can of corn and snapped his glove shut around the last baseball to be used in the 1976 World Series. McEnaney had set down the Yankees in the ninth inning on nine pitches. Illustrating the reliability of the Reds' bullpen, he'd allowed one base runner, on a base on balls to Graig Nettles in the eighth, in two and a third innings. Unbeknownst to Foster, the final out was his eighth put out of the game, which tied a World Series record for outfielders first set in 1919 by another Reds fly hawk, Edd Roush. The Cincinnati Reds were World Champions again and the first National League team to win back-to-back titles since the 1922 New York Giants. George Foster was so happy, so elated, so proud, and so filled with gratitude towards all the people who'd helped him get to this point in his career ... people like Giants scout George Genovese who signed him to his first pro contract, his manager at Indianapolis Vern Rapp, Reds hitting coach Ted Kluszewski ... that all he could do was grin from ear and ear ... and sprint as fast as his long legs could carry him for the safety of the Reds' dugout and their adjoining clubhouse where a rather subdued, bittersweet celebration was underway.

As the Reds filed into their clubhouse they hugged and clapped each other on the back. The obligatory champagne was there and they helped themselves to it, spraying around the room as much of it as they drank, as was the custom with World Series winners. They were happy, of course, because they'd just defended their title, something that is always harder to do than winning in the first place. And they'd done so in a convincing manner, without a loss in the post-season, sweeping the Philadelphia Phillies in the National League Championship Series before sweeping the Yankees in the World Series to win all seven games they'd played. Winning in 1975 had felt like a break through. They'd finally proved, after disappointments in 1970, 1972, and 1973, that they had the stuff of champions. This repeat, and the fashion in which they'd pulled it off, had people immediately talking about them in terms of being one of the best teams in baseball history. Some observers were even beginning to compare these Reds favorably to the team most often accounted the greatest of all time: the 1927 New York Yankees. So they were as proud as new parents and exhausted too, for it's always a "long season" (as Reds pitcher-turned-writer Jim Brosnan had pointed out decades before), especially for the two teams left standing for the final confrontation. But something else besides elation and relief was there in the room, something that seemed out of place in a celebrating baseball clubhouse.

In one extremely important sense 1976 was the final baseball season of its kind: the last not to be roiled by free agency. Baseball executives could see free agency coming over the horizon like an unstoppable storm, and while a few of them whose teams resided in big markets may have regarded the new freedom granted to players as an opportunity, many other execs were worried. What would free agency do to the economic structure governing the industry and how would their teams compete for the best players who suddenly were in a position to demand and get increasingly exorbitant salaries? One executive with a clearly defined position was Cincinnati's Bob Howsam, the man who had assembled the Big Red Machine through shrewd trades and the development of both a productive farm system and an organizational-wide

1. The 1976 World Series

operational philosophy that addressed every facet of the business and the game on the field, even down to a ban on facial hair for the players. In Howsam's opinion free agency meant quite frankly the death of professional baseball. If bidding wars for players' services were to become the norm, baseball would quickly spend itself into bankruptcy and oblivion. Baseball had faced bidding wars in the past, but long ago an instrument devised to curtail players' excessive demands and owners' profligate spending had been adopted: i.e., the reserve clause, which bound a player to his team basically in perpetuity (as long as the team still wanted him), one year at a time. Through the reserve clause, a team had the right at the end of each year to renew a player's contract for another year. Previously, both owners and players had understood the clause to apply forever, year after year, but a court had ruled that the clause meant one year, and one year only. After that, a player was free to offer his services to whomever he pleased. Now that the courts had essentially abrogated the reserve clause, it was a whole new ballgame, and the balance of power had shifted dramatically in favor of the players.

Howsam believed that small market teams such as his Reds were simply financially incapable of joining the coming new system of auction-style player procurement. The Reds did not have and would never have virtually unlimited amounts of money to throw at players who were free to offer their services to the highest bidder, and it would be the height of irresponsibility for him to join the bidding wars that were about to erupt in the off-season. No, the Reds would hold the line, come what may; they would continue to live within their budget, attempt to hold ticket price increases to a minimum, and remain solvent. They would try to maintain their hard-earned status by doing the things that had gotten them to where they were, the pinnacle of success; but Howsam realized that the odds were now stacked against him and the Reds. During the celebration in the Reds' clubhouse when an interviewer asked for his reaction to the Reds' victory, Howsam glumly mused, "We may never see what we had before." The players were not as pessimistic or as melancholy as Howsam, but even some of them sensed that the moment might be not only fleeting but unrepeatable. Reds second baseman Joe Morgan, who would win his second consecutive National League Most Valuable Player Award for his performance during the 1976 regular season, said, "How can you have a much better team than this one?" It was a fitting if unintended requiem.

2

Spring Training 1977
Human Nature and Hubris

On October 22, 1976, the day after the World Series ended, more than 10,000 fans jammed Cincinnati's downtown Fountain Square and its environs in 39-degree weather to celebrate the Reds' victory over the storied New York Yankees in four straight games. (After the Reds' triumph over the Boston Red Sox in the 1975 World Series, the Fountain Square celebratory crowd had been estimated at 30,000.) Reds fans would bask in the warmth of the team's repeat championship for months to come and optimistically look forward to spring 1977 and to what they assumed would be the beginning of another successful defense of the Reds' crown as the best team in baseball. However, while Cincinnati sports fans passed the time following the exploits of the NFL Bengals and the University of Cincinnati and Xavier University basketball teams, two Reds player movements over the winter would prove disastrous: one a free agent defection and the other an ill-advised trade.

The free-agent defector was Don Gullet, a left-handed pitcher who'd been the Reds' ace the past four seasons. A broad-shouldered farm boy out of Lynn, Kentucky, Gullet had been a three-sport star at McKell High School in South Shore, Kentucky. He'd once scored 47 points in a McKell basketball game and 72 points in one high school football contest on 11 touchdown runs and six kicked extra points. Gullet shone even brighter as a high school pitcher, rarely losing and once pitching a perfect game, striking out 20 of 21 batters. The Reds drafted him in the first round of the 1969 amateur draft and signed him to a $25,000 bonus. He spent one year in the minor leagues, at single-A Sioux Falls, striking out 87 batters in 78 innings. He made the big league club the next year out of spring training, on nothing but a blazing fastball, control, and a precocious amount of poise. Those things ... and the Reds' desperate need for pitching.

Sparky Anderson fell in love with Gullet from the beginning and could hardly refrain from singing the kid's praises every chance he got. In fact,

2. Spring Training 1977

Anderson quickly branded Gullet a future Hall of Famer with one caveat: as long as the quiet, conservative, God-fearing young man could stay healthy. And that indeed turned out to be the gist of the matter. Gullet became a starting pitcher in 1971 and turned in a year that stamped him as the stud of the rotation: a 16–6 record for a league-leading winning percentage of .727 and an ERA of 2.64. A bout with hepatitis caused Gullet to slump to a 9–10 record the next year, and starting in mid-season 1975 a succession of injuries slowed him down: a broken left thumb, a muscle spasm in his neck, inflammation in the muscles in his left shoulder, a dislocated ankle tendon. Despite these setbacks, Gullet always managed to win far more games than he lost, and his season records (1973–76) of 18–8, 17–11, 15–4, and 11–3 kept him at or near the top of the National League winning percentage rankings for pitchers every year. In fact, it was his dependable winning percentage that elevated him so highly in the estimation of his manager.

In 1974 after Gullet added a forkball to his repertoire in order to keep hitters from sitting on his fastball, Sparky Anderson voiced a laudatory assessment of his star pitcher. Referring to Gullet and the Reds' superstar catcher, Johnny Bench, he said, "It's the only Hall of Fame battery active in baseball today." The way Sparky saw it, "barring an injury, he [Gullet] is almost sure of making the Hall of Fame. With Gullet's body and the way he stays in shape, I know he's going to pitch until he's at least 35. So, doing that you know he's going to win at least 250 games with the start he has. And anything over 250 has to rate a pitcher serious consideration for the Hall of Fame." Anderson's often exaggerated player assessments aside, his prediction about Gullet was not far-fetched at all. At the end of the 1976 season Gullet was only 25 years old, yet he'd already accumulated 91 major league wins against only 44 losses. The three greatest left-handed pitchers of the previous generation were Warren Spahn, Whitey Ford, and Sandy Koufax, and all three would be voted into the National Baseball Hall of Fame. None of them came close to producing the fast start turned in by Gullet. At the end of their age 25 seasons, their major league win totals were eight (Spahn), 27 (Ford), and 36 (Koufax).

Gullet had always hated the process of negotiating a new contract, with good reason. Prior to free agency it had been an almost totally one-sided process, with all the power residing with the team owners and their representatives (usually the teams' general managers). Beginning in 1976 the scales had suddenly tipped in favor of the players. If a player was dissatisfied with his ballclub's final offer, he could invoke his newly acquired right to not sign his contract and play for the same amount of money the ballclub had paid him the previous year (or at a maximum pay cut of 20 percent). The payoff for the player to do what has become known as "playing out his option [year]" came at the end of the season, when he would become a free agent and be entitled to sign a contract with any team he wished. This is what Gullet had done in 1976.

Gullet had hired an agent, and a very effective one at that, to handle his contract negotiations: Jerry Kapstein. Reds GM Bob Howam and his lieutenant, the icy Dick Wagner, abhorred free agency and the new breed of business- and law-savvy professionals represented by the likes of Kapstein, and so no one was surprised when Gullet's contract could not get done. Media accounts reported that the problem was the Reds' balking at Kapstein's request for a multi-year deal for his client, even though the team had caved in and awarded the franchise's first multi-year deal (of two years) to Johnny Bench. The truth was that Reds management had decided Gullet was too much of a health risk to sign for more than one year. They also believed that the team could win without a pitcher who, after all, had accounted for only 26 wins in their two World Championship runs, just concluded: an average of 13 wins per year. Thus, a few weeks after the '76 World Series, Don Gullet became the first Reds player to sign with another team as a free agent. More than a dozen teams bid for Gullet's services, but in the end the New York Yankees landed the prize, giving Gullet a six-year deal worth $2 million. By comparison, Pete Rose ($185,000), Joe Morgan ($200,000), and Johnny Bench ($235,000) had all signed and played the 1976 season for considerably less. Gullet departed Cincinnati with a career winning percentage of .674 (91–44), which remains to this day the team record.

The trade that sent first baseman Tony Perez and relief pitcher Will McEnaney to the Montreal Expos on December 16 was anything but an early Christmas present for Reds fans. Perez was one of the most popular players in team history, and that fact alone should have given team management pause. But Perez was not just popular with the fans; he was the most popular player among the players, especially the young Latins who looked up to him and who looked towards him for fatherly advice. Perez was also the glue that held the Reds' clubhouse together, the "agitator" who kept big egos from becoming too swollen, the friend to all, who bridged relationships between other players who might have feuded with each other minus Perez's ability to defuse potential conflicts with his humor and endearing accent.

As Greg Rhodes explains in *Big Red Dynasty: How Bob Howsam and Sparky Anderson Built the Big Red Machine*, Reds management simply and severely underestimated Perez's intangible value to the ball club. In addition, Howsam acted under the same philosophy that had led a decade earlier to the other horrendous trade in team history, that of Frank Robinson to the Baltimore Orioles for pitcher Milt Pappas: the idea that it's better to trade a player a year or two too early than a year or two too late. (GM Bill DeWitt's rationale for the trade was encapsulated in his response to a sportswriter's pointing out that Robinson was only 30. "Yeah, but he's an old 30," said DeWitt. In his first year with Baltimore, the old Robinson won the AL Triple Crown, was unanimously voted league MVP, and led the Orioles to their first World Championship.) At the time of the trade, Perez was 34 years old, so Howsam appeared to have time on his side. But in planning for the future by making the trade, the Reds hurt their chances to win immediately, to take a third consecutive World Championship: a blunder that no major league team would make today.

There were other, extenuating circumstances that prompted Howsam's move. Just as the Reds in 1965 thought they had an able replacement for Frank Robinson's big bat in that of first/third baseman Deron Johnson, the Reds of 1976–77 believed that Dan Driessen, a part-time player and Anderson's favorite pinch-hitter since 1973, would be a capable replacement for Perez. While Driessen had batted only .247 with seven home runs and 44 RBI during the 1976 regular season, his performance in the World Series (.357 with a home run and a pair of doubles) had impressed team management. Heading into 1977 at 25 years old, the Hilton Head (SC) native was a decade younger than Perez, and the Reds thought he was ready for full-time play. According to *Big Red Dynasty*, Perez had resented being platooned with the left-handed Driessen, even though only three other players (all at the top of the order) had accumulated more at bats in 1976 than Perez. For Rhodes' book Howsam presents himself as doing Perez a favor by trading him so that he could avoid a platoon situation and play regularly, which implies that the Reds were planning on increased platooning with Perez and Driessen had Perez remained with the club. In any case, Perez certainly did want to remain a full-time player, who would willingly accept days off only when he clearly needed a rest. Finally, financial considerations were probably as big a factor as anything else. Players were suddenly getting very expensive, and the Reds' roster was full of stars who expected their salaries to be significantly boosted now that the first free agents were reaping previously unheard-of windfalls. Perez was one of those players with his hand out, determined to have it weighted down with cash, and the Reds calculated on big savings by trading him elsewhere. In addition, Perez too, if unhappy with the salary the Reds were willing to pay him, would be able to file for free agency the following year, and if he went that route the Reds would lose him without being compensated. So, from all these perspectives, the trade appeared to make sense. In hindsight, it was a costly mistake.

The lucrative contracts handed out to the first free agent class in late

1976 whetted the appetites of Perez's former teammates, who had no problem voicing their concerns. When the Reds and Joe Morgan came to an impasse over money, the two-time MVP complained, "I can't tell you what management is thinking. And right now, I don't give a damn." Shortstop Dave Concepcion said, "I think a lot of Reds will play out options, including me, if I don't get my million." Even the laid back George Foster played some verbal hardball, saying, "If push comes to shove, I'm thinking about playing out my option." It was clear that, despite the Reds' determination not to participate in any bidding for other teams' free agents, in order to keep their own best players, they were going to have to loosen the purse strings and begin to offer multi-year deals to players other than bellwether Bench. By March 1977, Morgan, right fielder Ken Griffey, and Foster had all received three-year deals with substantial raises, and Concepcion had somehow gotten his million bucks, wrangling a five-year deal on his own after firing his agent, the redoubtable Kapstein. Pete Rose remained unsigned.

As for Foster, his remark was more ploy than threat. He'd worked hard and overcome a lot to prove himself to be not only a bona fide major leaguer and a player deserving of a regular starting job, but a key component of a championship ball club. He'd grown comfortable in Cincinnati and was not interested in going anywhere, except back to another World Series. And, while there was not a lot of talk about it in the media, with Perez gone Foster knew that it would be up to him, more than anyone else, to pick up the slack when it came to driving in runs, to be the dependable bat in the middle of the order that pitchers feared and the Reds could count on. "Yes, when I signed my three-year contract I knew I could go to another club and make more money," he said. "But I wouldn't be happy. So I decided to stay with Cincinnati for less money and be happy. In fact, I hope this club can stay together. I want to establish myself in Cincinnati, like Rose and Bench have done. I want to stay here."

When the Reds re-gathered in Tampa, Florida, in late February 1977, their training camp was flooded with as much confidence as sunshine. Even without their two departed key pieces, they could count seven returning All-Stars on their roster; far more than any other National League team and the same as the previous year, if one wanted to include the starting pitcher acquired in the Perez deal, left-hander Woodie Fryman, who had been the lone All-Star representative from the Montreal Expos. (Perez had also made the NL All-Star team and walked in his lone at-bat, as a replacement at first base for starter Steve Garvey.) In Fryman's biography in the Reds' 1977 media guide, substantially longer than those provided for the team's established stars, Bob Howsam said, "We needed another lefthanded starter, and in

Woodie, we have a fine pitcher who knows how to pitch. He should be a real asset to our organization." Fryman was an experienced professional, but his lifetime major league record of 105–119 with four clubs was nothing to write home about. It was a stretch to think that Fryman would be an adequate replacement for Gullet.

Another new face in Tampa was 6'4" right-handed reliever Dale Murray, also acquired from Montreal in the Perez deal. Murray had led the league in appearances in 1976 with 81 and had saved 13 games. His claim to fame which was extolled in the Reds' media guide was the record he'd set (during the live ball era) over a three-year period (1974–76) of having pitched the most consecutive innings without allowing a home run: 247.1. His record in 1976 was 4–9, but his ERA of 3.27 compared to Will McEnaney's 4.87 made him appear to be an improvement over the departed Reds reliever.

The Reds opened spring training play on March 12 in Bradenton against the Pittsburgh Pirates, but the first exhibition to stir up excitement came on March 15 when they met the Montreal Expos in Daytona Beach. Far more important than the outcome of the game was the chance for Reds players and Tony Perez to re-unite and renew their friendship and for Perez to tell his side of the story. "Every year I play less and less games. I supposed to be tired when I am not," he told Bob Hertzel, the *Cincinnati Enquirer*'s Reds beat man. "You have a good year, like I had, and you get traded like that. You have to feel something. I feel something. I no go in and say I want to be traded. I say I not gonna sit down and play 100 games. They put it like I ask for trade. I ask to play." Perez went on to say that he missed Joe Morgan and Pete Rose sorely; that Perez's wife Pituka missed Karolyn Rose; and that Perez's sons Victor and Eduardo missed "Little Pete," Pete Rose, Jr. The later feelings were mutual. When Rose, reminding Reds management through the press that he might walk if not offered a suitable contract, asked Pete Jr., where he wanted to go if they left the Queen City, Little Pete said, "Montreal." Why? "Because that's where Victor and Eduardo are."

Don Gullet's absence was felt too when the topic of conversation was Concepcion's contract. Why couldn't the Reds have given Gullet a two- or three-year deal when they saw fit to give a five-year deal to Concepcion? "It's different. Gullet is a pitcher," said the Venezuelan shortstop. "He can get hurt more easy than me. I want the long contract so I can be around Griffey, Foster, Morgan the next three years and guarantee we win the division all three years."

While the Reds A squad was playing in Daytona Beach, down in Dunedin the B squad took on one of baseball's newest teams, the expansion Toronto Blue Jays. Rose and Morgan, rounding into playing condition slowly, made their spring training debuts in the game, won by the Jays 9–8 "in 11 ridiculous innings." The next day before the Reds beat the New York Mets 7–4 in Tampa, Dan Driessen revealed that he wasn't feeling any pressure to replace Tony Perez. "I will do what Driessen can do, not what Perez can do," he said. "I can hit, run, and field." So far, in four games, Driessen was doing just fine, batting .500 (8–16) with two home runs and a triple. In the win over the Mets Foster turned in his best performance of the spring, going 3–4 with a pair of doubles.

On March 17, as the Houston Astros visited Al Lang Field in Tampa, the Reds upped the pressure on Pete Rose to sign by renewing his contract under the option year clause. By doing this the club was supposedly signaling that it would be okay with them if Rose became a free agent at the close of the 1977 season.

As befitting a two-time defending champion, the Reds were a hot ticket that spring. On Friday, March 18, they played and lost 6–4 to the Minnesota Twins in Orlando before their fifth consecutive road sellout crowd. Twins fans got to see two Reds hitters tearing the cover off the ball: Driessen, batting .550, and a young buck named Ray Knight, pasting the ball at a .524 clip. They'd rather have seen Johnny Bench, out with a sore left knee, and Pete Rose, sitting because of a sore elbow, which he'd woken up with one day in December. Back in Tampa the next day Cincinnati lost again to the Kansas City Royals 10–9. Sparky Anderson gave Hertzel a long interview, during which he expressed his desire to "stay with the Reds forever" and to surpass Walter Alston's 23-year tenure as manager of the Dodgers; a run which had ended with his retirement with four games left in the 1976 season. As expected, Dodgers coach Tommy Lasorda had immediately taken over for Alston. When asked about his penchant for relieving starting pitchers at the first sign of trouble, Anderson gave a lengthy reply that revealed his major worry for the upcoming season. "I don't like to go get 'em," he said. "They won't believe that. And I'll tell you something else the pitchers won't believe. I really care for my pitchers. I don't really care for my regulars because they'll take care of themselves. You just put them out there and let them play. But the pitchers are my real concern. I told [Reds pitching coach] Larry Sheppard the other day. 'We can win if we don't make mistakes in our pitching.' I really mean that. Pitching is what we have to be right in our decisions."

Continuing to stumble, the Reds lost to the Astros 10–8 on Monday, the 21st, in Cocoa; minor league second baseman Ron Oester's two errors contributing to the defeat. Anderson described the team's performance simply as "horrible." He later tried to alleviate the severity of his reaction by saying, "I'm only interested in conditioning the players, not in winning games."

On Wednesday the 23rd the Dodgers nipped the Reds 2–1 in Tampa, provoking the mini-headline over the box score in the *Enquirer*, "Enjoy It Now, L. A." The taunt implied that the Dodgers, who'd finished second to the Reds four times in the decade already, wouldn't win very often against their betters when the games counted. The encouraging part of the loss was the pitching of Santo Alcala, the 6'6" Dominican whose 11–4 record had made him one of seven Reds pitchers to have won in double figures in 1976. The Dodgers scored both runs off Alcala, but his surrendering only five hits over six innings demonstrated he was on track to make another major contribution in the upcoming season. The Mets' Tom Seaver also made news that day, involving the two teams expected to fight it out for the National League's West Division title. The Mets' refusal to compensate Seaver fairly and their classless airing of salary-negotiation dirty laundry in the newspapers had thoroughly soured the great pitcher who was so important to the Mets that he was known as "The Franchise." At this point, many people, including Seaver himself, had begun to think the unthinkable: that Seaver might be traded away from the team. Seaver, who had no-trade rights because of his tenure with the Mets, came right out and said that he would accept a trade to the Los Angeles Dodgers or the Cincinnati Reds. "It might be nice to know that I would pitch for a team that averaged five or six runs a game," he said.

The next day the Reds traveled to the Dodgers' famous training complex in Vero Beach where they won a slug fest 11–9. Back in Tampa the following day, the 25th, Woodie Fryman turned in another good outing, as the Reds edged the Minnesota Twins 2–1.

The strangest game of the spring came on the 27th when the Yankees stormed into Tampa to meet the Reds for the first and only time in Grapefruit League play for 1977. The Yankees were obviously so intent on winning what the Reds regarded as merely a glorified workout that the waggish Hertzel dubbed the meeting "Game 5 of a four-game World Series." The intensity with which the Yankees were going to play the exhibition became evident in the very first inning when catcher Thurman Munson attempted to steal second base. Perhaps Munson was still smarting from the remark Anderson made after the Series, when asked to compare the Series' two backstops. "Don't embarrass any catcher by comparing him to Johnny Bench," Sparky had said. At any rate, Bench threw the plodding Munson out easily, prompting Concepcion who applied the tag to say: "You crazy. You try to steal a base." Concepcion was only joking, but umpire Nick Colosi thought he was angry and stepped between Concepcion and Munson to prevent any further escalation. This move caused Munson to think that Concepcion *was* angry, which did make Munson want to fight. Back in their dugout, the Reds laughed at the mixup.

The day only got worse for the Yankees' great catcher. In the third he tagged and tried to score from third on a line drive to right field. Ken Griffey threw him out at home, Bench making an amazing "El Toro!" one-handed sweep tag. Later, when Morgan lofted a foul pop near the screen, Munson couldn't locate it. The newest Yankee, Don Gullet, came racing off the mound and was in position to make another amazing play, but at the last moment Munson called him off ... and then dropped the ball.

It wasn't only Munson who badly wanted to knock the Reds down to size. In the bottom of the tenth inning with the game tied 3–3, Yankees manager Billy Martin intentionally walked George Foster, a move rarely made in spring training games. Afterwards Anderson said, "By walking George, you could tell Billy wanted to stay around a while." Despite the hard feelings on exhibit, the game ended not with a bang but a "whimp-out." Rookie Ray Knight came to bat after the intentional walk to Foster. With utility outfielder Champ Summers on second base, Knight hit a single into center field where Reggie Jackson, nursing a sore arm, fielded it and held onto the ball. Summers pulled a hamstring rounding third but limped into home safely nevertheless with the game's winning run, as Jackson trotted off the field holding the baseball in his glove. After the game Anderson couldn't mask his feelings about Gullet, the former favorite son, who'd pitched fine: allowing seven hits and three runs in six innings of work. "I don't want to hear his name again," Sparky said. In a parting shot, Anderson implied that Gullet had abandoned the Reds over a difference of $20,000; a claim that was certainly ridiculously untrue.

As the Reds continued to lose more often than they won, Rose's contract status became the daily focus in the media. By March 30, negotiations were at a standstill; Rose and his agent, local lawyer Reuven Katz, asking for $400,000 per year, the Reds not budging past $325,000. With it beginning to look as if 1976 might be his final season in his home town, Rose shrewdly said he was dedicating the season to the fans. Responding to the Rose team's deadline of meeting his salary demand by Opening Day, tight-fisted Dick Wager responded: "If he wants to do that, perhaps he should buy the ball club and run it himself. Then he can pay himself whatever he wants.... At some point in this we have to decide whether one person is more important than the franchise, more important than the town, the ball park and the ball club." Rose responded by offering to let an arbitrator decide the matter, saying that he'd play the season for $50,000 if that's what the arbitrator thought was fair. Wagner, of course, declined the offer.

Sparky Anderson sprouted a few more gray hairs when Gary Nolan, a workhouse of the Reds' rotation in previous years, was raked for 15 hits and 11 runs in four innings by the Texas Rangers on March 29. During this shellacking, a blister the size of a silver dollar on Nolan's right foot burst. The foot remained extremely tender and would keep Nolan anchored to the bench as the regular season opened. The next day Johnny Bench finally got untracked and hit his first two home runs of the season, but the Reds lost another game, 6–4 to the Baltimore Orioles to run their record on the spring to 8–12. In a burst of bravado, Anderson shrugged off the loss, saying, "The guys we got are so good that they just want to get their work in down here. Hit and run. They don't even want to go out there in the games. I don't even feel like managing. It'll be different when we open up for real." The game's sportswriters agreed with Anderson. In a poll conducted by *The Sporting News* they picked the Reds to three-peat. They picked the Philadelphia Phillies, New York Yankees, and Kansas City Royals to also win their respective divisions again.

After the game, while speaking with the press about the pair of homers he'd hit against Baltimore, Bench ruminated on the 17 home runs he'd hit in 1976; attributing such a low output to injuries, bad habits, and his lingering divorce case. Revealing that he was shooting for 30 home runs in the upcoming season, he said, "The home run is still my game." Asked if he thought he could win another home run title, he said, "I could but it isn't a goal of mine. You have to remember Schmidt and Kingman are power grooved." The Mets' 6'6" Dave Kingman, who'd played on the same Little League All-Star team in Hawthorne, California, as George Foster, was a threat to knock the ball over the fence every time he came to bat; and Mike Schmidt of the Philadelphia Phillies had won the NL home run crown each of the previous three years with totals of 36, 38, and 38. It didn't occur to Bench to mention his teammate George Foster in the discussion.

On the last day of March, after the Reds fell to the Chicago White Sox 4–2 in Tampa, the club cut five players, reassigning them to the team's minor league camp: catcher Don Werner, first baseman Dave Revering, and pitchers Paul Moskau, Joe Henderson, and Manny Sarmiento. While Nolan was not placed on the DL (disabled list), it was clear that because he was still recovering from the terrible blister on his foot, the Reds would not be counting on him being ready for the first two weeks of the season. With Nolan unavailable, then, Anderson announced that the Reds would open the season with a four-man rotation, consisting of Fryman, Pat Zachry, Fred Norman, and either Alcala or Jack Billingham. A stocky rubber-armed left-hander the Reds had acquired from San Diego in 1973, Norman cemented his slot in the rotation by pitching six hitless innings against the White Sox. The 34-year-old had gotten married over the winter, increasing his motivation to have a good year on the mound.

The Reds began April on a good note when they traveled to Sarasota to complete their home-and-away series with the White Sox. Backup catcher Bill Plummer and Ray Knight homered for Cincinnati, and Billingham gave up only two runs in seven innings, but the 5–2 victory did not fool Anderson, who groused, "We're just going through the motions. We're not eager to play. Nobody's doing nothing." The Reds' lackluster performance the next day in St. Petersburg on April 2 bore the Reds' skipper out. Tom Seaver and Skip Lockwood held the Big Red Machine to three hits, as the Mets sent the Reds to their 14th defeat of the spring (against nine wins). Meanwhile, the Reds became so frustrated at the lack of progress in negotiations over Rose's contract that they took the unprecedented step of using paid advertising in the press to state their position and attempt to win the public relations battle. In the Sunday, April 3, edition of the *Cincinnati Enquirer* they published a half-page open letter "to explain some things we feel have not been reported with complete accuracy and explanation in the Cincinnati newspapers." "A Special Message to Reds Fans" went on to say that "some newspapers have tended to state half-truths and misrepresent our endeavors, so we feel we must alter our usual approach [between club & player or representative in confidence] and speak out on some points." After complimenting Rose on his playing ability, the letter stated, "But we'd like our fans to remember that it was the ball club which recognized Pete's talents and signed him to his first contract." In a letter purporting to set the record straight, this assertion was ironically mendacious. In truth, the Reds had not considered Rose to be a prospect and signed him only as a favor to Rose's uncle who worked for the team at the time as a bird dog. The letter cited several reports concerning salary negotiations (both those of Rose and other players as well) the team considered to be inaccurate, and these were followed by three long paragraphs about the figures being tossed around in the Rose negotiations. According to the letter, the Reds had upped their offers to Rose several times, but Rose and his agent kept moving the goal posts; leading the team to question whether "Pete wants to stay in Cincinnati." After reiterating the need for all parties to work together as a family in order to provide a good product for the fans and to ensure the financial success of the club, the letter concluded: "We simply cannot permit one player to jeopardize all this. Reds baseball means too much to Cincinnati." The *Enquirer*'s contribution to the escalating feud was to run a "Yes/No" poll asking readers questions, such as "Are Pete Rose's demands in excess of his value?" and "Can the Reds win without Rose?"

Back in Tampa that Sunday afternoon (April 3) the Reds beat the Phillies 7–6, as George Foster hit a three-run home run off Tom Underwood in the first inning. It was Foster's first long ball of the spring in 61 at bats. In the fourth Ken Griffey, Foster's roommate, hit a grand slam, also off Underwood. During the game David Rose got into a fight with a foul-mouthed fan who was heckling his older brother. The last straw, according to Dave, came when the fan cursed the Rose boys' mother. "It was all I could take," said Rose the younger, who was escorted along with the obnoxious fan from the ballpark. Dave's older brother was angry too, about the advertisement that had appeared the day before in his hometown's newspaper. "They are trying to force me out of Cincinnati," Pete said, "but not until I have one more good year." Hertzel, trying only half-successfully to maintain a neutral stance, wrote, "Perhaps on Opening Day, both Rose and Dick Wagner should be introduced to the sellout crowd and let the applause meter decide which side is right." That night Bob Howsam went on the team's "RedsLine" radio program to try to explain the club's position. When a caller demanded to know the salaries of Morgan and Concepcion, Howsam said that the club's policy was not to reveal player salaries. He asserted that Rose's salary was comparable to those of Willie Stargell and Carl Yastrezemski, both of whom were "going downhill." Rose, he added, was also going downhill; an opinion the caller disagreed with. Clearly failing to convince the caller, Howsam cited the salaries of other players in both leagues, saying that the figures were inflated by free agent bonuses. He then pointed out that Rose was not a free agent, an irrelevance which only served to highlight the weakness of the Reds' arguments.

The Reds concluded their Grapefruit League schedule by splitting a pair of games with the Detroit Tigers. Their win came in the finale on Tuesday, April 5, at Tampa, a 10–3 cake walk built upon homers by Driessen, Foster, and Griffey. The homers by Driessen and Foster came back-to-back in the fourth inning. The team's 11–15 final ledger was Cincinnati's worst spring training record in 11 years. Afterwards Anderson talked about what his players had said in a pre-game meeting: "They told me they are going to turn it on again. It's nice to know this is a team that can turn it on just like water 'cause the faucet's been running cold all spring. I wasn't pleased with the spring training we had. We did not get into it mentally. They just couldn't get into the mood to play. I mean, these guys have played so many big games that this just hasn't meant much. We're the favorites and we should be. We will show the league why we're the favorites." Anderson acknowledged that the Los Angeles Dodgers, who were openly gunning for the Reds, would be the Reds' only serious challenger, but he also said he didn't believe they could make up the ten-game differential by which they'd lost the 1976 pennant. He concluded by saying that he wanted to do what no National League team had ever done before: win three consecutive World Championships. For any Reds fans truly listening, it was unsettling to hear him add confidentially: "I don't think the players want that as much as I do."

The Reds broke camp with one rookie, Ray Knight, and four other new players: outfielder Champ Summers and pitchers Woodie Fryman, Dale Murray, and Mike Caldwell. The team had acquired Summers on February 16, in a trade with the Chicago Cubs and Caldwell on March 29, from the St. Louis Cardinals in exchange for Pat Darcy; the relief pitcher remembered for surrendering Carlton Fisk's dramatic fair-by-inches walk-off home run that won the sixth game of the 1975 World Series for the Boston Red Sox. Knight forced his way onto the Opening Day roster by virtue of his performance in the spring (four home runs and 12 RBI; both marks second only to Griffey's five homers and 13 RBI).

Late Tuesday night the Reds ended their stalemate with the team's most popular player, signing Rose to a two-year deal estimated to be worth $375,000 per year with no deferred money. In the *Enquirer* the next morning both camps sounded as if the acrimonious negotiations had been as light and fluffy as discussions conducted by a Jane Austen book club. Howsam's henchman Wagner was quoted as saying, "I felt it was a real challenge to do it before the opener so we could go on the field with no animosity." Flush with cash, Rose was even more forgiving, opining that the negotiations had been carried on "in a truly professional manner. Both Reuven and Dick were professionals. They stuck to their guns and we stuck to ours." Now that his money problems were over (for the time being), Rose said he was bothered that the media was still obsessed with his contract business instead of who the Reds' starting pitcher for Opening Day would be. Summing up his contentment, number 14 gushed, "This is THE place to play. I have the right team, the right fans, and the right people running the show."

Rose clearly was ready for another Opening Day. The question was: Were the rest of the Cincinnati Reds?

3

April 1977
A Pair of Slow Starts

Opening Day of the major league baseball season is a major, major holiday in Cincinnati, Ohio, second in importance and the anticipation with which it is beheld to Christmas only. Opening Day is second because Cincinnati is still a town where the majority of the citizens (including the suburbs and Northern Kentucky) are still of Irish-German descent and Catholic heritage. Not everyone in Cincinnati is an Irish-German Catholic, of course, but one has to look pretty hard to find long-time residents who don't have at least a passing interest in the City's major league baseball team. And when the Reds win it all ... well, everybody gets excited to say the least. Consider the headlines on the front page of the *Cincinnati Enquirer* on the morning of Wednesday October 9, 1940, the day after the Reds beat the Detroit Tigers in the seventh game of the World Series. The main headline shouted, "REDS ARE WORLD CHAMPIONS" in big block letters, and below that appeared the secondary headline: "Whole City 'Goes Wild' After Victory." News about America's impending entry into the on-going World War II took a back seat to the baseball news, at least for the moment.

Each year the City welcomes the team back to town with a huge pregame downtown parade sponsored by an inner-city merchants association, and teachers expect any of their students lucky enough to have tickets to the game to be absent from school on that day. The Reds historically hosted the first game of the National League season by themselves so often, while the remaining teams sat idle for a day before also beginning the new season, that many Cincinnatians believed the honor had been officially bestowed on the team as a way of acknowledging the franchise's status as baseball's first openly professional team. In 2004 Greg Rhodes and John Erardi debunked this notion in their wonderful book on the subject (*Opening Day: Celebrating Cincinnati's Baseball Holiday*), attributing the schedule makers' favoring of Cincinnati to a combination of "geography, opportunism, tradition and money."

In 1977, of course, Reds fans still labored happily under their misconception and, if anything, felt that their team deserved the honor of being the first to host a game in the new season by virtue of their team's recent dominance. Sparky Anderson certainly had the team's legacy in mind as the advent of the first pitch of 1977 rapidly approached. "Now I can see why the Yankees won so many times back in the '50s and '60s," he said. "Winning breeds winning. You hunger for more winning. People talk about the Reds being the team of the '70s and we sure want to keep that going."

The Reds were set to open the 1977 season on Wednesday afternoon, April 6, at 2:30 against the San Diego Padres. While four inches of snow fell and softly covered the artificial playing surface of Riverfront Stadium that morning, Tom Boswell of *The Washington Post* published a column that portended a rainy downpour on Anderson's aspirations. Entitled "Psst! Suspicions Around League Reds Can Be Had," the column cited the loss of Perez, Gullet, and McEnaney plus the slide of Johnny Bench as a power hitter as reasons for this new attitude towards the Reds. "The Reds are still a traveling Hall of Fame preview," wrote Boswell, "but they are no longer so superfluously powerful as to seem able to shrug off any injury, and individual slumps or any opponent."

Of course, nothing so negative appeared in the *Cincinnati Enquirer*, not on Opening Day, when the home team is greeted with overflowing optimism every year, even in those years when the ball club is coming off a dismal finish the previous fall. Now that the 1977 season was upon them, the Reds felt they were ready to get down to the business of defending their consecutive World Championships; and fans in the entire region, just as confident as team members themselves, were ready to root them on their way.

Interestingly, the paper did include a prescient article about the unsung Reds player from whom the Reds now needed an even bigger contribution than he'd made before if they were to continue their winning ways: left fielder George Foster. Turned in by a writer named Norm Clarke, the piece was an upbeat profile despite its initially misleading title, "Foster Recognizes the Face of Failure." Writers had always been attracted to Foster's clean-cut image, and Clarke too began with a description of Foster as the atypical ballplayer: "He shuns fast company, never smokes, doesn't drink, thrives on health food and credits a hypnotist with turning around his career." Foster's explanation for this description, which was accurate and not a facade, was "I've been lucky to be guided by the right people in my life." Asked about his having seen a hypnotist in 1973 during the summer of his demotion to AAA Indianapolis, a topic which never failed to intrigue writers, Foster said, "I went to him as a last resort. I had to regroup. I had to do something to regain my confidence. He helped me change everything around. That summer was the turning point of my career." The gist of Clarke's story was Foster's unsuccessful run at the Triple Crown the year before (1976) and what, if anything, he'd learned about his efforts to achieve such a lofty goal. When winning the Triple Crown had appeared as a possibility, Foster lagged most in home runs, so he began intentionally swinging for the fences. His over-swinging led to a 4–44 slump during August, which in addition to not boosting his home run total also depressed his batting average. Foster wound up leading the National League in one of the Triple Crown categories, RBI, with 121. He finished fourth in home runs with 29 behind Mike Schmidt (38), Dave Kingman (37), and Rick Monday of the Chicago Cubs (32); and 11th in batting average (.306), significantly behind winner Bill Madlock (.339) of the Cubs. Four of the players ahead of Foster in the Top Ten were teammates: Ken Griffey (.336), Rose (.323), Morgan (.320), and center fielder Cesar Geronimo (.307). "We were far enough ahead at the time, I said why not go for it," he told Clarke. "Something like that doesn't come along too often. It was my choice, but it didn't work out. I was too materialistic. I look back on it now and know it was better to happen then, rather in April or March when it could have changed the standings. My objective was to go as hard as I could as long as I could. I don't think of the negative anymore. I know I can be better and better."

As disappointed as Foster had been at not winning the Triple Crown, he'd also been disappointed at not winning the NL Most Valuable Player Award, which had gone to teammate Joe Morgan for the second year in a row. When someone asked Foster what he thought about the writers' choice, he replied angrily, "I should have won it." Such jealousy was totally out of character, and ashamed at displaying it, he almost immediately retracted the statement, apologized for it, and congratulated Morgan. The article by Clarke demonstrated that Foster was a man who learned from his mistakes, and it contained a pithy comment about positive thinking which nicely summed up what George had learned: "Failure is success trying to be born in another way." It wasn't the type of comic one-liner typically uttered by Pete Rose, who was well known for saying things like "I'd run through fire in a gasoline suit to play baseball"; but it was characteristic of a thoughtful man who felt an obligation to help other people by being a good example.

Foster was not a stuffed shirt, however, and by 1977 he had learned the value of humor in connecting with people and winning them over. When, in referring to Foster's most unusual facial feature, Clarke asked George where he'd gotten his "mysterious eyes" Foster replied: "I went to Japan in 1970 and purchased them over there. They give me a better slant on things." Another time, when a reporter asked Foster why he was using a black bat, an oddity at the time, George replied, "I'm integrating the bat rack."

Thanks to Dick Wagner, the game on Opening Day went off as scheduled. When the Reds were still down in Florida, having worked their way through half the spring exhibition schedule, Wagner had been studying weather forecasts for Ohio in the first week of April, which called for snow. He'd alerted the Reds' grounds keeping crew, giving them a mandate to be prepared to do whatever might be necessary to have the playing surface ready for the afternoon game. Expanded by 60 extra members, the grounds crew shoveled and hauled away snow all morning, so that by game time very little of the white stuff was visible in Riverfront Stadium. As usual Riverfront Stadium was sold out for the game, but several thousand ticket holders chose to stay home rather than endure the 39-degree cold for a couple of hours.

For the first time in eight years Johnny Bench was not in the Reds' starting lineup on Opening Day. His knee was so stiff, he joked, that he almost hadn't been able to stand up and walk off the plane from Florida when it had landed in Cincinnati. Bench's caddy, Bill Plummer, replaced him and had a day to remember, going 2–4 and giving the Reds a 1–0 lead in the second by singling in Concepcion who'd doubled and stolen third base. After the game Plummer said, "My first opener. I really had the adrenalin flowing. I got to the park and figured I'd be freezing in the same corner of the dugout that I've been in the last six years."

With Bench sidelined, Foster batted in the cleanup spot, and he also came through. After catcher Gene Tenace had put the Padres ahead with a two-run double in the top of the third, Foster tied the game 2–2 with an RBI triple in the bottom of the inning. Following a Geronimo two-run home run that regained the lead 4–2 for Cincinnati in the fourth, Foster provided an insurance run in the fifth with a sacrifice fly. The 5–3 final was an encouraging start to the season, especially considering the work turned in by Reds pitchers. Starter Woodie Fryman earned the win in his first appearance as a Red, allowing three runs and seven hits in five and a third innings; however, the true pitching star of the day was Rawley Eastwick who shut down San Diego over the final three innings on one hit. It was an especially gratifying outing for Eastwick who'd had a bad spring and been booed while warming up in the bullpen by fans critical of his desire to wrestle contract concessions from Reds management. While being vague about exactly how much money he wanted, Eastwick had asked for a five-year contract. When the Reds would not budge off their offer of a three-year deal, Rawley decided to remain unsigned for the season, take a 20 percent pay cut, and play out his option.

Always dazzled by the home run, the sportswriters considered Geronimo to be the star of the game. When asked about his game-winning dinger, Geronimo, regarded as one of the best center fielders in the game, reminded them that he never tried for home runs. "In fact, I wouldn't be surprised if that is the only home run I hit this year," he said. The comment was too modest by far, as the slender Dominican would go on to hit ten homers in 1977, achieving what would turn out to be his career high. Over the length of his 15-year major league career, Geronimo would hit 51 home runs.

The next day the Reds and Padres sat while the rest of the National League sprang into action. A minor uproar still erupted around the Cincinnati Reds though, and it involved George Foster who suddenly was getting more attention than he wanted. The April 1977 edition of *Sport* magazine hit the newsstands, and it contained a story by Stu Black based on an interview he'd conducted with Foster. Part of the piece was a reiteration of the lessons Foster had learned the year before when he'd allowed himself to focus more on outcomes than the process. "I got away from the goals I had set for myself," he told Black. "I had wanted to be more durable, more consistent. All of a sudden, I was going for the MVP, for the Triple Crown. The more people talked about it, the more I thought about it." Nobody had a problem with Foster diagnosing self-inflicted problems, but he opened a potentially nasty can of worms when he appeared to accuse the Reds of racial bias: "I didn't bat fourth this past season until Bench went to the man and said he wasn't hitting, a change should be made. They wanted Bench to bat fourth as long as he wasn't mortally wounding the team. They wanted a white man knocking in the runs. It's good for attendance, they figure."

Of course, it was incumbent upon Bob Hertzel to get Foster's reaction to the publication of the story; and, of course, Foster was mortified when he realized how the story made him sound. He told Hertzel "The man took everything out of context. It got so I didn't want to read on for fear of what it might say.... They made it sound like I was mad that I didn't bat fourth. That wasn't the case and it wasn't what I said. I was glad to be batting anywhere. Sure, I said that white players are built up. Look in the stands. Most of the people are white. It is good business." Black had made no attempt to characterize Foster's comments as symptomatic of any general racial problems extant in the Reds' organization; and because the Reds were known for enjoying one of the most racially harmonious clubhouses in the majors, in the end the story did nothing more than raise a few eyebrows. Sparky Anderson's dismissive reaction to the issue raised by Foster probably represented the opinion of most observers. "It is ridiculous to think I would make any decision because a man is black or white," he said. Sparky also pointed out that Bench was better at taking pitches, which was important for the Reds' cleanup hitter to do in order to give Joe Morgan the opportunities he needed to steal bases: a huge part of the Reds' offensive strategy.

Meanwhile in Los Angeles, in the Dodgers' first Opening Day game with Tommy Lasorda at the helm, Don Sutton gave up a home run to the Giants' Gary Thomasson on L.A.'s very first pitch of the season. Sutton allowed only three more hits all day to beat the Giants 5–1. The ball hit by Thomasson was donated to the National Baseball Hall of Fame & Museum in Cooperstown, as it was the first baseball made by the new supplier, Rawlings, to be hit for a major league home run.

The Reds got back into action on Friday night facing more frigid weather as well as Brent Strom and the Padres. Strom, who would go on to serve as the pitching coach of the 2017 World Champion Houston Astros, got himself into trouble by walking the bases loaded in the first inning. The Reds then took a 2–0 lead on successive ground ball force outs by Foster and Concepcion, who each were credited with a run batted in. Especially bothered by the cold, Joe Morgan decided to bat without a batting glove after drawing a walk in the first. "I like to feel like the bat is part of me, an extension of my arm," he said after the game. To keep Morgan's bat warm, Anderson and hitting coach Ted Kluszewski took turns holding it over a stove in the dugout. Wielding his pampered stick, Morgan drove in the remaining four runs of the Reds' 6–3 victory; hitting a three-run home run in the fifth and a sac fly in the seventh. Relying on his curve ball and throwing 129 pitches ("too many," according to Anderson) Jack Billingham went seven and two thirds innings to get the win with help from ex–Expo Dale Murray. While Billingham shut out San Diego for six innings, all three of their runs were charged to him.

The weather in Cincinnati warmed up on Saturday (to the low 60s) and so did the Padres. They tied that afternoon's game by plating three runs off Reds starter Fred Norman in the sixth and then won it in the ninth by scoring three more off Eastwick, the big blow being a two-run triple by Mike Ivie. Right-hander Dave Freisleben, taken by the Padres in the fifth round of the 1971 amateur draft out of Sam Rayburn (Pasadena, TX) High School, held the Reds to four hits over seven innings; and Rollie Fingers finished off San Diego's 6–3 win with two hitless innings of relief. Making his first appearance of 1977, Bench started behind the plate and went 0–4.

On April 10, as the high climbed to near 70 degrees, Cincinnatians were treated to the results of the Pete Rose poll in their Sunday morning *Enquirers*. Around 500 citizens had turned in ballots and the results favored Rose by a 5–4 margin; with comments ranging from "Keep Pete at all costs" to "If Rose is hurting for money, he should sell his Rolls Royce." The breakdown was as follows:

Is the money Rose seeking in excess of his value? Yes 45%, No 54%;
Should the Reds agree to his demands? Yes 56%, No 44%;
Has Rose been underpaid in the past? Yes 55%, No 42%;
Can the Reds win without Rose? Yes 50%, No 43%;
Should Rose be the highest paid Reds player? Yes 52%, No 42%;
Have the Rose negotiations reduced your regard for the Reds? Yes 56%, No 43%;
Are athletes overpaid? Yes 48%, No 45%.

As Rose and the Reds had already come to terms by this time, the results of the poll might have been considered to be moot by some, but the Reds would face Rose across the bargaining table again in the future. And the poll clearly demonstrated that a majority of the Reds' paying customers thought the team had been wrong, that they had not treated Rose fairly, and that they had, in fact, underestimated his value to the team. Unfortunately for their fans, as history would show, Reds management did not put much stock in the poll. In December of 1978 Rose would leave the only team he'd played for since 1963, signing a free agent contract with the Philadelphia Phillies.

Sunday was get-away day for the two teams, and the Padres left Cincinnati on a high note, trouncing the Reds 12–4 to earn a split of the four-game series. Utilizing a big curveball as his out pitch, a left-handed rookie named Bob Shirley out of the University of Oklahoma struck out 11 Reds and gave up only four hits in eight and two thirds innings. An *Enquirer* editor poked fun at the apparent "David over Goliath" triumph of Shirley with the headline: "Hill Rookie Puts Little 'u' in Reds Sheepish Champs." Attempting to explain the Reds' lackluster performance, Morgan said, "We are not yet awake. We're not playing right. We don't have the life we should have." Then, in an angrier tone, he directed his remarks towards the Padres and Shirley: "Let's just say they owed us some professional courtesy and did not give it to us. Things like 3-2 breaking balls with a 12-0 lead. That's the kind of thing that can wake us up." The Reds did score four runs in the bottom of the ninth, and Dave Tomlin had to come out of the Padres' bullpen to get the final out of the ball game. But complaining about not receiving "professional courtesy" was a bit rich, coming from a member of a cocky team (the Reds) which had dominated the weaker team (the Padres) in the previous year's season-series 13–5. Rookie Shirley stayed away from any controversy, merely saying, "All I wanted to do was keep from embarrassing myself." It was mission accomplished for Shirley but not so for Reds pitchers. The starter, Santo Alcala, was knocked out after surrendering four runs in two and two thirds innings, and the bullpen efforts of Pedro Borbon, Mike Caldwell, and Murray (who threw two wild pitches) were even more embarrassing. As the Reds began their flight to Houston to start the season's first road trip, Sparky Anderson had plenty to worry about.

Awaiting Cincinnati in the "Eighth Wonder of the World," the Houston Astrodome, was a team which had finished 22 games behind the Reds in 1976. The 1977 Astros roster looked pretty much the same as the 1976 roster; but the current Houston team had a new attitude and they swept the three-game series 4–3, 4–3, and 7–6.

In the first game Houston jumped on Fryman in the bottom of the first inning for four runs, the scoring capped by a two-run homer off the bat of left fielder Cliff Johnson. It was all the runs needed by the Astros. Trailing 4–2, the Reds rallied in the ninth to cut the lead to one run on singles by Driessen, Concepcion, and Rose; but Joe Niekro, who pitched three and two thirds innings in relief of starter Doug Konieczny, retired Griffey on a fly ball to center to end it. Driessen's base hit was his first of the season after he'd gone 0–15 in the opening series against San Diego.

The next night the towering J. R. Richard took the mound and stymied the Reds for seven innings, allowing one run on five hits. Richard was a 6'8" giant of a man, an intimidating pitcher, whom the Reds for some reason usually had no trouble besting. He'd won 20 games in 1976 but had gone 0–4 against Cincinnati. Muscle spasms prevented the big flame thrower from going out for the eighth, so Ken Forsch replaced him. Pat Zachry finally made his 1977 debut and went six innings, giving up four runs ... again, all the runs the Astros would need. The Reds again rallied in the ninth inning, but this time a bad break would do them in. With the Reds behind 4–1, Bench and Foster singled to put runners on the corners with no outs. Shortstop Roger Metzger booted Driessen's ground ball, allowing Bench to score. After Concepcion's sacrifice bunt moved the runners to second and third, Geronimo hit a line drive headed for center field. It never got there. The ball hit Forsch and bounced right to Metzger who threw to first to retire Geronimo for out number two as Foster crossed the plate, closing the gap to 4–3. Forsch then retired pinch-hitter Champ Summers on a 5–3 ground out to end the game. Afterwards, Astros first baseman Bob Watson said, "In the past, when we played Cincinnati, we'd go out in the eighth inning and wonder what they were going to do to beat us. This year we don't look for those things to happen in the eighth and ninth innings. I feel like it's different this year than in other years."

The finale, played on Wednesday April 13, was the worst Reds defeat yet, as Cincinnati managed to blow a 6–0 lead. Billingham gave up only two runs through five innings but couldn't register a single out in the sixth; departing with a 6–2 lead and the bases loaded. Murray came on and four batters later the Astros had tied the game 6–6 on three hits and a run-producing ground ball double-play. The Astros won it in the bottom of the ninth, scoring their seventh run against Borbon. With two outs, Jose Cruz doubled into the left field corner. Borbon pitched carefully to Watson with first base open and wound up walking him. He worked Willie Crawford into a 1–2 hole but then made too good a pitch, which Crawford lined into center field. Geronimo's throw home was on line but too slow to nab Cruz who sped across the plate with the winning run. The loss was the Reds' fifth in a row, their worst stretch since early 1975 when they dropped six consecutive games. It dropped the team (2–5) into last place in the West Division behind Houston (5–1) and Los Angeles (4–2) and also marked Houston's first sweep of Cincinnati since 1972. Anderson was clearly troubled, saying, "You just hate to see it. I mean, every year it happens and no one worries. They figure class will tell and that when they get it together they'll win it all. Okay, so far that's the way it's been. But one year it won't work out. They won't be able to muster it."

"It's a little early to be reaching for the panic button," said a defiant Rose.

On Thursday as the Reds traveled to San Diego on an off-day, Anderson announced a mild lineup shakeup. Bench, who'd had another 0-fer in Wednesday's game and didn't hit a ball past the pitcher's mound, was 2 for 19 on the season. He had two singles and no RBI to his credit so far. He was being dropped as the team's cleanup hitter to bat fifth against left-handers and sixth against right-handers. The player promoted to the cleanup spot: George Foster.

With no game to report on, the *Enquirer* had sports columnist Mark Purdy take a look at the Reds. For the column entitled "Reds Woes Explained," Purdy interviewed Thomas Tutko, the author of a book called *Sports Psyching: Playing Your Best*. If there were a definable reason for the Reds' subpar performance so far, Tutko's explanation made as much sense as anything else: "The Reds have always seemed to be a family unit, but with Tony Perez and Don Gullet gone, and the troubles they had signing Rose, and the fact Rawley Eastwick has not signed yet—all of these things have tended to disrupt the family. It doesn't take that much to remove the little extra feeling that you're going to win, no matter what." Tutko also had quite a bit to say about Pete Rose which sounded a bit like long-distance psycho-analysis: "Although he says he's over the hassles with the club and is going to give 110%, he has a covert hostility toward the management for what happened, maybe because of the ad that the club took out in the newspaper. So while consciously he thinks he's playing hard, on the subconscious level he wants to pay management back for what it did. And how can he accomplish that? By playing poorly. That is the bad news for those who sell Pete Rose posters. The good news is that hostility and disruption generally clear up without treatment. I expect Rose will realize what is happening, and then go through a period of feeling guilty about it, and then start working even harder. My guess is that he will bounce back. As I expect the Reds as a team will stabilize and reach their full potential. They have a good manager in Sparky Anderson. He pretty much believes as I do that games are won off the field as well as on the field." Tutko may have been an expert in his field, but it was clear to Reds fans who read Purdy's column that the expert sports psychologist did not understand Pete Rose. Whatever one might think about Rose as a human being, one could not, with any credibility, accuse him of not hustling, of not going all out to win, of not caring about playing the game the right way at all times.

As if he were offering a rebuttal to Tutko's analysis, Rose reached a milestone the next night in San Diego when he played in his 500th consecutive game; the longest such streak among active players. Rose had last missed a game on September 26, 1973, when he took a day off to rest up for the playoffs.

The Reds took the opener of the series 9–5, after once again blowing a big lead (5–0 after two and a half innings). For once, the bullpen, in the persons of Borbon and Eastwick, did their job and held the Padres scoreless over the final four innings while the Reds' offense continued to hack away; scoring runs against all four of the San Diego pitchers who toed the rubber: Strom, Freisleben, Rollie Fingers, and Butch Metzger. During his post-game chat with the media Anderson revealed that he'd appealed to "my big guys" to exert their leadership. "With Rose, Morgan, and Bench talking to the guys," he said, "it is one player to another. He's his friend. Sometimes they don't believe the old man. They don't want to hear me. They have to be stronger. When you're losing, the big guys have to step in and say, 'Everything's gonna be all right.' That's why they get the big money." Morgan echoed Anderson's comments, saying, "There shouldn't be any pressure on Davey or George. We have a Rose, Bench, Morgan. We know what to do." Whether Anderson's appeal had anything to do with it or not, the big guys did come through. Morgan went 3–4 with a two-run home run, and Bench got two hits, including a double and his first home run of the year. Although it was little noted, George Foster also hit his first home run of the year, a two-run shot to left in the ninth inning off Metzger to seal the Reds' win.

One problem plaguing the Reds in the early going had nothing to do with "the big guys," and that was the unreliability of the bullpen. On Saturday night, the 16th, the bullpen blew another lead in a 5–4 loss. Fryman was nursing a 4–1 lead as he began the seventh inning. A single by Jerry Turner and a walk to Bill Almon prompted a call to the bullpen for Dale Murray, who immediately gave up a bases-clearing triple to Dave Winfield. After George Hendrick struck out, Gene Tenace lifted a fly ball into right deep enough for Winfield to come home and tie things up 4–4. In the top of the ninth Cesar Geronimo tried to score from second on a base hit to left by Griffey, but Turner threw him out at home to end the inning. Joe Morgan, who'd hit a three-run homer in the third, was the on-deck batter who helplessly watched Geronimo slide into catcher Dave Roberts' tag.

Geronimo redeemed himself in the bottom of the inning by making what Hertzel called "the most miraculous play of his major league career." Leading off the inning against Rawley Eastwick, Dave Winfield drove a ball deep into the right-center field gap. Winfield thought he had his second triple of the game, but Geronimo unleashed a laser-like throw that zoomed over the head of cut-off man Concepcion, traveled some 300 feet, and two-quick-hopped right into the waiting glove of substitute third baseman Doug Flynn. After Flynn applied the tag, there was nothing for the surprised Winfield to do but tip his cap towards Geronimo.

The respite was only temporary. George Hendrick and Tenace singled, and one out later Roberts ended it with a liner (credited as a double) into right-center. It was Eastwick's second loss and Murray's second blown save of the young season. Foster's elevation to cleanup hitter also got off to a stumbling beginning. In the first inning Morgan, who had forced Griffey at second, took off for second on a steal attempt. Foster swung at the pitch and hit a line drive caught by shortstop Almon, who then easily doubled Morgan off first. "I'm really confused," Morgan said afterwards. "I don't know when to run. But Sparky told George to go ahead and hack if he gets a fastball."

It was hardly any consolation, but other teams and players expected to do well were also off to disappointing starts. In the American League the Yankees had scored 22 runs in eight games and had lost five of six to the upstart Milwaukee Brewers. On Saturday they had stranded 11 runners while being shut out 2–0. Milwaukee pitcher Bill Travers gloated: "Now the Yankees are in last place. That's a good place for them, the way everyone picked them to run away with it. It shows you anything can happen in this game. We're playing good baseball and our pitching has been super. Now people will have to think about us." The plight of ex–Oriole pitcher Wayne Garland who'd been given a 10-year, $2.3 million deal by Cleveland also showed that giving free-agent signees guaranteed big money contracts did not guarantee big time performance. Garland lasted five innings in his debut in the Indians' home opener Saturday night, and the press had already labeled him a "Million Dollar Bust." Garland went from winning 20 games for the Orioles in 1976 to leading the league in losses with 19 in 1977. Garland gamely struggled against an arm injury, but when the

Indians had finally seen enough by 1981, their payoff from Garland for such a huge investment was a total of 28 wins against 46 losses.

The Padres made the final game of the series on Sunday afternoon a going-away present for the Reds by making two errors that led to a three-run first inning. Griffey and Morgan both reached on misplays of their ground balls, and Foster, who went 2–4, drove them home with a single. Pat Zachry went all the way in the Reds' 4–1 win, the team's first complete game of the season. Scheduled to meet the Reds back in Cincinnati now that their 2–4 road trip was concluded: the Los Angeles Dodgers who in less than a decade had become their most bitter rivals.

The series with L.A. was a baseball scheduling oddity: a two-game set with an off-day between the two games. Prior to Monday night's contest, the Reds announced that Gary Nolan, who'd yet to throw a pitch in a real game because of a foot injury, was now suffering from mononucleosis. The length of his absence due to the disease was "undetermined." Sparky Anderson also issued a challenge of sorts, saying, "If the Dodgers are gonna beat us tonight, they're gonna have to score six or seven runs. We're ready." It might have paid Sparky to check the Dodgers' batting averages before speaking out as he did. Coming into the game, six Dodgers regulars were batting over .300, while only two of Anderson's regulars were Griffey (.326) and Rose (.306). First baseman and glamor-boy Steve Garvey was not one of the Dodgers over .300, but he was the hitter in particular who made the night a miserable one for the Reds and starting pitcher Jack Billingham. Garvey started the Dodgers' scoring in the fourth by doubling with two outs and coming home on an error by Rose. He led off the sixth with a single to center, stole second base, went to third on a fly to right by Dusty Baker, and then scored on a wild pitch with Steve Yeager at the plate. Garvey's three-run home run in the seventh rounded out his 3–5 night, finished Billingham, and gave L.A. a 7–0 lead which they rode home to a 7–3 win. At this point in his career, Pete Rose had the potential to tie or break a record just about every time he stepped on the field. His eighth-inning two-run home run only reduced the Reds' losing margin; but, as the 135th homer of his career, it did have the distinction of tying Rose with Rip Collins for the most career home runs by a switch hitter in National League history.

On the Tuesday off day Steve Garvey told the press: "I think this may be the best team we've had in ten years. I think they [the Reds] realize we have the offense we haven't had before." He was right on both counts, although the Dodgers' hitters had hardly changed at all. Garvey, Dave Lopes, Bill Russell, Ron Cey, Reggie Smith, Dusty Baker, Steve Yeager ... they were Lasorda's regulars, and they'd been Alston's regulars the year before too. The only difference between the 1976 and 1977 Dodgers was outfielder Rick Monday, who replaced Bill Buckner. L.A. had acquired Monday January 11 along with pitcher Mike Garman in a trade with the Cubs for Buckner, Ivan DeJesus, and Jeff Albert. Monday was hardly an offensive improvement over Buckner. A bad back would limit him to 118 games in 1977, and he'd bat .230 with 15 home runs and 48 RBI on the season. Buckner had put up stats of .301/7/60 the year before, and he'd bat .284 with 11 homers and 60 RBI for the Cubs in 1977. Monday *was* a big improvement over Buckner in center field, when he was out there; and the Cubs, well aware of Buckner's limitations as a fly chaser, shifted him to first base where he played the rest of his career.

It's difficult to know exactly what Garvey was basing his statement about the Dodgers' improved offense on. At that point in the season he didn't have much experience or data to go on. In hindsight, it appears that the Dodgers somehow over the winter had matured into a bunch of power hitters. In 1976 third baseman Ron Cey had led the club in home runs with 23. In 1977 four Dodgers would wind up hitting 30 or more homers: Cey (30), Baker (30), Smith (32), and Garvey (33). L.A.'s total as a team jumped from 91 to a league-leading 191, an enormous increase. Even with Foster's 52, the Reds would finish ten homers behind, with 181. There's also the distinct possibility that the Dodgers' new manager had something, perhaps a lot, to do with the team's improved play. Lasorda's rah-rah, player-hugging style was mocked by some; but there was no question that the players, many of whom had played for Lasorda in the minor leagues, were responding positively to his whole ebullient "I bleed Dodger blue" shtick.

Whatever Garvey meant, the Dodgers used the home run to beat the Reds again on Wednesday, 3–1. Lopes hit the second pitch of the game (from Fred Norman) over the fence, and Cey slugged a two-run homer in the sixth. Don Sutton went all the way for L.A., holding the Reds to seven hits. The loss, which dropped the Reds with their 4–8 record back into last place, 5½ games behind the front-running 9–2 Dodgers, gave Sparky Anderson another sleepless night. Before the game he had given the media and, indirectly, his ball club an earful: "This is the maddest I've been since I've been managing. It isn't the losses that do it. There's a way of losing and there's an atmosphere of losing." Echoing Garvey's sentiment from the previous day, he continued: "This is the best L. A. club in the ten years I've been in the big leagues. But that doesn't mean they're supposed to win it all. I mean, who are the World Champions? Last Monday night I had the feeling we were respecting them more than they were respecting us. That is a horrible feeling just after getting a ring that says you're the World Champions. Okay, we've got the fight of our lives on our hands. But let's make a fight of it, not just roll over. Sure, the

Dodgers are good but the things they're saying about the Dodgers now is what they are supposed to be saying about us. I mean, we've got Hall of Famers over here. Hall of Famers!" Anderson dropped the Dodgers for a few moments to interject a boyhood basketball story about him throwing the ball at his coach because the coach took out the first string too early before ensuring the team's victory. Returning to the present, he concluded the tirade, saying "Losing is for other people. It ain't for me. If I have to lose, the people with me will be living in hell."

While Anderson was venting his frustrations, New York Yankees manager Billy Martin used an entirely different, "what the hell" approach. Heading into Wednesday night's game against the Toronto Blue Jays, the Yankees had lost five straight. Martin made up the game's batting order by letting outfielder Reggie Jackson pick names out of a cap. Whether the ploy really had anything to do with it or not, the Yankees suddenly shifted into high gear. They beat Toronto 7–5 and then went on to win six straight and 16 out of 18, by which time they had risen from last to first place in their division.

After the Reds' loss, more Dodgers players spoke of the tangible differences being felt by members of the two ball clubs. "They just weren't as up as they usually are against us," said shortstop Russell. "They look dead; we can see it. They're like we were last year. They sit on the bench and don't say anything. They look half-asleep."

"I think Tony Perez meant an awful lot to them," said Cey. "The Reds are struggling without him. He is being missed right now. I don't mean to sound derogatory about Dan Driessen, because he is a good ballplayer. But he's got a heavy burden to carry. Perez drove in 90 runs or more for ten or 11 years … there's not a handful of those kind around."

The Reds' scheduled off-day in Chicago on Thursday, April 28, turned into a two-day vacation when the first game of the three-game series on Friday was postponed due to weather. The game time temperature at Wrigley Field was a nippy 48 degrees; but wind gusts of up to 26 mph made it feel a lot colder, and the umpiring crew decided the conditions were unsuitable for the playing of a major league baseball game. A clubhouse meeting on Thursday accomplished nothing as the Cubs won both of the remaining games, each an afternoon affair: 2–1 on Saturday and 7–1 on Sunday. On Saturday Bill Bonhan held the Reds to five measly hits over eight innings. Pete Rose drove in the Reds' only tally in the third inning with a single to left field. When Foster, 1–3 on the day, opened the ninth with a single, Cubs manager Herman Franks brought in sinker baller Bruce Sutter to finish it off. Trying to shake off his slow start, Johnny Bench continued experimenting with altered stances and a new swing. It didn't help. He went 0–4, moaning, "This is getting frustrating." The losing was getting to the editors at the *Enquirer* too, who fashioned another sarcastic headline: "Big Red Faces."

There was another clubhouse meeting on Sunday (with the same result), during which Anderson announced a lineup shuffle. The struggling Bench,

With eyes focused on the pitcher's release point and his black war club in the launch position, George Foster was a terrifying sight for NL pitchers to behold. Pitcher Frank Riccelli told Cincinnati sportswriter John Erardi that Foster scared him more than any other major league batter because "he hit the ball so damn hard!" Above, Foster is batting against the Chicago Cubs at Wrigley Field in 1977, the year he hit 52 home runs. Five of the homers came against Cubs pitchers.

hitting .175, took a seat on the bench, and Concepcion who'd gone 3-4 the day before, was moved up to the second spot in the order behind Rose, with everyone else moving down a spot. This made Joe Morgan the cleanup hitter. If the *Enquirer* thought Saturday's game was embarrassing, Sunday's debacle rendered them speechless. The traditionally hapless Cubs, who hadn't played in a World Series since 1945, batted around in the first inning. They scored five runs against starting pitcher Woodie Fryman who gave up five straight hits, including two home runs, without registering an out before he was relieved by Mike Caldwell. Ray Burris turned in a complete game for Chicago, permitting only one run to score despite allowing 13 hits and a base on balls. The Reds hit into two double plays and left nine men on base, but the most embarrassing play of the game involved an out on the bases. In the top of the sixth with the Reds trailing 7-1, Foster tried to score from first base on a double by Driessen. With Murcer having trouble corralling Driessen's line drive, Foster rounding third ran into George Scherger in the coaching box and fell down. Second baseman Manny Trillo took the relay throw from Murcer and fired it to third baseman Steve Ontiveros, forcing Foster to run home. Ontiveros threw him out easily. After the humiliating loss, Morgan said, "If I have to bat fourth, we're in trouble."

Anderson practically insulted the team in explaining a change in his managing strategy. "I'll be bunting more now," he said. "Playing for one run. I've always said I ride with the tide and right now the tide is going the other way."

Pete Rose wasn't conceding anything. "Somebody is going to pay for our slump," he huffed.

The Reds next opened a three-game series in Atlanta on Monday, April 25. The Braves racked Jack Billingham for 17 hits and nine runs (five of them earned) over eight innings but still managed to lose the game handily because of atrocious pitching and defense.

Since moving to Atlanta from Milwaukee after the 1965 season, the Braves had rarely been competitive. In fact, under the ownership of Ted Turner they'd become something of a laughing stock. Their farm system was unproductive and Turner's trades and future free agent signings seldom panned out. Worst of all, Turner exhibited little respect for the baseball knowledge and abilities of the management people he hired; a debilitating state of affairs which would reach its absurd culmination 30 games into the season when the cable television mogul would replace veteran baseball man Dave Bristol as manager of the team with himself. Thankfully, National League president Chub Feeney with the backing of Commissioner Bowie Kuhn would see to it that Turner's reign in the Braves' dugout would last only one game;

just as American League president Will Harridge had immediately banned Eddie Gaedel from appearing in another major league baseball game after Bill Veeck had sent the midget up to bat in a 1951 St. Louis Browns-Detroit Tigers game. In short, these were not the Atlanta Braves of Greg Maddux, Tom Glavine, John Smoltz, Kevin Millwood, and Denny Neagle; but the Braves of Phil Niekro, Dick Ruthven, Buzz Capra, Andy Messersmith, and Eddie Solomon. Niekro was a quality pitcher who would ride his unpredictable knuckleball to the Hall of Fame but he was overworked in 1977. He started a league-leading 43 games in 1977 and wound up losing 20 of them, also the league high. Once a good pitcher, by 1977 Messersmith was a has-been, and the Braves' other three main starters were simply mediocre.

As Rose had predicted, the Braves caught the Reds at a bad time and paid a high price for doing so. Atlanta had dropped their previous game to Los Angeles 16–6, and the Reds were poised to continue the onslaught of the Atlanta pitching staff. Niekro started and lasted two thirds of an inning, allowing six runs. Jamie Easterly came on to allow eight runs in three and a third, and Mike Beard gave up nine more runs in three innings. Ten walks and six Braves errors contributed to the 23–9 massacre. The 23 runs were as many as the Reds had pushed across in the previous seven games combined, and their 12-run fifth inning matched a club record set on May 4, 1942, against the New York Giants. While the entire Reds lineup feasted on Braves pitching, two Reds players had particularly significant days at bat. Bench broke out of his slump with a 4–6 day, including a pair of homers, to bring his average up to a more palatable .239, and George Foster went 4–4, with a walk, a pair of home runs, and seven RBI. Foster hit a three-run blast off Niekro in the first and another three-run job off Beard in the fifth. After batting twice in the fifth inning, during which the Reds sent 16 men to the plate, Foster was given the rest of the evening off and was replaced by Ed Armbrister. Foster's perfect day raised his batting average to .321. More importantly, the two home runs, his second and third of the season, proved he was getting down the timing he needed to hit the long ball with consistency. The rest of the league had no idea what his big day portended.

Even after the big win, the Reds at 5–10 remained behind the 8–8 Braves in the standings; apparently unable to escape the shadow of the departed Tony Perez. Hertzel quoted an unnamed player, identified only as "one of the more important players," who said, "If he were here, things would be different. Right now, we're afraid to get all over each other. But if he were here he'd get it started."

The Reds used the momentum created by the laugher in the opener to sweep the series in Atlanta, winning 9–1 on Tuesday and 3–1 on Wednesday.

Norman (three hits in sixth innings) and Eastwick combined on a three-hitter in the second game, while Pat Zachry pitched a complete-game five-hitter in the third contest. Rose (3–5), Griffey (3–4), Driessen (3–5), and Foster (2–5) accounted for 11 of the 14 hits the Reds tallied in Tuesday's game, with Driessen shining brightest of all. Driessen's miserable start (0–17) had prompted him to moan, "I can't hit my grandmother right now"; but he'd recovered nicely and boosted his average to .250. On Tuesday night he hit a pair of homers and drove in 6 runs, making him 7–11 with 10 RBI for the first two games against Atlanta. Sparky Anderson jumped on the Driessen band wagon, predicted he'd hit 20 home runs on the year, and pronounced that the baton had officially been passed on to Danny: "This is a game for the kids. If they've got talent they're supposed to play. Sure, players like Perez have great moments, but the great moments pass on. Perez, he's gone. They [the players] like the man. They did more than like him. They loved him. But that's it. Bye bye baby. He was stealing from this boy." Informed of Anderson's comments, the modest Driessen said, "I just hope Sparky is right." Driessen stayed hot, going 2–4 and driving home the go-ahead run in the first inning of Wednesday night's game. Afterwards, he had another, more amusing comment on his predecessor: "I can't be Tony Perez. I'm not even Spanish." Anderson's most pointed remark after the welcome sweep was aimed at the front-running Dodgers who had jumped out to a 13–3 record, 6½ games ahead of the 7–10 last-place Reds: "They've got a lot of guys running their mouths and having a lot of fun. Let's see what happens in July and August."

While the absence of Don Gullet did not loom over the collective consciousness of the Reds as did that of Tony Perez, it was Gullet who made the news during the Atlanta series. On Monday night in Baltimore he slipped on wet grass while fielding a bunt by Orioles catcher Rick Dempsey and injured his ankle, shoulder, and neck: all on the left side. He returned to New York for evaluation and treatment.

Thursday the 28th of April was a scheduled off-day for the Reds, but they still played a game, in Detroit, and lost 6–4 to the Tigers on a walk-off home run by Jason Thompson. The exhibition was one of two so-called "Kid Glove Games" scheduled on a home-and-away basis with Detroit for 1977. Begun in 1949, the program was designed to raise money to support youth baseball, and the April contest raised $116,000 for amateur baseball in the Motor City.

The following night the Reds opened a five-game home stand at Riverfront Stadium, their longest of the season so far. Before the game, the starting pitcher, Woodie Fryman, a bit humbled by the recent pastings he'd been absorbing, wondered aloud, "Am I finished as a pitcher?" Joe Morgan sarcas-

3. April 1977

tically supplied the perfect answer which caused everybody within earshot, including Fryman, to laugh: "Just keep throwing strikes. Sooner or later you have to get *somebody* out."

Fryman did better than that, retiring 26 Chicago Cubs before giving way to Eastwick, who snuffed out a Cubs rally in the ninth with help from George Foster. With two outs, catcher George Mitterwald doubled and was then replaced by pinch runner Joe Wallace. After Fryman got behind pinch hitter Gene Clines 2–0, Anderson brought Eastwick out of the bullpen, which caused Cubs manager Herman Franks to pinch-hit the left-handed Larry Biittner for his previous pinch-hitter Clines. The move appeared to work when Biittner lined a pitch into left field, but the ball was hit so hard that the Cubs, respecting Foster's arm, held Wallace at third. The Cubs left runners on the corners and lost 3–2 when Eastwick then enticed Ivan DeJesus to lift a routine fly to Foster for the Cubs' 27th out of the ball game. Asked about the Cubs' decision to not test his arm, to keep Wallace from trying to score on the play to tie the game, George said, "If he had tried, he would have been out." It was a good day for Foster, whose RBI single in the sixth inning put the Reds ahead to stay. It was also the Reds' first win of the season by a margin of one run.

The Reds got an even more well-pitched game the next night, April 30, from Jack Billingham, who twirled a five-hit shutout, the 22nd of his career, to run his record to 3–1. The hitters made it easy for Billingham, giving him an early cushion to work with, scoring six runs off Cubs starter Ray Burris and sending him to the showers before he could get out of the second inning. When reporters in the post-game interviews asked him why he'd brought both his jacket and parka to the dugout bench, Billingham joked, "I just wanted to make sure I was ready for 23 runs again." It was Billingham who'd benefited from the Reds' 23-run rout of the Braves but who also had had to spend an inordinate amount of time cooling down on the bench while the Reds' batting barrages went on and on in several innings. Billingham went on to say that throwing strikes was the key to his success: "When I'm locating my sinker and throwing my curve for strikes I can beat anybody, especially with the runs this team usually scores for me." "Seems like we always score runs for Jack," mused Anderson in his office.

A 2–5 day with a pair of RBI enabled George Foster to end the first month of the season batting .329 with 20 RBI and three home runs. The 8–0 final on the 30th was the Reds' fifth win in a row, a streak which enabled them to finally climb over four other clubs into second place in the National League West Division. This was an encouraging note on which to end the month. Nevertheless, the Cincinnati ball club was still staring up at the

Dodgers whose phenomenal 17–3 start out of the gate and .850 winning percentage, both by far the best in all of baseball, gave them a 7½ game cushion over the Reds. If the Reds were going to catch the Dodgers, they would have to keep the momentum going. George Foster was about to pick up his own pace in an attempt to help the team do just that.

4

May 1977
Getting Untracked

George Foster went into the month of May with an eight-game hitting streak, Pete Rose with one of 16. Foster had not shown much of his usual power yet, and years later he told *Enquirer* writer Marc Hardin that Anderson had considered sitting him down for a while; but he was hitting for average and driving in runs so he continued to play. Even hotter than Foster and Rose was Ron Cey, L.A.'s All-Star third baseman known affectionately to Dodgers fans as The Penguin, for his squat physique and waddling-like running style. Cey entered the second month of the season hitting .403 with nine home runs and a new record for RBI in the month of April. His 29 RBI in the "cruelest month" eclipsed the old record of 27, which had been shared by Willie Stargell (1971) and Reggie Jackson (1974).

The Chicago Cubs were still in town for the finale of their three-game series, but it was the Los Angeles Dodgers who were still on everybody's minds. Before Sunday afternoon's game Anderson provided yet another assessment of the task that lay before Cincinnati. "We've given 'em a seven-and-a-half game spot," he said. "That's just about right. That doesn't bother us. They come back to us every year in July. Don't ask me why, but they always come back. They ain't gonna play no .750 ball. They ain't gonna play .700 ball or .680 or .650. If we play .650 ball, we'll win."

Jack Billingham, the Reds' most effective starting pitcher for 1977 so far, basically agreed with Sparky while putting it a slightly different way. "The Cincinnati Reds will win their games," he said. "We'll win our 95. If the Dodgers win 105, they beat us. But they ain't that good."

After admitting that the team had played poorly so far and were lucky to be as close to the front runners as they were, Joe Morgan chimed in with some braggadocio that sounded a little bit like whistling past the graveyard. "Those years [1972–75], chasing and catching the Dodgers, were the most fun I've ever had in baseball," he said. "When you're out front, you're always looking back. But when you're behind there's no way to look but up. Being behind makes you play harder and better. That is the big thing. We don't worry about what the Dodgers do. We don't look at what the Dodgers do. We know that if we go out and put up our wins on the board we'll catch them. If we win we've done our job. They will lose."

The most level-headed comment came from Rose, who said, "The Dodgers are off to a big start and there's nothing we can do about it. We just have to play our game and see what happens."

The preoccupied Reds failed to sweep the Cubs, who salvaged the finale 4–1 behind a quality start from Rick Reuschel (one run in 5.2 innings) and superb relief work from Bruce Sutter, who held the Reds scoreless over the final 3.1 innings. The 24-year-old Sutter from Lancaster, Pennsylvania, was at the beginning of a brilliant career that would earn him the honor of being the third relief pitcher inducted into the Baseball Hall of Fame. Sutter had been drafted out of high school in 1970 by the Washington Senators but attended Old Dominion University for one semester before dropping out. A Cubs scout found him playing semi-pro ball and signed him to a pro contract. Sutter reported to Bradenton, Florida and hurt his elbow before he could pitch more than 12 innings. He underwent surgery and discovered when he returned to the mound that his pitches were no longer very effective. The Cubs almost released him, but a minor league pitching instructor named Fred Martin taught him to throw what at the time was a revolutionary pitch: the split-fingered fastball. The new pitch, which looked like a normal fastball coming in but dropped straight downwards as it reached the plate, transformed him as a pitcher and saved his career. Despite Sutter's effectiveness at a succession of higher and higher levels, it took the Cubs until early 1976 to promote him to the big leagues. Although he didn't win the National League Rookie of the Year Award, Sutter turned in a year worthy of the honor; posting a 6–3 record with 10 saves and an ERA of 2.71 over 83 innings. That impressive debut was only a warm-up for the dominating season Sutter would have in 1977: 31 saves, an ERA of 1.35, and only 69 hits allowed in 107 innings. Speaking about the split-fingered pitch which he used to baffle the entire league, as he did the Reds on Sunday, Sutter said, "If they [the hitters] are going to hit me, they have to hit that pitch." Despite the loss, the Reds lost no further ground in the standings because the Montreal Expos managed to end the Dodgers' eight-game winning streak on Sunday; winning 6–2 on the strength of Steve Rogers' complete-game seven-hitter and home runs by Gary Carter and Del Unser.

The Reds' brief five-game homestand concluded with a split of a pair of games against the St. Louis Cardinals; the games scheduled, again most

4. May 1977

unusually, with an off day between them. The Reds took the first game 3–2 in dramatic, comeback fashion, scoring two runs in the bottom of the ninth. George Foster got things started against rookie reliever John Urrea by hitting a long fly ball to right that outfielder Joel Youngblood never got a glove on. When Foster, rounding first base, saw the ball hit the ground and take a high bounce off the artificial turf of Riverfront Stadium, he took off for second. Youngblood's throw beat him to the bag, but Cardinals shortstop Gary Templeton couldn't handle the throw and Foster slid in safely, with what the official scorers ruled a double. "I was going all the way," Foster said afterwards. "That guy [Urrea] was throwing good. You gotta take chances." After Bench popped out to the catcher in foul ground, Geronimo beat out a ground ball to short with Foster alertly going to third on the play. Pinch hitting for Doug Flynn, who'd entered the game as a defensive replacement for Rose at third base, left-handed batting Mike Lum quickly got behind in the count, taking a fastball and then a slider for strikes. "I didn't know what to look for," said Lum about the Cards' rookie who entered the game with a 0.66 ERA. Urrea threw another fastball and this time Lum swung the bat, smashing a low line drive to the right side that ate up second baseman Mike Tyson. As the ball caromed off Tyson's knee into right field, Foster scored easily, tying the game, and Geronimo headed for third. Youngblood made a good throw to third, but as third baseman Hector Cruz applied the tag the ball squirted out of his glove for an error and started rolling down the left field line. Geronimo scrambled to his feet and headed for home. Cruz retrieved the ball, but in drawing back his arm he dropped it, and Geronimo scored the winner without a throw. Considering the misplayed fly ball and the botched tag play at third, it was what is popularly known as an "ugly win," but Sparky Anderson was having none of that. "This game was important for us," he said. "It was the first game all year we came back to win and that's been our tradition. It showed, too, that we're not backing off, even though we've been losing."

As readers of the *Cincinnati Enquirer*'s Tuesday, May 3, edition enjoyed the paper's account of the Reds' come-from-behind victory over St. Louis, they were also treated to a cartoon by the inimitable Jerry Dowling about Ron Cey and his scorching first month of the season. Dowling was a caricaturist of the first order, an artist who skillfully exaggerated facial features yet still made the subject totally recognizable … and a humorist who provoked laughter and gently criticized without ever crossing the line into cruelty or character defamation. Born in Windsor, Ontario, Dowling graduated with honors in advertising design/illustration from the Ontario College of Art in Toronto in 1962. After stints as a package designer for Hiram Walker Distillery and as an editorial cartoonist for the *Windsor Herald* and later the *Detroit*

News, he landed at the *Cincinnati Enquirer* in 1967; where he soon began to labor at the vocation he was born to follow: that of sports cartoonist. His timing was perfect as he went on to chronicle the rise and fall of The Big Red Machine. It was his cartoon creation, in fact, that became the public image of the nickname for Cincinnati's world-beater ball team: that of a gargantuan, red, baseball-firing, bat-wielding, tractor-treaded, armor-plated, tank-like vehicle, driven by Sparky Anderson and manned by uniformed Reds players.

Dowling's cartoon for May 3 was titled "The Penguin Who Hates the Cold!" and it featured a big-toothed grinning Cey holding a blow torch, using it to melt the "Reds Wall of Invincibility" made of blocks of ice. The Reds' ice block wall is being lifted to a level where Cey can melt it by a tidal wave of water labeled "Big LA Lead." The flame issuing from Cey's blow torch is tagged "April RBI Record." In the background, peering around a rock formation, can be seen silhouettes of the famous comic book characters Batman and Robin; one of whose nemesis was a villain named the Penguin. Robin says, "Holy smoke Batman, the Penguin's on fire!" Batman replies, "He sees Red, Robin!" To complete the scene, a rodent named "Dirty Rat" sticks his head out of the water in the bottom right-hand corner. "Dirty Rat" was Dowling's ubiquitous device for editorial commentary, and in this cartoon he states the artist's subliminal message for the people in the Cincinnati clubhouse: "The Reds don't have it on ice!"

In complete sympathy with Dirty Rat, the Cardinals handed the Reds an 8–1 loss when the teams resumed play Wednesday night. Bob Forsch, the ace of the St. Louis pitching staff, twirled a complete-game four-hitter, running his record to 5–1. Woodie Fryman was victimized by the long ball, surrendering solo home runs in the first (Tony Scott), third (Templeton), and sixth innings (Lou Brock). His record dropped to 2–3. George Foster took the collar, ending his hitting streak at ten games.

Perhaps because of the Cardinals' barrage against Fryman, the *Enquirer's* baseball coverage included a story about suspicions that a livelier or "juiced" baseball was in use in the major leagues in 1977. As evidence of a possible alteration in the baseballs being supplied to major league teams, the story cited a 400-foot+ shot over the center field fence of Riverfront Stadium that had been hit by Braves catcher Biff Pocoroba, a player with two career homers; and the fact that lightweights such as the Phillies' Larry Bowa and Terry Harmon both already had two homers on the season. In a poll of 20 Reds players about whether or not the ball was livelier, 12 said "Yes"; six said "No"; and two were undecided. Sparky Anderson was among those voting in the affirmative. "The way some guys are hitting you can tell the thing is juiced-up," he said. "Pocoroba hitting one over the 402-foot sign? Balls are going out when the hitter is jammed. Little guys hitting home runs. You can't tell me something ain't screwy."

Understandably, Fryman agreed with Sparky, saying, "There's no doubt about it. You hit the ball halfway decent and it goes out of the park." Freddie Norman agreed too. "The ball is smaller and harder. You can feel it," he said.

Reds hitting coach Ted Kluszewski, the man who held the team record for home runs in a single season with 49, was not so sure. He said, "Not until I see some long home run will I believe the ball is livelier. The only thing I've noticed is that the balls seem to be going through the infield a lot faster this year." Johnny Bench agreed that the balls might be traveling farther than in the past, but he had an explanation for that other than a change in the ball itself. "Younger people, stronger people are hitting the ball," he said. "This is a new generation swinging the bat and that's why the balls are going out." George Foster also weighed in on the topic, and his comments indicated that as he spoke, he had his tongue firmly lodged inside his cheek. "Livelier? To me, there is no life in a baseball," he said. "It is inorganic. It doesn't breathe, and it has no soul." Nobody could argue with that opinion, but the debate about the baseball would continue all season, with no definite conclusion ever being reached.

As preoccupied with the L.A. Dodgers as they were, the Reds had another bitter rival in the National League: the Pittsburgh Pirates of the East Division. The Pirates were loaded with All-Star caliber players, and they expected to win their division every year just as the Reds expected to win theirs. And both teams had come pretty close to doing just that since the start of the decade. Since 1970, Cincinnati and Pittsburgh had won their respective divisions five out of seven seasons. Every year, for seven years, at least one of the two teams had participated in the National League Championship Series (NLCS), and in three instances (1970, 1972, and 1975) the two rivals had squared off against each other; Cincinnati winning all three times. The often heated rivalry between the Reds and Pirates reached its ludicrous and potentially most explosive culmination on May 1, 1974, when Pirates pitcher Dock Ellis took the mound at Three Rivers Stadium in Pittsburgh with the intention of beaning every batter in the Cincinnati lineup.

Ellis, a counter-cultural maverick who once threw a no-hitter against the San Diego Padres while high on LSD, felt that the Reds lacked respect for the Pirates and that his teammates were intimidated by the boys in red and white. He decided that plunking every Reds batter would send a message to Cincinnati that the Pirates were no longer their patsies. Without even bothering to act out the pretense of getting signs from his catcher, in the top of the first inning Ellis threw at and hit Rose, Morgan, and Driessen with pitches to load the bases. He next tried to hit Tony Perez, but as he recounted in *Dock Ellis in the Country of Baseball* by Donald Hall "He did not dig in. There was no way I could hit him. He was *running*. The first one I threw behind him, over his head, up against the screen, but it came back off the glass, and they didn't advance. I threw behind him because he was backing up, but then he stepped in front of the ball. The next three pitches he was *running*.... I walked him." After everybody moved up a base, Rose scoring, Ellis went after Johnny Bench. He threw two pitches in the vicinity of Bench's noggin, after which Pirates manager Danny Murtaugh had finally seen enough and walked out to the mound to relieve him. Eleven pitches, no strikes, three consecutive hit-batsmen and a walk wilder than your normal base on balls: that was Ellis' performance for the day. Stunned Reds players could hardly believe what they were witnessing in the first inning, but Ellis' little stunt did not start World War III; and once Pirates pitchers started throwing the ball over the plate, the game proceeded without further incident, Cincinnati winning 5–3.

Dock Ellis was no longer with the Pirates in 1977—he'd signed a free agent contract with the Yankees after the 1975 season—but the Buccos who hosted the Reds for a three-game series May 6–8 were not any more intimidated by the current version of the Big Red Machine than Ellis had been. They swept the Reds 6–3, 12–10, and 6–4. In the first game on Friday night Anderson played Bench in left field to give the veteran catcher's knees a rest. Foster moved over to center field and Geronimo took a night off. Trailing 3–1, the Pirates socked the game away with a five-run fifth inning against Billingham that was highlighted by pitcher John Candelaria's two-run single to right. Any ideas the Reds had about rallying were rudely stuffed by Goose Gossage, who blew his smoking fastball past them the final three innings. Gossage entered the game after Rose led off the seventh with a base hit up the middle. He struck out Griffey and Morgan and got Foster to pop out in foul ground behind first base.

Saturday afternoon's game was played before a national television audience, and the teams kept viewers glued to their sets by putting on a slugfest that was in doubt down to the final out. The Reds gave Pat Zachry a 4–0 cushion in the first inning on the strength of back-to-back home runs by Driessen and Foster off Bruce Kison; but the reigning NL Rookie of the Year didn't hold the lead for long. The Pirates scorched him for three runs in the bottom of the first, two in the second, and three more in the fifth. His day was over after he opened the fifth by walking Dave Parker and then serving up back-to-back home runs to Al Oliver and Willie Stargell. With the loss, Zachry's record dropped to 2–4. Combined, the teams used nine pitchers who allowed 27 hits and six home runs. Perhaps, the most humiliating aspect of the loss was the fact that for the second day in a row, it was a pitcher whose hitting stopped the Big Red Machine dead in its tracks. Reliever Grant Jackson's double to left field in the seventh inning knocked in Pittsburgh's winning (11th) and insurance (12th) runs. Pete Rose collected two hits in the game for the fifth game in a row and extended his hitting streak to 20 games. Referring to the three runners his team left on base in the eighth and ninth innings, Anderson groused: "We don't never drive in the run when we need it, and we don't never get the key guy out." Asked what the Reds needed to do to turn things around and end their slump, he said, "There's no magic formula to get out of it. Just keep playing."

The Reds' loss on Saturday dropped their record to 10–14, which left them 10.5 games behind the Dodgers, whose record stood at 22–5, even after a 7–4 loss in Philadelphia in 13 innings. In an unattributed story in Sunday's edition, the *Enquirer* implied that the season was essentially over for the hometown team; referring to the game of April 16 when Morgan hit his last home run as "back when the Reds were still dreaming pennant." The story postulated that if Los Angeles were to win 100 games, the Reds could lose only 47 more for the entire season; meaning ... that Cincinnati would have to go 91–47 the rest of the way, for a winning percentage of .659. The story concluded that such a scenario was "not impossible, but then again, the Dodgers well could win more than 100."

The Reds beat themselves on Sunday afternoon. Clinging to a 4–3 lead, Norman gave up a single to second baseman Rennie Stennett to open the bottom of the seventh. Norman then fielded Phil Garner's attempted sacrifice bunt, but when he threw to first Morgan was slow in getting to the bag and the baseball sailed past first for a throwing error. With runners on second and third, Norman struck out catcher Duffy Dyer and retired pinch-hitter Tommy Helms on a fly to left too shallow to allow Stennett to tag up and try for home. After shortstop Frank Taveras, batting .222 coming into the game, walked to load the bases, pinch-hitter Fernando Gonzalez beat out a slow roller to third, allowing Stennett to score and tie the game. Pittsburgh's fifth and sixth runs scored moments later when Dave Parker blasted a double off the wall in right field. Nobody wearing a Reds uniform was more frustrated at getting swept again, for the fourth time so far in 1977, than Rose, whose 0–4 day ended his hitting streak at 20 games. When he lined into a 5–3 double play in his final at bat in the seventh inning, he slammed down his bat and helmet.

The battered Reds moved on to St. Louis, Missouri, for their second four-game series of the season. They lost the opener 6–5 on Monday, May 9, in an extra-innings game decided by bullpens and base running. With the game tied 5–5 at the start of the ninth inning, Cards manager Vern Rapp turned to his not-so-secret relief pitching weapon, Al Hrabosky, known as the "Mad Hungarian." Sporting a nefarious looking Fu Manchu and staring daggers the entire time he was on the field, Hrabosky went through a psych-out routine before facing each batter: walking off the back of the mound, turning his back to the plate, visibly seething with anger, and violently firing the baseball into his glove to signal that he was ready for combat. Hrabosky acted and looked scary, and maybe a little crazy, and it didn't hurt that he also possessed a blazing fastball. Intimidated or not, the Reds loaded the bases against Hrabosky with a pair of singles sandwiched around a base on balls. Those base runners only set the scene for The Mad Hungarian. Hrabosky reached down for some extra fury and struck out George Foster, Johnny Bench, and pinch-hitter Bob Bailey in succession to leave the bases loaded.

In the top of the tenth inning, Rapp made another move which helped determine the outcome; sending Mike Anderson in to play right field in place of Hector Cruz. Ray Knight singled with two outs and then tried to score from first on Griffey's gapper into right-center field. Anderson hit cut-off man Mike Tyson who relayed the throw to cut down Knight at home. The Reds' Anderson then called on Dale Murray to pitch the bottom of the tenth, a move which didn't turn out well at all. Murray pitched to exactly one batter, catcher Ted Simmons, who went yard to win it.

The loss put the Reds six games under .500—it would be their nadir for the year—and led to more soul searching. Joe Morgan, batting .259 coming into the game, said, "I've panicked. I'm swinging good. It's all up here [tapping his head]. I'm swinging at pitches I never swung at before." Anderson agreed with Morgan's self-analysis and urged all his charges to take more walks rather than chase bad pitches. Pete Rose, who never quit thinking about baseball and how best to win games, opined that Anderson wasn't using the Reds' bench as well as he might. "When he plays Bob Bailey or Ed Armbrister, it messes up the pinch-hitting power we have." Rose suggested starting Ray Knight or Doug Flynn at third base against left-handed pitching and moving himself to first base or to left field, or Armbrister to left field; the latter moves necessitating that Foster move to center field. Asked about Rose's suggestions, Anderson rejected them. He'd thought about them already, he said, and was more worried about the team's pitching than the everyday lineup. As well he should have been, judging by the pitching staff's overall ERA of 4.46. *Cincinnati Enquirer* sports cartoonist Jerry Dowling went even further than Rose dared to go by publishing a cartoon that lampooned the team's coaching brain trust. The cartoon depicts the pennant fight between Los Angeles and Cincinnati as a race to the moon. Assembled in the foreground are the Reds' "Fly

Us to the Moon Committee": Anderson and three of his coaches (George Scherger, Larry Sheppard, and Russ Nixon), who all appear befuddled as they stare at a drawing of a World War I–era prop plane, labeled the "Big Red Machine Plan to Win Every Time." On a wall behind them is a sign indicating "'The Geniuses' Are IN." Hitting coach Ted Kluszewski looming behind the other geniuses says, "... er, Fellas"; as he tries to call their attention to what is going on behind them in the background: a modern rocket labeled "Dodgers" blasting off from the earth. In the bottom left-hand corner Dirty Rat adds his two cents' worth: "Call it Sputternik." The cartoon probably made even suffering die-hard Reds fans laugh.

The Dodgers' Tommy Lasorda wasn't laughing yet, but he was certainly enjoying himself talking about his own ball club. He told reporters that the Dodgers had gotten off to such a great start because the players had worked so hard in spring training; they'd put in lots of extra running and gotten into top physical condition. And the eight regulars had done it all as a unit. They'd worked together, hit together, and played together all spring. "It's the hardest I've ever seen a bunch of guys work," he said.

Just when the Reds were at their lowest ebb, they got a big boost on Tuesday and from an unexpected source too. Gary Nolan, whose recovery from a foot problem and mono took longer than expected, finally made his 1977 debut. He held the Cardinals scoreless for five innings while

"Fly Us to the Moon." Jerry Dowling had the two essential qualities of all great cartoonists, in spades: he could draw and he was funny. Jerry named Sparky Anderson and his coaches here, but Reds fans would have recognized them from his renderings of them. Dowling was also artistically succinct. The rocket, the diagram of the bi-plane, the sarcastic reference to the "geniuses"—it's clear the Dodgers are leaving the Reds behind."

the Reds took a 2–0 lead, and Pedro Borbon and Eastwick finished off the 2–1 victory. Stacking his lineup with right-handed hitters against the left-handed Cardinals starter Pete Falcone, Anderson started Bob Bailey and Ed Armbrister in place of Dan Driessen and Cesar Geronimo. Bailey played first base and Armbrister left field, with Foster sliding over into center; just as Rose had suggested. Armbrister figured in both Reds runs. He scored the first run in the second, after singling and coming home on a sacrifice bunt by Nolan and a single by Rose; and he drove in the game-winner in the fourth with a sacrifice fly to deep center field. Foster went 3–5 and made an important defensive play. Tony Scott led off the bottom of the ninth with a shot into the left-field corner. Given the placement of the ball, it should have been a double, putting him into scoring position, but Scott hesitated just enough rounding first base that Foster's strong throw into second nailed him. The win ended the Reds' five-game losing streak, and with the Dodgers losing in Montreal, Cincinnati picked up a game on Los Angeles for the first time since April 22.

The Reds won again on Wednesday, May 11, 5–1. Rose, Morgan, Foster, and Concepcion all went 2–4, and Billingham and Mike Caldwell managed to limit St. Louis to a single tally despite allowing 11 hits and six bases on balls. Vern Rapp tried to out-maneuver Sparky Anderson again; this time with negligible results. In the seventh the Cardinals loaded the bases against Billingham with one out and Garry Templeton due to bat. Rapp pinch-hit the left-handed batting Lou Brock for Templeton. Countering Rapp's move, Anderson brought left-hander Caldwell in from the bullpen to face Brock. Countering Anderson's move, Rapp then sent right-handed batting Mike Anderson out to pinch-hit for pinch-hitter Brock. Rapp's chess moves went for naught as Anderson grounded into a routine, inning-ending 6–4–3 double play. The back-to-back wins elated the Reds. "That's the first two of 19 in a row," said the Reds' manager. "We're riding the crest of a big wave. I can feel the salt spray in my face." Pete Rose agreed, albeit a little less poetically. "We'll be within six games [of first place] by next Friday," he predicted.

There's an old saying in baseball about the need to take the long season one day at a time, and the Reds got a painful reminder the next day of the truth of that saw when they suffered a 10–1 loss that ended the series tied at two games apiece. The loss was not only a lopsided one but a strange one as well. Three Cardinals pitchers held Cincinnati to one hit on the day, and the Reds were no-hit for 7.2 innings before Griffey doubled into the left-field corner, after Buddy Schultz, on in relief of starter John D'Acquisto, had retired 11 straight. The Reds scored their only run in the first without a hit on a walk to Rose, a wild pitch, a ground out, and a sac fly by Driessen. The Cardinals put the game away with a six-run sixth inning, keyed by a bad-hop base hit.

4. May 1977

With the bases loaded and two outs, it appeared that Reds starter Pat Zachry was going to get out of the inning with no runs scoring when he induced Don Kessinger to hit a ground ball to Joe Morgan. Kessinger had been the Cubs' outstanding starting shortstop for a decade, but his distinguished career was nearing its end at this point. Lady Luck smiled on him at this moment, as his grounder hit the lip of Busch Stadium's Astroturf carpet and bounced over Morgan's head and into center field for a double. Two runs scored on the play; and before reliever Dale Murray, who came on after Scott singled off Zachry, could get the final out of the inning the Cards had pushed four more runs across the plate.

In Atlanta, the Braves broke out the champagne and celebrated; not because they clinched the division but because they finally won a game after losing 17 straight. Owner Ted Turner, who'd acted as manager of the team the night before, had been barred from doing so again by NL President Chub Feeney, so it was third base coach Vern Benson who guided the team to victory. The Braves' real skipper, Dave Bristol, who'd been forced two days earlier to start a ten-day leave of absence so that Turner could pull his little charade, was also summoned back to Atlanta to resume his tenure. The Braves issued a face-saving release (which didn't fool anyone) stating that Bristol was being brought back from a "special scouting mission." Despite being unceremoniously deposed, Turner was happy about his team's 6–1 win over the Pittsburgh Pirates. Over the loud music and raucous jabber of the clubhouse, he said, "Geez, it sounds like Christmas Eve ... the war is over." Third baseman Jeff Burroughs said, "Let's play again right now. We're hot!"

The hero of the game for the Braves was their little (5'10", 145 pounds) Mexican starting pitcher, Max Leon, who drove in three runs and combined with reliever Rick Camp on a four-hitter. It was also Leon, employing his basic mastery of the King's English, who best encapsulated the reason for the seemingly exaggerated response to a single victory. "You win, you happy," he said. "You lose, you sad. You lose 17 times, you very sad."

If the Reds were going to get back into the race they had to start winning series, if not sweeping them. And for the moment at least, they were being handicapped by the absence of Johnny Bench whose knee problem was becoming more serious. The injury was described as a sprain, and team physician George Ballou said that the "problem seems to be centered above the knee joint." Bench said he could hear a clicking sound whenever he moved up or down on the knee and that "surgery is a real possibility." The Reds were home for eight games in ten days (May 13–22), and they managed to get the homestand off on the right foot by taking two of three against the San Francisco Giants during the first weekend. Bench sat out all three games.

The Giants started veteran Jim Barr on Friday night, and the Reds knocked him out of the game by scoring five runs in the first inning. Dispatching Barr so quickly proved especially satisfying because he'd been tough on the Reds in the past, posting a 4–0 record against them in 1976. Fred Norman, who evened his record at 2–2, shut out San Francisco for six innings and survived the grand slam which Randy Elliott hit off him in the seventh with two outs, after Eastwick came on to shut down the Giants the rest of the way. The only controversy in the 6–4 Reds win came in the second inning when Larry Herndon, beating the tag by catcher Bill Plummer, scored from second on a base hit to left by Marc Hill. He scored, that is, before an alert Driessen noticed that Herndon had stepped on Plummer's catcher's mask, not home plate. Driessen told Plummer what he'd seen, Plummer appealed to plate umpire Terry Tata, and Tata called Herndon "OUT!" Television replays showed that Driessen was right. Afterwards, Herndon disputed the decision, saying, "I stepped on the plate. If I had stepped on the mask I would have broken my ankle." Without implying anything on Plummer's part, Bench offered an interesting perspective from his years of experience: "I know a lot of catchers who put it [the mask] there [atop home plate] on purpose. They'll even put the bat there, too, so the runner can't slide."

The Giants evened the series Saturday night, winning 4–3 before the largest crowd (32,682) at Riverfront Stadium since Opening Day; by scoring twice in the top of the ninth, the winner coming on, of all things, a perfect suicide squeeze. After the Giants had tied the game 3–3 on a bases-loaded single by shortstop Tim Foli, Pedro Borbon went to work on catcher Mike Sadek. Borbon's first pitch was up and in. His second was very low, just what the doctor ordered for the Giants. Larry Herndon was already running from third as Sadek got down a perfect bunt to execute the rarely-used, heads-up play. Foster, who went 1–4 at bat, had momentarily preserved the Reds' lead in the seventh when he threw Johnnie LeMaster out at home. LeMaster, trying to score on a single by Bill Madlock, ran over Plummer, knocking him head over heels; but Plummer held onto the baseball for the out. Plummer suffered a bruised left biceps on the play. Pete Rose got the 2,800th hit of his career, putting him within sight (80 more hits) of the all-time record for hits by a switch-hitter, held by Frankie Frisch.

The extent to which Rose represented the team for many Reds fans was apparent in the first installment of the "Tank McNamara" comic strip which the *Enquirer* ran in its Sunday, May 15, edition. Written by Jeff Miller and drawn by Bill Hinds, the strip was already carried by 150 newspapers around the country. For their debut in Cincinnati, Miller and Hinds gave the strip a decidedly local flavor. In an office setting, the topic of conversation is the possibility that Pete Rose might leave the Queen City in the near future if his salary demands aren't met. An unconcerned female worker says, "So what?" Speaking on behalf of all the beer-drinking sports fans the comic strip was aimed at, her male counterpart says, "So the quality of life in this town goes down to ZIP, that's so what!!!!"

The *Enquirer*, which loved conducting polls of its readers back then, also published in the Sunday edition the results of another one they'd recently completed. Back in late April, city councilman David Mann had tried to rush through an "emergency" ordinance to rename Riverfront Stadium after Charles P. Taft, the 79-year-old who'd resigned on February 24 from Cincinnati City Council after 30 years on the job. A former butcher named Joseph P. Walsh filed suit to stop Mann's plan, insisting that the Stadium should be named after a ballplayer, not a politician. Judge William S. Mathews ruled against Walsh, declaring that the voters of Hamilton County would have to be the ones to stop Mann's measure at the polls. The issue interested the *Enquirer* enough that they wanted to see what the public thought. Should Riverfront Stadium be named after Charles P. Taft? they asked. Should the Stadium be named after anyone? And, if so, whom should it be named after?

In regard to the first, main question, the poll produced a landslide response. Ninety-eight percent of respondents said, No, Riverfront Stadium should not be named after Mr. Taft. Slightly less than ten percent said that the Stadium should be named after anybody at all. And then, of those who favored renaming Riverfront, there was widespread opinion as to whom should receive the honor. Interestingly, the top two vote-getters were Powell Crosley, Jr., former owner of the Reds and the man whom the Reds' previous ballpark had been named after; and Pete Rose. Crosley received 31 votes, Rose 29. The other suggestions: Queen City Stadium (12), former teammate of Babe Ruth and Reds radio broadcaster Waite Hoyt (11), local pol Eugene P. Ruehlmann (10), Taxpayer Stadium (7), Citizens Stadium (3), former Reds manager and courageous cancer victim Fred Hutchinson (3), Tony Perez (3), Redland Stadium (2), local entertainer and philanthropist Ruth Lyons (2), Cincinnati Stadium (2), and former Ohio Governor James Rhodes (2). In the end, the name Riverfront Stadium remained in place until 1996, when the local utility company paid to have the name changed to Cinergy Field. Many fans refused to ever accept the name change and insisted on referring to the place as "Riverfront."

The Reds took the series against San Francisco with a 6–2 victory on Sunday afternoon; getting another strong outing from Gary Nolan who allowed only four hits in seven innings. Both runs given up by Nolan came on solo home runs in the third by Bill Madlock and then Terry Whitfield.

After the game, it wasn't Madlock or Whitfield who were on Nolan's mind but Willie McCovey, the Giants' 39-year-old slugger. McCovey wasn't the terrifying force he'd once been, but he was still dangerous, a threat to hit the ball out of the park every time he swung the bat. Nolan had walked McCovey twice, before striking him out in the sixth inning. Nolan said that he'd had McCovey set up. After throwing Willie seven straight pitches away, he struck him out on an inside fastball. Discussing McCovey reminded Nolan of the history that existed between them. During his rookie year in 1967 when the 19-year-old had burst upon the National League scene, Nolan struck out 15 batters in 7.2 innings against the Giants on June 7 in a game at Crosley Field. The great Willie Mays whiffed four times that night against Nolan, and McCovey went down swinging three times himself. But Big Mac also clubbed the three-run homer in the eighth inning that beat Nolan and the Reds 4–3. Nolan remembered the moment as if it had happened the day before: walking off the mound to a standing ovation after McCovey's shot had caused manager Dave Bristol to relieve him. "I wanted to tip my hat," he said. "I couldn't. I was crying. It's a thrill I'll never forget."

Monday was an off day for the Reds, and while his teammates caught up on their rest, Johnny Bench sprang into action … as a DJ. "Lucy's in the Sky," a popular nightclub located in the downtown Holiday Inn, billed itself as the place "where the stars meet the stars." To support their claim, the hot spot took out an ad in the *Enquirer* informing the public that Bench, the club's latest "Celebrity Disc Jockey" would "program and play the music" on Monday night. A photo of the hip catcher, sporting long side burns and wearing a checked double-knit jacket, accompanied the text of the advertisement.

Bench was back in the Cincinnati lineup on Tuesday but went 0–4 as the Pirates bested the Reds 3–0, John Candelaria (eight innings) and Goose Gossage combining to limit the Reds to one extra-base hit and seven hits overall. The game wasted a good effort by Billingham, who surrendered five hits and one run in eight innings. Willie Stargell's two-run homer in the ninth against Mike Caldwell iced it for Pittsburgh. The win gave the Pirates at 23–9 a two-game lead over the Cubs in the East Division. Pirates manager Chuck Tanner was gracious after his club's decisive victory. "You better believe they are the World Champs," he said. "The season is not over for the Cincinnati Reds."

No, the season wasn't over, and as if to corroborate Tanner's remark, the Reds bounced back to spank the Pirates the next day 8–3. Sparky Anderson himself got bounced in the sixth inning by first base umpire Paul Pryor. Sparky objected to Pryor's not calling a balk on Pirates relief pitcher Terry Forster, who was stepping towards home while throwing to first to keep Reds runners close to the bag: a tactic clearly against the rules and punishable by a balk

4. May 1977

penalty. "Your eyes are in Hawaii," Anderson jeered towards Pryor. "Why don't you come sit next to me right here? You're not doing much out there." After Sparky made a few more comments and threw a helmet onto the field, Pryor had enough and gave the Reds' manager the thumb. With a fine already ensured, Anderson then went onto the field to get face-to-face with his adversary in black to get his argumentative money's worth. Speaking to reporters after the game about his first ejection of the season, Anderson said, "I knew it [his explosion] was coming. It was building up. I've been sitting there, holding my tongue. And let me tell you, we've had some stinking calls."

Neither Bench nor George Foster played in the game. Because the Pirates started left-hander Jerry Ruess, Foster was scheduled to play center field in place of Cesar Geronimo, but George sustained a minor injury warming up before the game. While leaping for a high throw, he came down awkwardly and strained his back. Asked if would play in the Reds' next game on Friday, he said, "I hope to. I don't mind the soreness. I just wish the pain would go away." Forced into the starting lineup, Geronimo went 2–4; and he and Bob Bailey, being platooned at first base, each drove in two runs in the first inning to give the Reds a 4–0 lead that was all Norman and Borbon needed to defeat Pittsburgh.

On Thursday the Reds took a break from the grind of the National League schedule to play their home game in the Kid Glove series with the Detroit Tigers. The exhibition attracted more attention than usual—two Detroit television crews were on hand—because Mark Fidrych was scheduled to make his first appearance of 1977. The young right-handed pitcher had injured his left knee while shagging batting practice flies during spring training and subsequently had it operated on. Nicknamed "The Bird" due to his resemblance to the famous "Big Bird" Sesame Street character, the lanky, mop-topped Fidrych had taken the major leagues by storm the previous year, his rookie season, by virtue of his talent, personality, and antics on the diamond. A humble, happy-go-lucky, unselfconscious kid from Worcester, Massachusetts, Fidrych had employed a fastball with tremendous, late movement on it to compile a 19–9 record with an ERA of 2.34. His outstanding pitching was only half of it; he also put on a unique side show each game, undertaking his own manicuring of the mound by hand, giving whispered instructions to the baseball, cutting the air with his hand to give his pitches directions, and running off the mound to shake hands with teammates who made good plays behind him. No one had ever seen anything like his act before, and people of all sorts, not just baseball fans, loved him. Every time Fidrych started a game, a sellout crowd was anticipated; and with the injury to his knee all that was in jeopardy. Vern Ruhle started for the Tigers and went two innings. Fidrych then came on and pitched the final seven innings of the Tigers' 4–1 win, allowing only two hits. It was an encouraging beginning to what seemed as if it might be a full recovery, but the star-crossed hero later hurt his arm and flamed out after several years of unsuccessful comebacks. Fidrych ended his five-year career with a record of 29–19. Sadly, Fidrych, one of the most beloved players to ever wear a Detroit Tigers uniform, died an accidental death in 2009 at the age of 54 while he was working underneath his dump truck.

Joe Morgan took advantage of the off day to have his eyes dilated and to undergo an eye exam, which he initiated himself. "I'm just missing pitches," he explained. The exam disclosed that the vision in his right eye had deteriorated slightly, and he was fitted for contact lenses which would not be ready until the Reds returned from an upcoming road trip to the West Coast. Morgan sat out the first game of the four-game series with the New York Mets that started Friday night.

The Mets came into Riverfront Stadium struggling mightily, seven games under .500 at 14–21. They still had 11 carryovers from the team that had won the East Division just four years earlier, in 1973: pitchers Tom Seaver, Jerry Koosman, Jon Matlack, Craig Swan, and Bob Apodaca; catchers Jerry Grote and Ron Hodges, shortstop Bud Harrelson, second baseman Felix Milan, first baseman Ed Kranepool, and outfielder-first baseman John Milner. But their current roster had too many holes, and the team was going nowhere. In fact, manager Joe Frazier would last with the team only ten more games before being canned and replaced with one of his own players: 36-year-old Joe Torre, who would begin a career as a major league skipper that would eventually land him in the National Baseball Hall of Fame. The Mets would play better under Torre but not nearly well enough, and they were destined to finish in last place, 37 games out of first. If the Reds were going to bully any team, as they'd often done in the past few years, these Mets were a good outfit to start with.

And the Reds did almost pull off a sweep, only a one-run extra-inning loss in the fourth game preventing it. The Reds began the series in style on Friday night, beating the great Tom Seaver 6–2. For some reason, the Reds had Seaver's number. They'd defeated Seaver 18 times and lost to him ten times, making them the only National League team with a record over .500 against him. Twice pitching out of trouble (two on, one out, heart of the order up), Gary Nolan won his third straight game, with two innings of scoreless relief help from Woodie Fryman, relegated to the bullpen by his lackluster starting pitching. While Morgan rested his eyes and the rest of his anatomy, George Foster returned to the lineup. He went 1-3, his first inning double into the left field corner driving in a run to give the Reds a 2-1 lead.

4. May 1977

The Reds won again on Saturday night 8–7. Both teams got into the opponent's bullpen early, and the game came down to a strange situation that did not reflect well on Mets manager Joe Frazier. With the tying run on third base and two outs in the top of the ninth inning, Mets reliever Skip Lockwood's spot in the batting order came up. Frazier had plenty of hitters available to pinchhit but no other relief pitchers available to work should the game continue into the bottom of the ninth; so he let Lockwood hit for himself. Lockwood grounded out, pitcher to first base, and the game was over. Even though Lockwood had been 2–2 at bat on the season, batting a pitcher in a game-deciding situation like this one was inexcusable. Dale Murray pitched perfect fifth and sixth innings in relief and finally picked up his first win in a Cincinnati uniform. Rose, 2–4 on the day, hit safely in his 30th (out of 33 games) game of the season, and Johnny Bench's two-run homer keyed a four-run fourth inning that tied the game 4–4 after the Mets had scored four runs themselves in the top of the inning. Morgan celebrated his return to the lineup with a pair of hits and a pair of stolen bases; the second of which broke the team career record of 320, which had been set by outfielder Bob Bescher who'd played in Cincinnati around the turn of the century (1908–13).

After the game the Reds announced the trade of pitcher Santo Alcala to the Montreal Expos for two players to be named later (those players would turn out to be pitchers Shane Rawley and Angel Torres). In comments to the media Alcala gave the Reds low grades for the way he had been handled. He said that the team put extra pressure on him by taking him out of the starting rotation when he had a bad outing. Then, they gave him no instructions on how to prepare for and adjust to relief pitching, a role he had no experience with. Nevertheless, he was looking forward to a fresh start in Montreal. "They trade me, good for me," he said. "This is my life. I try to do good over there. I have a long way to go. I know it. Now I go to the mound every fourth day and I learn a little bit more." To immediately replace Alcala on the roster, the Reds promoted 24-year-old right-hander Tom Hume, who'd posted a 3–2 record and 2.05 ERA with the Indianapolis Indians, Cincinnati's top farm club.

The Reds played their first, scheduled doubleheader of the season on Sunday, winning the first game 8–1 and dropping the nightcap 4–3 in 11 innings. Billingham outpitched Jerry Koosman, a tough left-hander, in the opener to run his record to 5–3, and Bench's three-run homer in the first provided all the run support Billingham needed. At this point in the season, Bench led the team in homers with seven; Driessen in RBI with 26. Relief pitching decided the second game, and the Reds' bullpen blinked first. After Nino Espinosa (five innings) and Skip Lockwood (four) got the Mets through the first nine innings, Frazier turned the game over to 25-year-old right-hander Jackson Todd, a lymphatic stomach cancer victim who'd been given a 30 percent chance of survival after being operated on in 1974. Borbon pitched a scoreless tenth inning for Cincinnati, and Todd did the same for the Mets, wiggling out of a one-out bases-loaded jam. The Mets took a 4–3 lead in the top of the 11th on a double by Dave Kingman and a single by Mike Phillips, and then Todd stranded the tying run on second in the bottom of the inning to win it for New York. Dave Concepcion lead off the inning with a single and then stole second base, but Todd bore down to pop up Bench, strike out Bailey looking, and retire Rose on a grounder to short. Rose went 0–10 in the doubleheader. Foster went 0–5, capping a miserable series for him; a 1–12 stretch with three strikeouts, four walks, and one RBI that lowered his batting average from .309 to .289. For National League pitchers facing Foster, it would be the calm before the storm.

Another scheduling aberration, two consecutive days off (May 23 and 24), gave the Reds a chance to rest before embarking on a trip to the West Coast, where they traditionally had trouble winning consistently. The importance of the trip caused Bench to postpone getting a blue dye injection into his bothersome left knee to facilitate x-rays. "We have a big series coming up this weekend in San Francisco and Los Angeles," he said, "and I don't want to have this thing on my mind, thinking about what the tests showed. Plus, if there WAS a reaction, I may not be able to play or else be hampered."

The Reds dropped both games in San Francisco by the same score, 6–5. For two-time defending World Champions they didn't get much of a reception; 7,041 fans showing up for Wednesday night's game, 5,702 coming out for Thursday's. The two teams themselves were part of the problem. The Reds obviously were not playing like champions, and the Giants were well on their way to a losing record of 75–87 and a fourth-place finish in the West Division. A bigger problem was the Giants' ballpark, a non-descript monstrosity, rushed to completion and plagued by cost-overruns and shoddy workmanship, built in the worst possible location. Positioned on Candlestick Point, an open piece of real estate that absorbed the full brunt of cold, damp, and fierce winds blowing in from the Pacific Ocean on a nightly basis, Candlestick Park was a terrible place for a picnic, a ballgame, or just about anything else other than possibly a field trip to collect meteorological data. The Giants' blunder in adopting the site for their new stadium after relocating from New York happened only because shrewd developers showed owner Horace Stoneham the site on a calm sunny morning before the wild nighttime winds had begun to howl. Candlestick Park quickly became notorious as a place where anything hit into the air was an adventure, and even more quickly it became a least-favorite ballpark to play in and the butt of countless jokes. San Francisco writer Herb Caen called it "the ninth blunder of the world." When Giants outfielder Jack Clark was asked what would improve conditions at Candlestick, he supplied a one-word answer: "Dynamite." Pirates pitcher Jerry Reuss said, "This wouldn't be such a bad place to play if it wasn't for the wind. I guess that's like saying hell wouldn't be such a bad place if it wasn't for the heat." And no less a savant on all things baseball than former Mets manager Casey Stengel said, to explain a pop up not caught by his team, "I have to think the wind got hold of it. Otherwise, my mind tells me my fielders would have been running towards it instead of away from it." The ultimate embarrassment over Candlestick Park came in the 1961 All-Star Game played there, when Giants pitcher Stu Miller committed a balk because the wind "blew him off" the pitching mound. (Actually, the wind caused Miller to step off the rubber mid-windup, but it sounds funnier to say the wind blew him off the mound, and the latter is how the event is usually reported. And, to the point, he *was* guilty of a balk because the wind made him lose his balance.) Years later Miller attempted to downplay the severity of the wind but his explanation hardly helped. "I knew about the wind," he said. "After all, it was my home park. But I wasn't ready for that one gust." Giants ownership tried for years to improve Candlestick Park before San Francisco finally got a new ballpark in 2000; but, as Robert F. Garratt says in his trenchant study *Home Team: The Turbulent History of the San Francisco Giants*, nothing could disguise "the fact that the place was at root both unsuitable for baseball and inhospitable for fans." Candlestick Park was so bad that Garratt identifies it as the main cause of the Giants' most serious problems during the period of the stadium's usage: the recurring poor attendance, the team's subpar performances, and, worst of all, San Francisco's near-loss of the franchise to another city on three different occasions.

What did the Reds in Wednesday night had nothing to do with where the game was played but was mainly the pitching of Tom Hume, making his major league debut with his mother and brother from St. Petersburg, Florida, part of the slender crowd at Candlestick. After working leadoff hitter Derrel Thomas to a full count, it was all downhill for Hume. Thomas scratched out an infield hit on a grounder knocked down by Morgan and was then driven in by a double into the right field corner by Bill Madlock. Darrell Evans knocked in Madlock with a double to center, which brought pitching coach Larry Shepard to the mound for a little chat while Woodie Fryman got hot in the Reds' bullpen. After walking Terry Whitfield, Hume finally got an out, retiring Willie McCovey on a fly ball to center. But after getting Gary Thomasson into a 1–2 hole, Hume made a mistake which Thomasson deposited into the right field upper deck for a three-run homer and a 5–0 Giants lead. Hume departed having completed ⅓ of an inning and with an ERA of 135.00.

The Reds' comeback efforts were led by the suddenly rejuvenated George Foster and were thwarted by Fryman who "walked the ballpark" in the fourth inning. Foster recaptured his home run stroke and hit one over the left field fence with one out and nobody on base against starter John Curtis in the second inning. He hit another one off Curtis, his sixth homer of the year, in the fourth; this time with Johnny Bench, who'd doubled, on base. Cincinnati added single runs in the sixth and seventh innings but still came up a run short. After pitching well for three innings, Fryman lost it in the fourth and loaded the bases on walks. His fourth base on balls in the inning, to Darrell Evans, forced in the Giants' sixth and ultimately winning run.

Revealingly, Sparky Anderson's mind was still on the Dodgers. "I still feel we're gonna catch the Dodgers," he said in his post-game remarks. "I know it sounds ridiculous but it's the way I feel. Why do I think we're gonna catch the Dodgers? I'm hanging it on one thing … my luck. What I'm hoping, and I hope you understand this, is that we go into Dodger Stadium and are embarrassed. I mean we're gonna go in there and they will be cocky. There'll be an air there that we usually throw out. Each guy on our team will have an embarrassing feeling and, if I know my players, they won't like it one bit. If anything is going to turn us around, that will do it. We have never felt embarrassed before. But now, with 50,000 people in there taunting us … well, I just believe we'll react."

As Sparky should have realized, the Cincinnati Reds were in no position to be looking ahead to a team they continued to regard as unreal as Big Foot; a mythical creature who was suddenly in the news. The Royal Canadian Mounted Police in Mission, British Columbia, reported that they'd unmasked a couple of men from Vancouver in their early 20s "who had for a time [three years] fooled some of the leading experts on the phenomenon." One of the men confessed to having dressed up in a large monkey suit and sauntered up to a local highway just as an intercity bus, driven by his partner in the hoax, passed by. The bus driver made sure that his passengers caught sight of the creature, and the pranksters imprinted distinctive 15-inch footprints into the ground nearby with heavy plaster molds. According to the Police, it was "the quality of the prints which had convinced the experts that the sightings should be taken seriously."

The Reds should have taken the Giants, as well as the Dodgers, more seriously. The Giants scored single runs in six different innings, including the bottom of the eighth, to edge the Reds again, 6–5. Oddly, despite scoring five runs, the Reds were 0–10 for the game with runners in scoring position.

Cincinnati's tenth one-run loss of the season (out of 22 losses) elicited a cryptic comment from Joe Morgan, which he refused to elaborate on. "I know what is wrong," he said, "but I can't say what it is publicly."

Sparky was right about one thing: Dodgers fans couldn't wait to watch their heroes take some long-in-coming retribution against the Reds, and 53,055 of them showed up on Friday night, May 27, at Dodger Stadium to do so. They weren't disappointed, as the Dodgers built a 5–0 lead against Pat Zachry over the first three innings and then salted the game away with a five-run eighth inning against Eastwick and Caldwell. The Reds were outhit 17–6 and outscored 10–3. The only highlight for Cincinnati was George Foster's seventh home run, a line drive into the right field bleachers against L.A. starter Tommy John to lead off the fourth inning. It was the Reds' fourth loss in a row. Bob Hertzel wrote a lead for his *Enquirer* story about the game that summed up the way things looked from the press box: "The 1977 season now appears to be over as the Cincinnati Reds, having put themselves in a must-win situation, didn't and now trail the Los Angeles Dodgers by 13½ games."

Perhaps it was the Dodgers who relaxed next, and who could have blamed them, considering their huge lead so early in the season? In any case, the Reds rebounded the next day and hung a 6–3 loss on Dodgers ace Don Sutton, his first defeat of the season after six victories. Foster got the Reds' decisive five-run rally in the second inning going with a one-out home run into the left field bleachers, his eighth homer of the year. It gave him the team lead in homers by one over Johnny Bench. Pete Rose hit a single on a Sutton hanging curve ball to drive in two runs, and Ken Griffey got hold of another one to drive in two more runs on a soaring homer to center. "I've been waiting to do something with that curve ball of Sutton's," he said. "Sometimes it just drops off the table, and there is no way to hit it. This one hung up there in my eyes and I really got it." Although the Reds didn't need it, Foster hit another homer the very next inning, also off Sutton. It was his fifth home run in four days and his ninth of the season. The 2–4 day also got Foster's batting average back over the .300 mark, at .305. It wouldn't drop under .300 again the rest of the season. Los Angeles manager Tommy Lasorda had seen enough of Foster. When Foster came to bat again in the fifth with two out and one on, left-hander Al Downing was on the mound. Downing was rolling right along in relief of Sutton, but Lasorda was taking no chances with the hottest hitter in the league. He brought in a right-hander, Elias Sosa, to pitch to Foster, and the move worked. Sosa struck Foster out, looking.

Jack Billingham, who was turning into the team's most reliable starter, went seven innings, allowing three hits, to pick up the win with help from Borbon and run his record to 6–3. "I was very fortunate," he said afterwards.

Reds manager Sparky Anderson visiting the mound to talk to or to replace a pitcher was a common sight in 1977. A lack of consistent starting pitching was probably the team's number one problem all year. On this night at Dodger Stadium at the end of May, veteran right-hander Jack Billingham kept the Bums in check for seven innings, even though, as he said, "I didn't have anything [on the ball]." Catcher Johnny Bench had a comeback year in 1977, hitting 31 home runs after only 17 the year before.

4. May 1977

"I didn't have anything. It was one of those days when my body and arm just wouldn't work together." Probably because his trust in the Reds' bullpen was wearing thin, Sparky Anderson asked Billingham after he'd finished the seventh if he wanted to continue. "That amazed me," said Billingham, "and I didn't say anything. He could see I was struggling, and this was a big game for everyone. We both knew I had to come out."

While admitting that the Dodgers were the best team in the league, at that time, Joe Morgan took up the rationalizing burden for the Reds. "You can't win the pennant in April and May," he claimed. "It's like an NBA game. You can't win it in the first quarter. There's too much time left after that. It's the same way with the Dodgers. This is an indication that we can put everything together, and when we do, it will be a different ball game. We won't quit. No matter how far behind we get we won't give up. They crushed us yesterday but we were at the bottom. When you're at the bottom, there's no way to go but up. You can bounce up or climb up, and I think we've started climbing."

In Cincinnati the win over the Dodgers was totally obliterated the next morning by news of a devastating tragedy that had occurred the night before, on Saturday, May 28. The ritzy, extremely popular Beverly Hills Supper Club, located in Southgate, Kentucky, about ten miles south of the Ohio River, had caught fire and burned to the ground. Originally the site of an illegal gambling house as far back as 1926, the Club had been expanded several times between 1970 and 1976 in a haphazard, uncoordinated way so that by 1977 it was a sprawling complex of bars, stages, and dining and banquet rooms; connected by a confusing maze of corridors, hallways, and service spaces. Worse, substandard electrical work abounded in the place; fire code room capacities were blithely ignored; flammable construction and decorating materials existed throughout the building; there was a serious lack of exits; and basic building protections, such as smoke detectors, alarm systems, and fire-suppression and sprinkler systems, were non-existent. In short, the Club was a catastrophe waiting to happen.

No one knows for certain what started the fire, but it was first noticed in a smaller room called the Zebra Room around 9:00 pm. The fire spread and grew quickly, and if not for the courageous decision of a young busboy to interrupt a comedy act in the Cabaret Room, where famous singer/actor John Davidson was scheduled to perform, in order to calmly ask the patrons to exit the building, the subsequent loss of life would have been even worse. Overcrowding contributed greatly to the tragedy. Altogether about 3,000 patrons were in the building, double the capacity. At least 900 people had crammed into the Cabaret Room, meant to accommodate about 600. When the building lost power and the lights went out shortly after the fire started, panic ensued and a stampede towards the Cabaret Room's one exit not already blocked by fire caused a crush of humanity that trapped many people in the smoke and fire. Most of the fire's 165 fatalities occurred to people who could not escape the Cabaret Room. The devastating loss of life would affect people in the Cincinnati area for decades and lead to numerous laws intended to prevent such disasters in the future.

A somber Reds team took the field at Dodger Stadium on Sunday afternoon to play the rubber match of the three-game series; Fred Norman (3–2) facing off against Rick Rhoden (6–2). A member of the Dodgers' Big Five rotation, Rhoden was an interesting guy. He'd overcome the bone disease osteomyelitis as a youngster and still had to wear a brace on his left knee on occasion. Signed out of Seacrest High School in Delray Beach, Florida, and possessing what scouts described as a Sandy Koufax–like fastball, he'd sped through the minor leagues, arriving in L.A. in mid–1974. He started 1976 8–0, made the NL All-Star team, and finished the year 12–3 with a league-leading winning percentage of .800. A good hitter, Rhoden would later have with the Pittsburgh Pirates an 11-game hitting streak, during which he batted .500 (16–32). On June 11, 1988, with the New York Yankees he would become the first pitcher to start a game as the Designated Hitter; he grounded out and hit a sacrifice fly. After baseball, he became a professional golfer and played in 34 tournaments on the PGA Champions Tour for Seniors. So Rick Rhoden was a savvy, formidable opponent, but May 29, 1977, was not his day.

Before a third huge crowd (52,880), the Reds played Home Run Derby against Rhoden and the Dodgers, all of their runs in the 8–1 victory coming via the long ball. Although Rhoden pitched into the seventh inning, the game was essentially over after the second. After loading the bases on singles to Rose and Griffey and a walk to Morgan, Rhoden challenged Johnny Bench with a fastball on a 3–1 count. Bad idea. Bench hit it into the left field grandstands for a 4–0 Cincinnati lead. The next inning Griffey hit a two-run homer. Not to be left out, George Foster hit yet another homer into the center field bleachers in the eighth inning off Stan Wall, giving him six homers in the past five games. Morgan capped off the barrage in the ninth with the Reds' fourth dinger of the day.

In the ebullient visiting clubhouse after the game, it was the fired-up Morgan whose tongue wagged the most defiantly. "We can't just be beating people now," he said. "We have to start beating up on 'em." Asked why the Dodgers had never caught the Reds in a pennant race before, he said, "We're a different breed than they are. That's why, when we get in front, they never catch us. It's in their minds that we caught 'em before. They know we won't quit." Asked why he'd stolen a base the day before when the Reds already had a 5–0 lead, an unwritten no-no in professional baseball, Morgan said it was in retaliation for some of the "minor league antics" the Dodgers had been pulling, such as standing at home plate to watch balls they thought were going out of the ballpark. Morgan added that Dodgers catcher Joe Ferguson hadn't said a word to him during Sunday's spanking about the previous day's stolen base prohibited by the tacit ballplayers code of conduct.

Winning the final two in Los Angeles salvaged the trip to the West Coast, and the defending World Champions headed back to the mid-west, licking their lips in anticipation of immediately beginning a seven-game home stand against the lowly Atlanta Braves. According to script, the rejuvenated Redlegs swept the three-game series.

Tom Hume redeemed himself and gave Anderson six pretty good innings in his second major league start. In allowing three earned runs in six innings his ERA, still in its incubator stage, dropped to a more palatable 11.37. George Foster, now absolutely "unconscious" at bat, blasted another home run, his 11th on the year and his seventh in six games. The solo homer to left came in the sixth inning off starter Andy Messersmith and tied the game at 3–3. Amazingly, it was the first of Foster's 11 home runs that he had hit at home, in Riverfront Stadium. The Reds put the game away with a four-run eighth inning, highlighted by Griffey's two-run triple off Rick Camp. The final score was 7–3.

After the game, nobody was in a hurry to leave the Stadium. Instead, a contingent of players lingered to watch the Dodgers-Astros game on television. The significance of the moment was not lost on Pete Rose, who said, "Look at that. A week ago I don't think you'd have seen so many of us sitting here watching the Dodgers. Early in the season we only played the Dodgers twice. We read about Ron Cey and Reggie Smith and how great they were going. But now we've been out there. We've played them and we know we can beat them. We know we're better than them…. Winning, that is what it's all about. I didn't play on a pennant winner until 1970. All the time before that was just building up statistics. I wish the '60s could have been like the '70s have been. It keeps you going, this winning. It keeps you enthusiastic, and that is what keeps you young. The older you get, the tougher it is. But when the World Series comes around and you're in it, well, that's what we're playing for."

The Dodgers, not the Atlanta Braves, were still on Sparky Anderson's mind too. "They're scared, very scared," he said. "The fans out there, they just can't forget the way we caught 'em in '73 and almost got 'em in '74. You can hear it on the sports call-in shows that they have. The players have the memory of it too, and if they blow it there won't be enough hiding places for those guys who have been through it twice before. If we can just get it to 5½ games by August. Then you'll see how hostile those fans out there can get. All I'm looking for is one shot at 'em. If we get it, we'll just see how all that charisma and bullshit they got over there helps them." Nobody needed to have it explained that Anderson's latter comment was a direct reference to the managing style of Tommy Lasorda. Nor did anyone point out that Lasorda's positive-reinforcement-on-steroids motivational methods were more similar to than different from those employed by Sparky himself.

On the last day of May the Reds used defense and timely hitting to beat Atlanta again. They turned five double plays and for the second game in a row put a crooked number on the scoreboard in a late inning. This time it was the guys at the bottom of the order who came through. The Reds' comeback got started with an umpiring controversy. With the Reds trailing 3–2 in the bottom of the eighth, Griffey opened the inning with a single to right against Braves starter Phil Niekro, who was having a forgettable season. He then stole second base on a play which led to the ejection of Braves manager Dave Bristol. The Braves believed that Griffey was out because shortstop Jerry Royster's glove with the ball inside it got between Griffey's foot and the bag as Griffey slid into second. Bristol ran out to argue the call, but base ump Lee Weyer who made the "safe" call was having none of it. According to Bristol, "He [Weyer] threw me out before I got there. He ran at me to throw me out. It was blatant. He [Griffey] slid into the glove."

In his post-game comments, Weyer neither defended nor explained the call; choosing instead to focus on Bristol's behavior. "Bristol bumped me," he claimed. "He knows it, and bumping an umpire usually carries a suspension. You can't take that. Bristol said to me, 'You haven't given us anything in eight years.' I told him I'm just out there to call 'em right."

Royster backed up Bristol all the way, saying, "He was out. His spike caught in my glove. The umpire called the play too quickly. It's a crime, amazing you can have a call like that in the big leagues."

Griffey's explanation didn't seem to clarify anything, perhaps intentionally. "I slid in and the front of my foot caught the base," he said. "When I got up, my back spike caught in Royster's glove. The glove was under my heel."

Whether the call was right or wrong, it came at a crucial time in the game, and fortunately for the Reds it went their way. The delay caused by the argument between Bristol and Weyer may have caused Niekro to lose his concentration or his rhythm or it may have been simply another case of a knuckleballer having trouble controlling his bread and butter pitch; but in any event after play resumed Niekro wild pitched Griffey to third. Morgan

4. May 1977

walked and advanced to second when Bench grounded back to Niekro; Griffey holding at third. The Braves intentionally walked Driessen to load the bases, and then Niekro induced Foster to pop out to short. With two outs, it all came down to Cesar Geronimo.

Two weeks earlier Geronimo had been struggling and his batting average had been sinking towards the "Mendoza Line": .200. Batting coach Ted Kluszewski told him that his batting stance was too wide, that it was robbing him of his power. Geronimo had been reluctant to change at first, but he finally tried it Big Klu's way and found that he liked the new stance. On Wednesday in San Francisco during his first at bat using the new stance, he homered, and he'd become one of the team's hottest hitters since then; adding 70 points to his average. He kept the good times rolling against Niekro, lining a single into center field to drive in Griffey and Morgan and put Cincinnati ahead 4–3. Concepcion then drove in Driessen with a single to left to provide the Reds with an insurance run. Murray, who held Atlanta scoreless in the eighth and ninth, got credit for the win for the second day in a row and ran his record to 3–1. He was thrilled to be the beneficiary of the late-inning scoring by his teammates. "We're getting those late inning runs, just like the Reds always did when I was pitching at Montreal. I'm gonna tell you, when you start winning, everything falls in place. We're doing it all now."

Geronimo too was feeling it, the sense of confidence throughout the Reds' clubhouse that was as palpable as the loud music blaring from the stereo speakers. "I believe we have gotten it all together," he said. "I believe we will catch the Dodgers."

5

June 1977
Gaining Momentum

The new month opened with news of Joe Torre's first win as manager of the New York Mets the day before on May 31, a 6–2 victory over the Montreal Expos. The Mets hired Torre as their "player-manager," but the title was a nominal one as Torre's career as a player essentially ended as soon as he grabbed the managerial reins. He appeared in only four more games the rest of the 1977 season. Under Torre's predecessor, Joe Frazier, the Mets had lost nine of the previous ten.

It was also announced that George Foster had been named National League Player of the Week for the week ending May 30. In that span of six games and 23 at bats, Foster had racked up seven home runs, nine RBI, and 31 total bases. He'd scored eight runs and driven in at least one run in each game. In addition to the recognition, he received a digital watch as an award. The *Enquirer* took notice of the honor by publishing a piece in its June 2 edition which attempted to give its readers some insight into Foster's personality and his thinking on various topics. According to writer Bill Braucher, Foster was a player who demonstrated uncommon devotion to his craft: "George Foster takes his 35 inch 36 ounce bat home to his downtown apartment for practice. 'I've found that if I want to excel, it has to be almost a 24-hour-a-day thing. I bring the bat home to check my swing and stance, visualizing myself at the plate, review everything in front of a mirror. I try to project myself into a game, to do something here that I'd do there.'"

Aware that the subject had been something of a sore spot for Foster, Braucher asked for the slugger's reaction to batting sixth in the Reds' lineup. Foster's reply began on topic but soon went in other directions. "Things are much different this year," he said.

> I'm batting behind the power hitters, not in front of them. So I don't get the kind of pitches I did before. Because I don't get as much to hit I have to be extra patient. I need to be more consistent with men on base, and one way to accomplish it is to avoid rush-

ing things. I know I can do it, and it's gratifying that consistency is starting to come. Still, I feel I can do better in the areas of concentration, discipline, and aggressiveness.

You have to take everything in perspective. Some guys just have more to say. If you feel inside you did the job, nobody has to pat you on the back or hand you an award. Awards should be the byproduct of goals. I got sidetracked last summer, at least subconsciously, when I was just three home runs behind Mike Schmidt and Dave Kingman. People started talking Triple Crown, and maybe I thought about it too. Certainly it's a great feat. Then, too, I wanted to see how strong I'd be if I played every day instead of sitting out some games. I wanted to play because it took so long to get the chance. I didn't get much exposure in school or the minors. Now that I've got the chance I want to make the best of it my own way. I can't sell myself like Reggie Jackson. He put a lot of pressure on himself at the same time, but in the end he'll produce; like Ali, who had to sell himself so people would pay attention. Then he backed up what he said.

In response to a question about the money he was making via his new contract, Foster said, "Some people don't understand. A player can be making $400,000 a year but comparatively little in cash; most of it in annuities or insurance policies or other benefits average workers take for granted. The money situation and the business end have taken over too much of the game. It's not as much fun as it was in the minors or when I played as a kid. But I still enjoy it and consider myself fortunate to be here. In the game itself I think of doing something to win. I want so desperately to do the best I can."

On Wednesday, June 1, the Reds completed the three-game sweep of Atlanta with a 5–2 victory; brought about in large part by the complete-game four-hitter tossed by Pat Zachry. It was Zachry's first win after four consecutive losses and upped his record to 3–6. During his losing streak he'd given up 27 runs in 25 innings of work. "It has been a long time between drinks," said a relieved Zachry afterwards. "It really has been a drought, a nightmare.... Seems like a year since I won a game." The Braves managed to keep the reigning NL Player of the Week in the ball park, but Foster still contributed to the win: getting on base three times via a HBP, a single, and a base on balls and scoring three of the Reds' five runs. The win leveled Cincinnati's record at 23–23, marking the first time in 51 days, since the fourth game of the season, that they'd been at .500. Sparky Anderson echoed the feeling of relief expressed by Zachry, saying, "At least it lets 'em know the coroner didn't get us."

The two-team home stand concluded with a four-game set against Houston, June 3–6. The Reds split the series, losing the first and third games and winning the second and fourth. The split left them at .500, a mediocrity they could ill afford.

On Thursday night it was the bullpen that once again let the team down. The Astros scored three runs in the ninth to tie the game and three more in the 11th to win it, 6–4, ending the Reds' five-game winning streak. Jack Billingham started and pitched very well but was handed a no-decision for his trouble. He went eight and a third innings and departed with two on and the Reds ahead 3–0; but Rawly Eastwick, brought in to relieve him, gave up a mammoth home run to the first batter he faced, first baseman Bob Watson, that tied the game. Players were still buzzing about the homer after the game, and most Reds felt that it was the longest fair ball hit so far at Riverfront Stadium. Strangely, it was never acknowledged in subsequent Reds media guides as a "Loge Level" or "Red Seat Home Run" (one hit into the Stadium's upper level of seats, made of red plastic); perhaps because the ball never landed in the seats but hit off the façade of the left field upper deck. Entering the 1977 season, four "Red Seat Home Runs" had been hit at Riverfront since its opening mid-way through 1970, including one hit on June 14, 1976, by George Foster. Reaching the red seats was considered a feat that only the most powerful of batters would ever accomplish.

As the game appeared to have hinged on Anderson's turn to the bullpen, the media asked him to justify the decision. "I thought Jack had had it," he said later in his office. It was an honest, obvious answer to one of the most unfair "second-guessing" questions routinely asked of professional baseball managers. If the manager leaves a tiring starting pitcher in and the pitcher winds up losing the game, the assumption is that a reliever should have been brought in. If the manager relives the same tiring starting pitcher and the relief pitcher loses the game, the media wants to know why the manager didn't stay with his starter. It's a "can't win," "gotcha" situation.

Eastwick, who had made two appearances in the past 13 days, had an explanation for his performance. "I don't know if it's the front office or what, but I haven't been getting enough work. Maybe it's the fact I haven't signed my contract." While he blew the save, the "overly-rested" Eastwick did not get saddled with the loss. That fell to Dale Murray, who gave up four hits and three earned runs in the top of the 11th. Still, Eastwick was part of an odd situation that brought a disgruntled attitude out into the open. With two on and two out in the top of the tenth inning, Eastwick appeared to get out of a jam by inducing Jose Cruz to bounce out. However, umpire Art Williams saw Anderson start out of the Reds' dugout just as Eastwick went into his limited "windup" and called "Time—no pitch," negating the play. The Reds, who had run off the field, had to go back out so that the left-handed Cruz's at bat could continue. Instead of letting Eastwick continue, Sparky called to the bullpen for Woodie Fryman in order to get a lefty-vs.-lefty matchup. Fryman got Cruz to ground into an unassisted force out at third to end the inning.

After the game, Fryman, who was not happy about being brought in to face one batter, announced that he wanted to be traded. He claimed he was not upset about being demoted to the bullpen but by the way it had been handled. "I listen to the radio and read in the newspaper that I'm in the bullpen, but no one came up to me and told me," he said. He went on to say that after eight days of not pitching he'd gone to Anderson for an explanation. "We had a long talk," Fryman said. "He told me I'd be a spot starter and used in certain situations." Apparently, despite his contention to the contrary, Fryman was upset at his reduced role on the team.

The Reds bounced back on Friday to win 4–0 behind the two-hit complete-game pitching of gutsy little Freddie Norman. Norman walked eight batters, was in trouble all night, and threw a total of 153 pitches. But he kept Houston off the scoreboard. A worn-out Norman told the media, "I made the pitches when I had to. I must have made 200 pitches. The walks just aren't me, and I am concerned about them. But, it is satisfying to pick the club up again and maybe get us going on another winning streak." George Foster and Johnny Bench accounted for all four Cincinnati runs. In the second inning Bench hit his ninth homer with Foster aboard to put Cincinnati up 2–0, and Foster hit a two-run double in the next inning to complete the scoring. Now that Bench was looking more and more like the superstar he'd been in past seasons, he was suddenly being mentioned in trade rumors involving Mets pitcher Tom Seaver. As the things that had taken a toll on Bench in 1976, *Enquirer* beat man Bob Hertzel included injuries, a lung operation, and the "mental torture of a marriage breakdown, ending in a divorce that became almost as much a circus as was his wedding."

Game three of the series on Saturday night drew a good crowd of 45,414 and was determined, as baseball games often are, by pitching. Good pitching by Houston and not so good pitching by Cincinnati. Second-year Dominican right-hander Joaquin Andujar held the Reds to six hits and one run over eight innings, and Joe Sambito closed the game out with a scoreless ninth. Andujar, 6–3 on the season, was a Reds-killer of sorts and had once belonged to the Reds. With the win on Saturday, Andujar improved his record against his former club to 4–0, and his ERA against them dropped to 1.57. The Reds had clearly made a mistake in trading Andujar for two other pitchers (Carlos Alphonso and Luis Sanchez) who never panned out, and Reds players understandably couldn't help wondering "what if" as Andujar kept them off balance all day. "They made a mistake, they trade me," Andujar said after the game. "Pete Rose, he say to me, 'Joaquin, if we had you we will easy.' I say to him. 'That's baseball.'"

Rookie Tom Hume started for Cincinnati and went two and a third innings, absorbing the 8–1 loss. Hume left with the score 3–1, but as he'd done so often thus far in the 1977 season, reliever Dale Murray gave up a hit to the first batter he faced. This allowed two inherited runners to score, both of which were charged to Hume. After getting one out, Murray then gave up a home run to Art Howe which allowed two more runs to score, giving Houston a "7" to hang on the scoreboard in the top of the third inning. Batting fifth, George Foster went 1–3, singling in the second to keep his 11-game hitting streak alive, but it was far too little to make any difference in the game's outcome. Playing shortstop in place of Concepcion, Doug Flynn (2–4) was the only Reds player to get as many as two hits.

The story of the Reds' 14–4 rout of Houston in Sunday afternoon's finale was the hitting of Johnny Bench, who clubbed two home runs and knocked in five runs while batting in the sixth spot in the order. The two homers gave Bench 11 on the season and tied him with Foster for the lead among Reds players. They both trailed the Dodgers' Ron Cey (13) and the Dodger's Reggie Smith and the Braves' Jeff Burroughs, who each had 12 homers to his credit. With 37 RBI, Bench had exactly half as many as he'd accumulated over the entire course of the 1976 season. He still trailed the Dodgers' Ron Cey who led the NL with 51 RBI, but his big day put him back into the conversation. "My objective is and always has been to win the RBI title," he said after the game. "Hitting .300 isn't a goal of mine. If I hit .234 like I did last year, what matters is when I get the hits. If I hit .280 with men on base, that's what's important." Bench also claimed to be unconcerned about where he hit in the batting order. "I have no complaints if I hit sixth or seventh. In fact, mentally, it is a bit easier. Hitting fourth you are under the gun right away. You have to think of two things: offense and defense. Further down in the lineup you don't have quite the pressure on you as a hitter and can concentrate more on handling the pitcher and calling the game." Gary Nolan, who was beginning to look like his old reliable self, picked up the win to go 4–0. He left after six innings having allowed six hits and one run. Borbon, in relief, gave up Houston's other three runs.

The game got out of hand quickly, as the Reds pounded J. R. Richard for ten hits and nine earned runs in three and a third innings. This beating avenged the handcuffing Richard had saddled the Reds with in the second week of the season. George Foster went 1–3 with two walks and two runs scored to finish the series 5–14.

In Chicago, the Reds' opponents in the previous year's World Series put on a power show yet to be displayed by the Big Red Machine in 1977. The Yankees beat the White Sox 8–6, with all their runs coming via the long ball; courtesy of Carlos May and Reggie Jackson who hit two-run homers, and

Thurman Munson, Graig Nettles, George Zeber, and Bucky Dent who all hit solo home runs. The win moved the Yankees at 29–23 back into a virtual tie for first place in the AL East Division with the Baltimore Orioles who stood at 28–22.

In another scheduling aberration, the Big Red Machine traveled to New York for a three-game series June 6–8 which comprised the entire road trip. The series was shortened to two games after the first game on Monday night was rained out. *Enquirer* beat man Bob Hertzel still had space to fill, so he wrote a feature story for Tuesday's edition on new manager Joe Torre, who'd led the Mets to six wins in his first seven games at the helm. The recent winning hadn't changed anything though. The team remained in turmoil due to the contract situations of Tom Seaver and slugger Dave Kingman, who was also unsigned; and Mets' management, embodied by Chairman of the Board Donald M. Grant, was taking a beating in the press. "The real question concerning the Mets," wrote Hertzel, "is whether Seaver or Grant will win the power struggle." It was pretty clear at this point that one of the two men would be leaving the organization in the near future.

Cartoonist Jerry Dowling supplied what commentary on the Reds was to be found in the paper that day. His latest effort, called "The Penguin Hunt," again featured the Dodgers' hot-hitting third baseman Ron Cey, leading the NL in home runs and RBI, and the two Reds players trying to catch him in both departments: Johnny Bench and George Foster. A grinning Bench is posed in the foreground, holding a bat over his shoulder marked "11 Homers, 37 RBI," and peer-

"The Penguin Hunt." Of the many Dodgers having great years in 1977, third baseman Ron Cey swung the hottest bat in the first couple of months of the season. Here Dowling plays off Cey's nickname, the Penguin, to illustrate Johnny Bench and Foster's challenge of Cey for leadership in the NL home run and RBI categories. While clearly a joke, Dowling's use of the idea of clubbing or "bashing" this baseball Penguin would not amuse animal rights activists today.

ing through binoculars. A reflection of the egg-shaped Cey appears in each lens of the binoculars. Behind Bench a grinning Foster thumps into his open hand his bat marked "11 Homers, 33 RBI." Bench says to Foster, "We're gaining on him George, get your club ready!" Foster replies, "It's [chuckle] ready John, let's get [chortle] on with the bash!" In the bottom left-hand corner, Dirty Rat squeaks, "Cey there!"

There was also news in the sports pages about the estimated crowd of 50,000 basketball fans who'd flooded the streets of Portland, Oregon, the day before to celebrate the recent accomplishments of the City's NBA franchise. It was the first time the Trail Blazers had ever made the playoffs, the first time they'd advanced to the Finals, and the first time they'd won the Championship. The Blazers had lost the first two games of the Finals in Philadelphia to the heavily-favored Seventy-Sixers and their spectacular super-star Julius Irving; but led by forward Maurice Lucas and center Bill Walton they'd stormed back to win the next four games in a row to claim the title. It remains the team's only Championship. Coach Jack Ramsay called the Blazers' unlikely run "maybe the greatest season that professional basketball has ever seen," and he praised the MVP of the Finals by saying: "I've never coached a better player. I've never coached a better competitor. And I've never coached a better person than Bill Walton."

In what was becoming a futile pattern, the water-treading Reds split the remaining two games of the series; getting shut out 8–0 by Tom Seaver on Tuesday night and returning the favor 5–0 on Wednesday night behind Jack Billingham who ran his record to 7–3. Seaver held the Reds to five hits (three by Geronimo and two by Driessen), while striking out ten. He victimized Pete Rose and George Foster three times each, and with his 2,397th whiff moved past Sandy Koufax into 13th place on the all-time list of strikeout leaders. Tom Terrific helped his own cause, hitting a sacrifice fly in the fourth inning and an RBI single in the eighth. Late in the game the crowd, demonstrating whom they favored in the power struggle tearing the team apart, repeatedly chanted, "Sea-ver, Sea-ver!" Foster's 0–4 day ended his hitting streak at 11 games.

In crafting his shut out on Wednesday night, Billingham allowed eight hits, all singles except for a double by second baseman Felix Milan to lead off the fourth inning. Batting cleanup because the Mets started left-hander Jerry Koosman, George Foster immediately put the failure of the day before behind him. With one out and two on in the first inning, he launched a long home run to left field "far into the fourth deck" of Shea Stadium. The three RBI started him on an impressive consecutive game RBI streak. Mets announcer and Hall of Famer Ralph Kiner, who himself had been a prodigious home run hitter, praised Foster, saying, "He hits a lot like Hank Aaron." The homer, Foster's 12th of the year, supplied all the runs that Billingham would need, but it wasn't his only contribution to the Reds' victory. Not especially noted for his glove, Foster made a great play in the fifth inning, which Hertzel described as a "shoestring, backhand catch while running toward the left-field line to retire Felix Milan."

Thursday, June 9, was an off day for the Reds, but there was plenty of excitement at Riverfront Stadium and in the Cincinnati media as the Montreal Expos and Tony Perez were scheduled to make their first visit of the 1977 season to the banks of the Ohio for a weekend four-game series. Dave Concepcion and Pete Rose were the first ones to get the ribbing of their beloved former teammate going. Concepcion said he couldn't wait to get to first base so he could tell Perez, "I only have two errors this year. It took me a long time but I finally get someone at first base who can catch bad throws." Third baseman Rose said, "Man, I played 12 years with him and I ain't seen him drop a bunt. You know I'm going to be way back." Sparky Anderson, on the other hand, was all business, saying, "I won't let him beat us. We'll walk him in game-winning situations. I'm not afraid of boos."

On Friday morning as a guest on a local television talk show named after the host, Bob Braun, Perez dished out some of the good-natured barbs he was well known for. He called Joe Morgan "chubby"; said that Johnny Bench was getting too old to catch next year; and told Pete Rose that he'd better play deep at third base or "I kill him with a line drive." Later, Perez visited Bob Howsam's office to pick up his 1976 World Championship ring, which his former teammates had already received. Speaking to reporters he said, "I hear there's going to be a big crowd tonight. I be here tomorrow to pick up my cut of the gate. That's why he [Howsam] trade me, so I can come in and get big crowds for him." On the field prior to the game Perez and Concepcion embraced, and later Johnny Bench came up from behind Perez and lifted him off the ground in a big bear hug. When Perez saw Joe Morgan, he kidded Morgan about having had his eyes examined. "Every place I go I read you can't see," he said. "Can't see?" replied Morgan. "I'm hitting higher than you." Ken Griffey added a barb that contained an ironic kernel of truth. "You had to leave Cincinnati to become a star," he said.

When the game began at 8:05, a couple of banners could be seen hanging from the railings in the grandstands. One said, "Welcome Home Tony." Another said, "We Love You Tony! Heet a Home Run!!" Perez came to bat for the first time leading off the top of the second inning and received a one-minute standing ovation from the crowd of 35,148. Perez's popularity was so great that the Reds' fans in attendance really did want to see him murder the

First baseman Tony Perez was the clubhouse leader of the Big Red Machine. He kept everyone loose and egos in check with pointed but good-natured barbs, and he mentored young Latin players on the team. Cincinnati management realized too late what a mistake it was to trade him to Montreal. Perez remained close to his best friends on the Reds, and every matchup between Montreal and Cincinnati in 1977 felt like a homecoming game.

ball, and they booed when Johnny Bench caught the high pop up hit by the "Big Dawg" against Reds starter Fred Norman. They booed even louder when Norman walked him in the fourth. By the time Perez came to bat and struck out in the sixth inning, the game was essentially over; the Reds enjoying a 10–0 lead which stretched to 13–1 by the end of the game. Norman and Pedro Borbon held Montreal to five hits, while the Reds pounded out seven extra-base hits: three home runs and four doubles. Pete Rose hit one of the doubles, the 500th of his career, which earned him the second standing ovation of the game. George Foster hit one of the homers, a two-run "slicing line drive into the foul screen in left" off Dan Warthen in the fourth inning; which, combined with an RBI single in the third, gave him three RBI on the day. It was Foster's 13th homer of the year. Dan Driessen also hit a homer and also drove in three runs to upstage Perez, his predecessor. A dejected Perez said afterwards, "They don't look like they need me." That was a debatable proposition which certainly had a different look to it 24 hours later.

Gary Nolan started Saturday evening's contest and, with "help" from Dale Murray, gave up all the runs scored by Montreal in the Expos' 6–4 victory. With a 2-4, 4-RBI night, Perez demonstrated why an entire city felt his absence. In the top of the first inning with one out and runners on second and third, Perez drove a Nolan pitch off the very top of the center field wall for a triple. Warren Cromartie then knocked Perez in with a single to give Montreal a 3–0 lead. Cognizant of what Sparky Anderson had said before the series began about his intention not to let Perez beat him, reporters later asked Perez if Sparky should have walked him. Perez said, "I not Babe Ruth."

In the fifth inning in the midst of another Montreal rally, Perez came through again. After Ellis Valentine doubled in a run to up the Expos' lead to 4–2, Anderson brought Murray in to face Perez with runners on second and third. In a repeat of a depressingly familiar outcome, Murray gave up a hit to the first batter he faced, allowing runs to score which were charged to the starting pitcher he replaced; in his case, Gary Nolan. Perez hit a sinking liner into right field that Griffey tried and failed to make a shoe string catch on. As Perez was not exactly known for sprinter's speed, Griffey was able to retrieve the baseball before it got too far past him and rifle a throw to Concepcion, who threw on to third base to nail the sliding Perez. But not before Perez had driven in two more runs.

After the game, Perez's mood was clearly brightened from the night before, and he directed some more "agitating" comments towards his former teammates. "I more loose, relaxed," he said. "After the standing ovation Friday night I try too hard. I got traded. I know that. I must face it. But this is fun." Asked about the hit taken away from him by Pete Rose who went to his left to make the play, Perez said he told Rose, "I never see you make a play like that before and then make a good throw." And, when asked to comment on the home runs hit in the game by Rose and Concepcion, he said, "They get home runs from two Judys. They supposed to lose." George Foster, one of the Reds' sluggers Perez kiddingly implied was a more appropriate batter to hit a home run, did not homer; but he did go 2–4, and he drove in a run in the fifth on a single to right field against starting and winning pitcher Jackie Brown. It was George's seventh RBI in three games.

A doubleheader was scheduled for Sunday June 12, and by then the focus was off Tony Perez and on what is always the most important thing in major league sports: winning. The Reds won both games but did it the hard way, overcoming a blown big lead in the first game and having to rally from 6–1 and 8–4 deficits in the nightcap. George Foster went 3–7 on the day and collected the game winning hit in each game. He also chalked up three more RBI to give him 43 for the year. He was quickly establishing himself as the most dangerous threat in the middle of the Cincinnati Reds' batting order … even when he wasn't knocking the ball over the fence.

The Reds led the first game 6–3 going into the ninth inning, but Rawley Eastwick could not close the game out. He gave up three hits and two runs before Anderson yanked him. He left with one out and the tying run on first base in the person of Larry Parrish. Pedro Borbon gave up a single to Andre Dawson which advanced Parrish to third; and then when Wayne Garrett, pinch-hitting for pitcher Dan Walker, flied out to center field, Parrish tagged up and came in to tie the score 6–6. George Foster came to bat in the bottom of the ninth with the bases loaded and one out. He hit a groundball to second baseman Dave Cash, who hesitated for a second before he threw the ball home. The split-second delay as Cash considered going to second for a try at a double play proved very costly, as it gave Ed Armbrister, pinch running for Doug Flynn, just enough time to beat the throw to Expos catcher Gary Carter. While Foster's at bat was scored a fielder's choice, it did produce the game-winning RBI. Despite the win, the Reds were dejected at almost having lost it, and Hertzel reported afterwards that "it [the dejection] showed" in the clubhouse between games.

Just as Tony Perez had done in the second game of the series, Rawley Eastwick redeemed himself in the second game of the Sunday doubleheader. After the Expos built an 8–4 lead in four innings against Jack Billingham and Dale Murray, Eastwick came on to hold them scoreless for the final five frames, as the Reds pounded five Montreal pitchers for 20 hits and an eventual 14–8 victory. After scoring four runs in the sixth inning to tie the game 8–8, the Reds pulled away with four more runs in the sixth; George Foster driving in the ninth and game-winning run with a single to right field. It was a triumph for Eastwick, but afterwards he was unable to hold back a torrent of unhappiness about his contract situation. He told Hertzel that on the advice of his agent, Jerry Kapstein, he was planning to enter the free agent market at the end of the 1977 season. Blasting the Reds with both barrels, he said, "I will never sign another contract here. Sparky, Howsam, and Wagner smile in your face and, at the same time, stick a knife in your back. You can put my name to that and spell it out. Someday the people will find out what kind of people are running this organization, and they are bleep bleep [i.e., 'horse shit']. Things will work out and the Reds'll get their due."

According to Hertzel, the Reds' position hadn't changed much. They said they'd offered Eastwick a three-year contract for fair money but had refused to guarantee it. They also claimed that Eastwick and Kapstein had never told them exactly how much money they wanted, and they said that they were now trying to trade the pitcher before Wednesday's upcoming trade deadline. While the Reds' front office may have been at their wits' end with Eastwick, they could take comfort in the team's having seemingly righted itself. In winning nine of the previous 12 games, the Reds had cut six games off the Dodgers' 13½ game lead. They were now 7½ games behind (six games behind in the loss column) with three and a half months of the season left to play. The Dodgers, who'd lost ten of their last 15, were definitely coming back to earth a bit, and catching them no longer looked like "Mission Impossible."

The Philadelphia Phillies next trotted into Cincinnati for a three-game series which would conclude the home stand. The Phillies were a good draw, and with school out for the summer attendance at Riverfront Stadium was starting to swell. Crowds of 27,147, 30,036, and 31,214 would show up for the three games: excellent figures for games played on Monday, Tuesday, and Wednesday nights. Coming in, the Phillies sat in fourth place in the East Division, 5½ games behind the surprising, front-running Chicago Cubs. The Phillies had won the Division the year before and were still expected to win it again in 1977, despite the good baseball being played by the Cubs, and by the Pirates and Cardinals, for that matter, who were also above them in the standings. The Phillies were led by three stars: left-handed pitcher Steve Carlton, third baseman Mike Schmidt, and outfielder Greg Luzinski. But they surrounded these stars with a strong supporting cast of savvy veterans, such as SS Larry Bowa, 2B Davey Johnson, OF Garry Maddox, C Tim McCarver, OF Jay Johnstone, and C Bob Boone. The Reds had to respect this conglomeration of talent, but they enjoyed an edge felt by the Phillies as well as themselves: the knowledge that they'd swept the Phils when it counted most, in the previous year's NLCS. Because of their places in the standings, both teams needed to win, if not sweep, the series.

Normally, in a game like this, both mangers would hand the ball to their aces. Danny Ozark did just that, starting the closed-lips, steely-eyed Carlton who commanded a tailing fastball and a devastating sinker. Sparky Anderson really didn't have an ace, at least not one the caliber of Carlton; so he simply turned to the guy he thought gave him the best chance of winning because he was the most rested, Woodie Fryman, who was returned to the starting rotation by default. It didn't start well for Woodie. Garry Maddox led off the game with a double, was sacrificed to third by Larry Bowa, and then, with Mike Schmidt at the plate, sauntered home on a wild pitch. When Schmidt blasted his 12th home run of the season, Fryman heard boos from the Cincinnati faithful. The left-hander recovered to end the inning without further damage, striking out Greg Luzinski and Davey Johnson.

The Reds immediately got Fryman off the hook, and it was George Foster most responsible for the rescue. Rose hit Carlton's first pitch of the game up the middle for a single. He stole second on the next pitch, the first of four Reds stolen bases on the day. An infield single by Ken Griffey put runners on the corners. When Joe Morgan hit a grounder to Johnson playing first base, Rose lit out for home but stopped and headed back to third after Johnson's throw to Tim McCarver had him beat at home. He was tagged out at third by Schmidt who took McCarver's throw. Carlton's reprieve was temporary though because he made a mistake: he gave George Foster something to hit. Foster slammed Carlton's pitch over the right field wall for his 14th homer of the year, and the Reds went on top 3–2.

After his rough beginning, Fryman settled down. He went seven innings, giving up only five hits and one more run while striking out ten. He pitched well enough to get the win but didn't because Borbon, who started the inning, allowed Philadelphia to tie the score 4–4 with a run in the eighth. The suspense didn't last long in the bottom of the ninth. Dan Driessen, who'd struck out twice in the game, led off and hit an opposite field home run against Wayne Twitchell to win it for the Reds, 5–4. All the laconic Driessen said about his dramatic, walk-off homer was "I was just glad to see something I could hit." Foster's three RBI gave him ten in six games.

Besides the Reds' resurgence, the big baseball news in Cincinnati revolved around the Tom Seaver situation and speculation that the Reds might be able to acquire him in a trade. Bob Hertzel published a four-column story on the subject in Tuesday morning's June 14 edition. Hertzel quoted Seaver, in Atlanta with the Mets, as saying: "Only one man makes me want to leave—Mr. Grant. It's taken 11 seasons but the man has taken the heart out of me. He blames me for everything that goes wrong. I just don't enjoy working for the man." The story explained that originally Seaver had said he would only accept a trade to the Cincinnati Reds, Los Angeles Dodgers, Philadelphia Phillies, or Pittsburgh Pirates, but that now he'd decided he would go anywhere. One trade rumor being circulated had Seaver coming to the Reds for Rawley Eastwick, utility infielder Doug Flynn, and minor league outfielder Steve Henderson, currently batting .312 for Triple A Indianapolis. The problem with that scenario was that with Eastwick being unsigned, the Mets might lose him to free agency after having his services for only the final three and a half months of the 1977 season. Even if Eastwick were not traded to the Mets as part of a deal for Tom Seaver, the embattled reliever did not expect to remain in Cincinnati much longer. "I'm sure I'm not going to be here after what I said," he admitted.

The Reds beat the Phillies again Tuesday night 3–2, but again the big news in the *Enquirer* the next morning had to do with the approaching trade deadline. On the front page of the sports section the game story appeared below a news story headlined: "Seaver Deal Cools. Eastwick Forcing Mets to Look Past Reds." After repeating the details of the Reds' hoped-for trade to obtain Seaver, the story stated that "Rawley Eastwick all but killed that deal Tuesday when he told NY Mets general manager Joe McDonald he is going to go through the 1977 season without a contract, no matter which team he plays for." The story also outlined some of the offers that had been made by other teams. Supposedly, Pittsburgh had dangled pitcher Bruce Kison and outfielder Al Oliver for Seaver; Philadelphia's offer of pitcher Tom Underwood and outfielder Jerry Martin was underwhelming and that was putting it mildly. Sparky Anderson implied that the Reds needed to play a bit of poker even if they were not in a position to seriously bid for the Mets' star pitcher. Sparky wanted the Reds to bid up Los Angeles so that the Dodgers would give away too much even if they did obtain the prize. He also claimed that the beleaguered and disgruntled Fryman wasn't going anywhere. Anderson felt that Fryman could still win 15 games for the ball club.

Fred Norman, Johnny Bench, and Joe Morgan took care of the Phillies in Tuesday night's 3–2 victory. Bench drove in all three Cincinnati runs with a homer, a single, and a ground ball. Morgan helped him get the third and game-winning RBI. With one out, the bases loaded, and the game tied 2–2 in the sixth inning, Bench hit a grounder to short. Running from first, Morgan took Phillies second baseman Ted Sizemore out on the play, knocking him into the air, so that his attempted double-play throw to first base was off line. Morgan's aggressive slide allowed Rose to score the go-ahead and eventual winning run from third. As for Norman, he pitched as if he were the ace the

Reds so desperately needed. His complete-game six-hitter prompted Anderson to say: "A couple of years ago in New York I told Norman he was the best left-hander in the league. I still say that. You hear about the guys like Matlack [the Mets' Jon Matlack]. They throw hard but they don't win. Fred wins. Check his record. There's no reason he shouldn't win 20 games."

Right before game time on Wednesday night, the Reds announced some shocking news: they had been able to consummate a deal with the New York Mets to obtain perhaps the best pitcher in baseball, the great Tom Seaver. To get Seaver the Reds happily parted with four players: Pat Zachry, Doug Flynn, Steve Henderson, and another young minor league outfielder, Dan Norman. The trade seemed to immediately shift the balance of power in the National League West Division, and it would be in the news for days. Tommy Lasorda's initial reaction was a calculated downplay of the potential effect the trade would have on the 1977 pennant race. "It's a helluva deal for the Reds," he said. "I hated to see Seaver go to Cincinnati but I have believed in my ball club all along and I still do." Dodgers second baseman Davey Lopes didn't like the trade one bit and was candid about his concerns. "This definitely makes them a stronger club," he said. "This has to be one of the biggest steals since the Babe Ruth trade. A trade is supposed to help both teams. But I don't think the Mets are as good a club as they were before. I can't see how they improved their team one iota."

When it was time to play ball, the excited and suddenly vastly improved Reds got the brooms out and swept the Phillies. The 8–7 comeback, extra-inning win was the team's gutsiest and most dramatic victory of the season so far.

Gary Nolan had his second bad outing in a row, and this time he didn't even get through the first inning. After a single and a fly ball out, Nolan surrendered a home run to Schmidt (who thus homered in all three games of the series), a double to Luzinski, another homer to Richie Hebner, and a single to Bob Boone before Anderson sent Larry Shepard to the mound to bring him back to the safety of the dugout. The Phillies tacked on another run in the second and two more in the fourth against Tom Hume, so that by the middle of the seventh they led 7–2. A four-run Reds rally in the bottom of the seventh cut the lead to 7–6, and that's where things stood until the bottom of the ninth. Gene Garber got two quick outs and only needed to retire George Foster to end the game. He couldn't do it. Not only that, he served up a pitch which Foster unloaded on with his black bat. The ball sailed on a tremendous arc high above the Astroturf playing field and landed five rows deep into the center field green seats to tie the game 7–7. It was Foster's 15th home run of the season. After Borbon held the stunned Phillies scoreless in the tenth, the Reds won it in the bottom of the inning in a most unexpected way. With two outs, Bob Bailey, pinch hitting for Borbon, singled into left field. The Phillies must have been waiting for Sparky Anderson to pinch run for the slow-footed Bailey because they were completely caught off guard when Bailey took off for second and slid in safely, stealing the base without anyone even covering the bag. Anderson then sent in a pinch runner for Bailey, reserve outfielder Champ Summers, who scored the winning run moments later when Pete Rose drilled a hit into right field. The win was characteristic of the Big Red Machine at their best. It was the kind of triumph that demoralized the opposition and planted doubt and fear in the psyche.

After the game it was learned that the Reds had made more deals than just the Seaver trade. They finally unloaded Rawley Eastwick, sending him to the St. Louis Cardinals in exchange for a young left-handed pitcher named Doug Capilla. And they sent Mike Caldwell to the American League's Milwaukee Brewers in exchange for two minor leaguers: pitcher Dick O'Keefe and infielder Garry Pyka. The latter deal proved to be totally one-sided, in favor of Milwaukee. O'Keefe and Pyka never made the Show, and Caldwell regained the form he'd flashed while winning 14 games for San Francisco in 1974. Caldwell went 5–8 for the Brewers in 1977, but he posted an ERA of 2.36 and won 22 games for them the next year. In seven and a half seasons with Milwaukee he would go on to win a total of 102 games. Although he wasn't informed of it until a 3:00 am phone call from Dick Wagner, Gary Nolan was also sent packing. He was swapped to the California Angels for 19-year-old minor leaguer Craig Hendrickson and a player-to-be-named-later. Although virtually nothing about it had appeared in the press in 1977, Nolan had been laboring for some time with a bad arm. He claimed that the Reds never regarded his problem as an injury but only as the typical soreness which pitchers have to work through. Perhaps the Reds finally believed that his problem was real and not merely psychological. In any event, they cut ties with him at the right time, as Nolan appeared in only five games with the Angels the rest of the season. The Angels released him the following spring, and he retired from baseball to become a blackjack dealer in Las Vegas. Finally, the Reds purchased infielder Rick Auerbach from the Texas Rangers.

All in all, it was a house cleaning which turned over 20 percent of the Reds' roster. Moreover, since the last out of the 1976 World Series, 40 percent of that roster was now no longer with the team. That night Johnny Bench looked around the clubhouse and said, "I feel like it's the end of the season, saying goodbye to everyone. Sometimes it's a cold business."

The next day, Thursday, June 16, was a travel day. The Reds were scheduled to visit the two East Division clubs they'd just hosted, and they headed to Montreal first. With no Reds game to report on, Friday's *Enquirer* focused on more reactions to the Seaver and Eastwick trades that had occurred Wednesday evening. Gordon Verrell of the *Long Beach Independent* reported that "the reaction here is that the Reds stole Seaver. The Dodgers offered Rick Rhoden in a three-player package. Rhoden thought the Mets were crazy for going for Zachry over him." Jack Lang of the *NY Daily News* reported that Seaver had broken down at an impromptu press conference held in front of his locker, and Lang characterized the trade as a big Mets mistake. "I think New York is a lot poorer and Cincinnati is a lot richer," he wrote. The Dodgers' Davey Lopes appeared to sing a different tune after having had a night to think about the Mets-Reds trade, declaring, "I don't care if he [Seaver] is pitching [for the Reds]. It's not any instant pennant." Sparky Anderson wasn't buying that attitude even for a second. "I would have to think in L. A. they'd be very sick at this time," he said. While Rawley Eastwick was no Tom Seaver, the Cardinals, according to Jack Herman of the St. Louis *Globe-Democrat*, were very excited to acquire him. "The Cardinals think they have the best bullpen in the majors now," he wrote. "And they think they can sign Eastwick. Vern Rapp is a close friend of his. Eastwick pitched for him for two years. I don't know if friendship means anything when money is concerned, but the reaction here was very good. The Cardinals think it's dynamite."

Back in 1969 when the expansion Montreal Expos went through their inaugural season, they played their home games at Jarry Park ("Parc Jarry" in the local parlance), originally a 3,000-seat recreational ballpark owned by the City. While it was expanded to accommodate 28,000 for the Expos, the place offered the lowest capacity of all major league stadiums and was inadequate in numerous other ways. A large municipal swimming pool just beyond the right-field fence, for instance, prevented the erection of outfield bleachers from foul pole to foul pole. Montreal tried to solve their ballpark problem by re-using a facility that had been built for the 1976 summer Olympics. Constructed at a cost of close to a billion dollars, Olympic Stadium ("Stade Olympique" among French-speaking natives) sported a futuristic look and seated nearly 60,000, so it did address the main concern; however, the concrete-like artificial playing surface was not conducive to baseball, and construction delays and problems plagued the place. It was supposed to have baseball's first retractable roof; but that roof, supported by a 550-foot-tall inclined tower, was not installed until 1988. The retractable roof was eventually abandoned because it was difficult to operate and slow to open and close, and Olympic Stadium became a domed stadium with a stationary roof. There was talk of building a replacement for Olympic Stadium closer to downtown Montreal, but such discussions became moot when the Montreal franchise was relocated to Washington, D.C., after the 2004 season and the team was renamed the Nationals.

The Cincinnati Reds played their first game in the new but unfinished Olympic Stadium on Friday, June 17, and 26,284 fans showed up to witness the matchup of Steve Rogers and Jack Billingham. Sitting on the bench in the Cincinnati dugout wearing a Reds uniform for the first time was Tom Seaver. George Foster christened the ballpark in style, at least from Cincinnati's perspective, by slamming a pair of home runs and knocking in four runs to lead the Reds to a 9–4 win. Rogers, the ace of the Montreal staff, was cruising right along with a 3–1 lead when Foster struck the first time. With two outs in the fifth inning, Rogers faltered, giving up singles to Joe Morgan and Dan Driessen. While advancing on Driessen's base hit, Morgan pulled his right hamstring and held at second base. He was able to gingerly trot home a few pitches later after Foster hit a "towering" home run over the left-field wall to put the Reds ahead 4–3. While leading off the ninth inning Foster hit a second home run for good measure against reliever Bill Atkinson to conclude the Red's scoring. At this point Foster had passed Ron Cey, Reggie Smith, Mike Schmidt, Greg Luzinski, his teammate Johnny Bench, and all other contenders for the league lead in home runs and RBI ... except for Jeff Burroughs of the Atlanta Braves. Burroughs also had a two-home run/4 RBI game on Friday, and his 18 home runs and 55 RBI gave him a slight advantage over Foster, who now had 17 homers and 53 RBI. Neither lead would last much longer. Rogers took the loss and saw his record drop to 8–5, while Billingham picked up his eighth win against three losses.

The next night Seaver got his first start as a Cincinnati Red, and he turned in a beauty, a three-hit complete-game shutout. Seaver struck out eight, walked none, and didn't allow any Expo to get past first base. He was so dominant that out of the 111 pitches he threw, only 33 of them were not strikes. Interest in Seaver's debut as a Red was so high that NBC rushed a crew up to Montreal in order to broadcast the game back to the New York City area. The 6–0 win was deeply satisfying to Seaver who afterwards said, "This is the start of my second career, and it is going to be a beautiful experience." Asked if thoughts about his chief tormentors, Mets chairman of the board Donald Grant and sportswriter Dick Young who'd carried water for Mets management, had crossed his mind during the game, he said, "I did not think of them. My thoughts were not to show those guys. I knew the game was on television in New York, and I just hope the people there who are Tom Seaver fans enjoyed the game." Seaver helped himself with the bat, going 2–4 and getting a key two-run single in the Reds' four-run eighth inning that put the game out of reach. Naturally, he appeared to be as elated about his hitting as his pitching.

"I hope Koos [Seaver's buddy, Mets pitcher Jerry Koosman] was watching when I got my hits," he said. "You can bet I'm going to call him."

George Foster did his part to welcome Seaver to the organization by hitting another home run, his 18th of the season. It came off starter and former teammate Santo Alcala in the fourth inning with one out and nobody on base. The home run extended the Reds' streak of hitting at least one homer per game to ten games. As for Foster, he was on a tear that appeared to have no end in sight. In the past 23 games he had produced 13 home runs and 32 RBI. This was exactly the kind of run support that Seaver had said he'd welcome from a new team, such as the Reds, before he was run out of New York. The Saturday night win was also the Red's seventh in a row and their 16th win in their previous 20 games. Nevertheless, they remained 6½ games back of the Los Angeles Dodgers, who refused to buckle to the pressure being put on them by their Ohio rivals.

As much as people in New York loved Tom Seaver, the New York Yankees managed to turn the spotlight away from him and onto themselves by dramatizing on a national television broadcast an ugly little morality play involving manager Billy Martin and outfielder Reggie Jackson. During the Yankees' 10–4 loss to the Red Sox in Boston on Saturday, Jackson loafed in pursuit of a checked-swing pop-fly double into right field by Jim Rice. An angry Martin sent Paul Blair out to right field to replace Jackson who was shocked at the hutzpah of Martin making such a substitution in the middle of an inning. As Jackson trotted off the field towards the Yankees' dugout, Boston fans jeered him lustily. In the dugout an enraged Jackson and incensed Martin both had to be restrained by multiple players and coaches from slugging it out, and the whole scene was shown to home audiences around America. After the game Martin told reporters: "Make your own observations. It's between Reggie and me. I don't make observations about my ballplayers to the press. I don't care if it was seen all over the world. I'm not going to let TV run my team. As a manager, I ask only one thing of a player—hustle. If a player doesn't hustle, it shows the club up, and I show the player up. That is the only thing I really demand. It doesn't take any ability to hustle."

In Seaver the Reds now had the hammer they'd been missing, but Sparky Anderson couldn't very well run him out to the mound every other day, or even every third day. No, a team needs a stable of dependable starting pitchers, and the lack of one was a problem still bedeviling the Reds. Three of the starting pitchers that had been counted on before the season began were now gone: Alcala, Zachry, and Nolan; and a fourth was hanging on but barely.

5. June 1977

Anderson had no choice but to put the game ball for Sunday's get-away game into his locker.

This first trip into Montreal was a home coming for Woodie Fryman, and the lefty was cheered when his name was announced as the starting pitcher for Cincinnati and again when he jogged out to the mound in the bottom of the first inning. The cheering continued but it was directed at the hometown Expos who knocked Fryman out of the game in the fourth inning via a pair of two-run home runs, by Gary Carter and Andre Dawson. Before the Reds could get back into the dugout, reliever Tom Hume gave up a three-run homer to Ellis Valentine to make it a seven-run inning that nailed it down for Montreal. The final was 8–4. Wayne Twitchell, a trade deadline acquisition from Philadelphia, pitched five innings to get the win, his first against the Reds after seven losses; but the real credit belonged to Don Stanhouse. He held the Reds hitless over the final four frames. George Foster missed another home run by inches and had to settle for a double, as his fourth-inning drive which knocked in Dan Driessen bounced off the left-field wall. Foster missed first base while watching the flight of the ball. He had to stop, go back and touch the base, and then "high-step it" (as he put it later) into second in order to reach the bag safely.

Elsewhere in baseball, the Cleveland Indians fired manager Frank Robinson and replaced him with bullpen coach Jeff Torborg. Robinson, the first black man to manage in the major leagues, said, "I definitely want to stay in baseball, and it doesn't have to be as a manager." Robinson would get several more chances to manage in the big leagues. In Los Angeles, the Dodgers not only beat the Cubs 3–1 to add a game onto their lead, they also won the brawl started when Cubs pitcher Rick Reuschel plunked Reggie Smith on the ankle with a pitch. Smith was ejected from the game, but so were Reuschel, his catcher George Mitterwald, and Cubs manager Herman Franks.

The three-game series in Philadelphia from Monday, June 20, to Wednesday, June 22, drew good beginning-of-summer crowds of 38,121, 45,091, and 47,148. It was also a disaster, as far as the Reds' starting pitching was concerned. No starter was able to go five innings, and the Phillies scored a total of 30 runs in the three games, an average of ten runs per game. Not even the high-powered offense of the Big Red Machine could be expected to score enough runs to overcome that kind of generosity.

Fred Norman saw his six-game winning streak come to an end in the opener, won by the Phillies 10–4. Norman's giving up a two-run homer in the first inning to Mike Schmidt was excusable, as it marked the fourth game in a row that the powerful Schmidt had homered against Cincinnati. His giving up a homer to banjo-hitting Larry Bowa in the second was not forgivable;

nor was his issuing three straight walks to force in a run in the third. Murray and Hume in relief were not much better than Norman, as the Phillies scored at least one run in each of the first six innings.

The Reds out-hit (17 to 13) and out-scored (10–5) the Phillies to take game two Tuesday night. Ken Griffey and Johnny Bench had three hits apiece; and George Foster, Dan Driessen, Dave Concepcion, and Cesar Geronimo each chipped in two hits. Foster capped the scoring in the top of the sixth, hitting a three-run homer, his 19th, off Warren Brusstar. It was not your garden variety long ball. According to the *Enquirer's* Hertzel, the blast to right-center field was a "mammoth home run that careened off the scoreboard some 440 feet from home plate, an area never before reached by a right-handed hitter." Including the run he drove home with a single in the first inning, Foster had four RBI on the day. His total of 60 was the high in both leagues. He also took over the lead in home runs in the National League.

As far as Sparky Anderson was concerned, the key take away from the victory was not the Reds' pounding of Phillies pitching but the major league debut performance of his starter, Paul Moskau. Nicknamed "Super-Rook," the 23-year-old Moskau came with impressive credentials: a 7–1 record for Triple A Indianapolis in 1977 before his promotion to Cincinnati and an overall minor league slate of 30–9. Moskau allowed eight hits, four walks, and four earned runs in four and two thirds innings against the Phillies, but Anderson saw enough to be encouraged, or at least hopeful. "I tried to force him onto the club [at the beginning of the year]," he said after the game. "Soon as I seen him, I liked everything he does. He's what you look for in the big leagues—an athlete. Let's face it, we're way back, even though the boys don't seem to think so. Moskau is very important to us. He has to pitch well this year if we're going to—in any way, shape or form—win it." Without even realizing it, Anderson may have been influenced in his evaluation of Moskau by the home run the kid hit in the game in his second major league at bat.

Wednesday night's game, a 15–9 romp in favor of Philadelphia, was the type of slugfest usually seen at Chicago's Wrigley Field on days when the Lake winds are blowing out. A total of eight home runs were hit—three by Cincinnati, five by Philadelphia—and Hertzel saw this profusion of power as de facto evidence of the juiced-up baseball some people believed was being used. The headline to his game report included a pun referring to the so-called "rabbit ball": "Phillies Win by 'Hare' as Reds Out-Homered." To emphasize how dominant the long ball was in the game Hertzel wrote, "Singles meant nothing. Dan Driessen collected four of them and a walk in the game and no one noticed."

Eight home runs were a lot, but without question, lackluster pitching was as responsible for the abundance of offense as much as livelier baseballs. The Reds pummeled Phillies starter Larry Christenson and reliever Ron Reed for 12 hits and nine runs in six innings. The Reds' Jack Billingham lasted four and a third innings and blew leads of 4–0 and 7–4. The Reds' bullpen, now almost a total wreck, wasn't any better as all four of the relievers who followed him gave up runs. The game hinged on the Phillies' seventh inning. Trying to keep the game tied at 9–9, Tom Hume started the inning by popping up the dangerous Mike Schmidt, who'd homered in the fifth and would homer again in the eighth. Hume then loaded the bases on a walk, a single, and another walk. In desperation, Sparky Anderson turned to the team's latest addition to the pitching staff, the 40-year-old Joe Hoerner; who had been traded from Indianapolis a couple of days before. Hoerner had once been an effective pitcher, even an All-Star selection one year, but those days were long gone. After the Texas Rangers released him at the end of the 1976 season, the Reds offered him a minor league contract as a player-coach. His even being in a Reds uniform indicated the chaotic state of the club's bullpen.

Hoerner immediately threw a wild pitch to Ted Sizemore which allowed Greg Luzinski to score from third base. He threw three more pitches wide of the plate to intentionally walk Sizemore and reload the bases. On his next pitch he finally threw a strike, but it was one Larry Bowa turned on and hit over the fence for a grand slam home run. Bowa was so thrilled he leapt into the air as he rounded first base. Of the eight pitchers who worked in the game, Tug McGraw was the only one to keep the opponent off the scoreboard. McGraw proved the old adage, that good pitching beats good hitting, by holding the Reds scoreless in the three innings (7th–9th) he pitched.

If there were a bright spot in the thumping the Reds absorbed on Wednesday or in their losing the Philadelphia series 2–1, it was the continued assault on NL pitching by George Foster, who was showing that he could not only be counted on to consistently produce runs but that he could also carry the ball club for significant stretches … if only the pitchers could keep the games close enough for his efforts on offense to matter. In the 15–9 debacle on Wednesday night Foster went 3–5, drove in four runs, and hit his 20th home run of the season. The homer to right-center field came in the top of the first against Christenson and gave the Reds a temporary 3–0 lead. In a story about Foster's importance to the Reds Hertzel checked off the slugger's personal and professional trademarks: his black bat (an exotic rarity at the time); the one-handed catches he made (to the horror of Little League coaches); the post-walk bat flip that looked, perhaps, a little arrogant; his penchant for stepping out of the box right before the pitcher began his windup; and his reliance in interviews on pet words, such as "somewhat" and "thusly." The latter was so frequent that *Enquirer* cartoonist Jerry Dowling noticed it and made use of it, having his Foster caricature utter the words. As for the stepping out of the batter's box, that was a habit that annoyed more than a few pitchers. Foster denied that he did it in order to upset or distract the pitchers. He claimed he stepped out to re-focus his own concentration; a statement which was almost certainly true. If it had the effect of also disrupting the pitcher's concentration, well ... that was just the breaks of the game.

Earlier in the season before Foster found his home run stroke and before he began driving in runs on an almost daily basis, Anderson had called his performance "the weakest .300 I've ever seen." For Hertzel's story Sparky explained more precisely what he'd meant. "Average is not important for him or Johnny Bench. I don't care what they do when no one is on base but they must hit when runners are in scoring position." According to Joe Morgan, Foster wasn't swinging for the fences even though he was in such a groove it looked like he was. "It's getting so that I can tell when he's going to hit a home run. He just looks so strong, determined standing in there. George Foster can hit 50 home runs in a season if he wants to. But he's concerned about hitting .300. I told him to go after those homers but it's hard to convince him." Apparently, Foster had learned his lesson from the year before. He wasn't going to run around like a chicken with its head cut off chasing numerical goals or awards. He wasn't, in other words, going to start over-swinging. Instead, he was going to stay focused on making the pitchers give him something to hit, and when he got something to hit he was just going to try to hit the ball as solidly and as hard as he could. He would let the baseball go where it would. And he was going to take the entire season one at bat at a time. He had what you'd call a good game plan, and he was going to stick to it.

With no game to report on, Thursday being on off-day around the National League, Friday morning's *Enquirer* focused on the major problem staring the Reds in the face: the sorry state of the bullpen now that Rawley Eastwick, last year's Fireman of the Year, was gone. The newspaper had received more than 400 letters about the situation from concerned fans; many of whom were not only dismayed that Eastwick had been traded but that he'd been traded, as Hertzel put it, "for virtually nothing" in return. Sportswriter Bill Braucher had no solution but sardonically predicted one effect of the situation: "Before the season ends Pedro Borbon's right arm may be on display in the Smithsonian." Phillies slugger Mike Schmidt weighed in with a couple of disturbing comments. "I think it's the nature of the Reds' pitching staff. With Don [Gullet] gone, they don't have the high hard fastball pitcher. Their pitchers are just comfortable to swing at." He also couldn't resist sticking in the needle, saying, "I bet Sparky would have liked to have Eastwick in this series."

Trailing as the Reds were, every series they began seemed important; however, games against Los Angeles were doubly important. When the Reds beat a team other than L.A., they had to rely on the team playing the Dodgers to win in order to gain a game in the standings. Until that happened, the Reds' gain was calculated as a half game. When the Reds beat the Dodgers themselves, head-to-head, no waiting, no contingency was involved; they gained a full game immediately. Added to that was the psychological benefit of defeating the main opponent, mano-y-mano: a factor that had aided the Reds considerably in years past. On Friday, June 24, the Reds opened a series at home that would give them a chance to knock four games off the Dodgers' lead. It was a chance, in other words, to make a major move in the pennant race.

Cincinnati fans certainly understood the significance of the series, and a standing-room-only crowd of 51,864 showed up for the Friday night tussle. An added attraction was the home debut of the team's new superstar, Tom Seaver. Oddly enough, Seaver went into the game saddled with a five-year losing streak at Riverfront Stadium. He hadn't won there since June 18, 1972. Even so, no one really expected Seaver's history pitching in Riverfront to be a factor in the outcome of the game on Friday night, and it wasn't. But the SRO crowd was. Afterwards Seaver said, "I was very nervous at the start. The big crowd, the pennant race, being in a new city, everything. It worked to make me more nervous than I thought I would be."

Benefiting from Seaver's butterflies, the Dodgers cobbled together a two-run first inning which helped them squeak out a 3–2 win. Leadoff man Davey Lopes drew a walk and then stole second base. He went to third on a single to center by Bill Russell; and after Russell moved to second on a Reggie Smith ground out to first, the Reds held a mound conference; indicating how seriously they were taking a Dodgers threat to score, even in the first inning of the first game of the series. After Seaver whiffed Ron Cey for the second out of the inning, Steve Garvey singled on a pitch which Seaver later said "wasn't in enough" to give L.A. a 2–0 lead. The Dodgers cobbled together the winning run in the sixth, Rick Monday delivering the game-winning run on another two-out single. "It was a combination of a mediocre pitch and a good hitter," said Seaver.

As for the Reds, they were stymied by the sinkerballs and changeups of left-hander Tommy John. The Reds hit no fly balls and grounded into four double plays. The only fair ball they hit into the air all night was Joe Morgan's two-run home run in the seventh inning. The Reds believed John was doctoring the baseballs, scuffing them to induce unnatural, difficult-to-hit downward movement, and they complained about it throughout the game. Home plate umpire Ed Sudol said, "Anderson showed me a couple of balls with scuff marks on them. But he was showing me the same two balls in the ninth inning as he showed me in the first. I asked him if he had any more, but he just walked away. Who knows who put the scuff marks on those balls? Sparky Anderson is a smart man and a great manager and I respect him. But who knows? The fact is that the Reds were swinging at bad pitches all night. If they would have laid off the bad pitches, like Joe Morgan did, they'd have done all right."

The victory was Tommy John's seventh win against the Reds in eight decisions. Johnny Bench, 1–4 on the night, expressed the frustration shared by many of his teammates. "I would rather face Tom Seaver than him. I hate hitting against him [John]," he moaned. Speaking for his teammates, John said, "It was a great game for me, for the team, to come in here with all the hoopla and best Tom Seaver in his first game." Attempting to salve the disappointment of losing while their new ace was on the mound, Morgan said, "In the long run it might be best for us. We learned he's [Seaver] not invincible. That is important. It just was a bad time to learn it." Sparky Anderson too refused to throw in the towel, saying, "Our mood is always the same. Kinda crazy. We don't change much day in and day out. We've been under the gun before.... World Series, playoffs. The attitude is 'You do, you do.' 'You don't, you don't.' The pressure is on them. They have to win. We were written off when we were in L. A. and thirteen and a half back. Look, a thirteen-and-a-half lead is a mortal lock. No one in the world can catch you. But we're nine and a half back. If they blow it, God help Dodger Stadium and everything around it."

One reporter, possibly thinking that a more realistic assessment might be forthcoming from the new guy used to dealing with the more sophisticated and cynical writers and readers of New York, asked Seaver if he thought the Reds were still alive. Seaver laughed and said, "That is the dumbest question I ever heard."

An update on the voting for the upcoming All-Star Game was published in Saturday morning's edition of the Cincinnati paper, and it showed that three Reds held leads for their positions: Johnny Bench at catcher, Joe Morgan at second base, and Dave Concepcion at shortstop. George Foster, who'd gone 3–4 against Tommy John in Friday night's game, was in second place among NL outfielders behind the Phillies' Greg Luzinski. Among third basemen, Pete Rose trailed Ron Cey by more than 150,000 votes for the starting role in the game; while Ken Griffey was in fourth place and Cesar Geronimo in sixth place among NL outfielders.

5. June 1977

Another big crowd of 50,062 turned out for Saturday night's game on June 25. Johnny Bench's mom and dad were in town for a visit; and the breakfast Mrs. Bench made Johnny, biscuits and "home run gravy," was just what the doctor ordered. Bench hit two home runs (numbers 15 and 16) and a double and drove in three runs in the Reds' victory which had a little bit of everything in it.

Solo home runs by Bill Russell and Dusty Baker in the first and second innings gave the Dodgers an early 2–0 lead and portended ill, but Woodie Fryman gave up only one more run in his six-inning stint and was able to claim credit for Cincinnati's eventual 7–6 win. "It was a whole lot of a struggle but I'll take it," he said later.

Bench's big day began with a double in the second inning. He homered leading off the fourth inning, and homered again in the fifth in odd circumstances. With one out and runners on the corners, George Foster hit into a 6–4 force out at second base that drove in Joe Morgan from third and erased Dan Driessen at second. Bench thought the inning was over with the out at second. After realizing the inning was still on-going, he settled into the batter's box in a daze, and with almost no focus on batting, swung at Sutton's first pitch and hit it over the left-center field wall for a two-run homer. Driessen's seventh-inning homer off Al Downing, his seventh of the year, put the Reds up 7–5 and proved to be the winning margin. The productive hitting by Bench and Driessen was crucial as Mr. Reliable, George Foster, went 0–4, although he did drive in a run with the force out.

Also contributing to the win was the Reds' defense, another traditional strength of the Big Red Machine which hadn't received much attention in 1977. In the fourth inning, L.A. hoped to add to their 3–2 lead by catching the Reds napping. They tried to squeeze Davey Lopes in from third with Bill Russell at the plate, but the Reds were ready for it. Fryman threw wide of the plate, and Bench easily tagged out Lopes, who according to Bench "accepted the tag." In the sixth inning Joe Morgan took a hit away from Rick Monday on a ground ball up the middle that he had to range far to his right to field. In the eighth Cesar Geronimo made a shoe string catch of Boog Powell's shallow pop into center field, and then in the ninth he speared Steve Garvey's shot to the warning track at the last second.

The two L.A. home runs left the Dodgers two short of their total for all of 1976 (91); and the five homers in the game added, in the opinion of Hertzel, "more fuel for those who believe the baseball is a joke." A skeptic of the rabbit ball theory, Bench nevertheless expressed surprise that his second homer made it over the wall. "I didn't think that one was going out," he said. "I thought it was just a fly ball. Then I saw the outfielders going back. I thought it might hit the wall and then I saw Baker watch it go out." Sparky Anderson couldn't have cared less about the debate over the baseballs. The win over the Dodgers was the only thing that mattered to him. "That saved our lives," he said. "To the Dodgers it was an important game. To us it was a lifesaver."

Another sellout crowd, this one of 51,715, jammed into Riverfront on Sunday, June 26, hoping the Reds could sweep a doubleheader and gain some ground on the detested Dodgers. On the strength of another quality start by Fred Norman (seven innings/three runs allowed) and home runs by Dan Driessen and Dave Concepcion the Reds won the first game 5–4. Between games Sparky Anderson said, "All that matters is what is in October. It is not over. Eight and a half games is not too much to ask if we were willing to go after them." An exasperated Anderson sounded a tad more pessimistic after rookie starting pitcher Paul Moskau gave up six runs while lasting exactly one third of an inning in the second game, won by L.A. 9–3. "People are tired of hearing us cry wolf, especially the Dodgers. We better do something in a hurry, or the party is over with," he said. "I won't cry. We knew we had a job to do. We knew we had to win three of four. We didn't do it. So we go after 'em again the next time we see them."

Considering that the Reds were outhit 26–14 in the double dip, they were probably lucky to walk away with the split. The meat of the Cincinnati batting order certainly did not have a good day; as Rose, Griffey, Morgan, Foster, and Bench went a combined 4–31, with one extra-base hit among them, Griffey's double in the first game. Foster did knock in one run in the first game to raise his RBI total to 65, but Steve Garvey hit two home runs and drove in three runs in the second game to give him a league-leading RBI total of 66. Hertzel's lead for the game story about the doubleheader split in Monday's *Enquirer* summed up the situation pretty well. "It is June. Not yet mid-season 1977. There is a pennant race. Or so it seems. The crucial time has come and gone and all that was decided was nothing has been decided."

Watching the Reds run in place was fine with the Dodgers. As Davey Lopes said in the visiting clubhouse afterwards, "We gained four games on them. That's four games out of the way, and eight and a half in front is not a bad position to be in with 90 left." The previous year the Reds had fashioned a 13–5 record against L.A. After the doubleheader, their record against them in 1977 was 4–5. There were nine more games on the schedule between the two clubs, four in August and five in September. Anderson said his ball club needed to win seven of those nine remaining games. In truth, the Reds would most likely need to win them all.

In baseball, as in life, things can always be worse, and they were worse for the Texas Rangers, who couldn't seem to keep a manager in the dugout.

5. June 1977

In one week, they went through four managers, a situation *Fort Worth Star-Telegram* beat writer Jim Reeves called "sheer madness." The Rangers started the season with Frank Lucchesi at the helm, but following a loss on June 21. that leveled the team's record at 31–31 owner Brad Corbett and team president Eddie Robinson decided to make a change. They hired former New York Giants second baseman Eddie Stanky who was coaching at South Alabama University to take over. When told of the impending change Lucchesi wept. Stanky's tenure was as brief as Ted Turner's had been: one game. That's how long it took Stanky to miss his family and realize he really didn't want the job. Some of the Rangers' players speculated that Stanky could tell he wasn't going to enjoy working with contemporary players and their modern attitudes and personal habits, such as pitcher Dock Ellis' wearing his hair in curlers. With Stanky's abrupt departure, third base coach Connie Ryan took over, making him the Rangers' third manager in three days. Ryan managed the club for almost a week until the brass settled on Orioles coach Billy Hunter as the man to guide the team the rest of the season. A strict disciplinarian, Hunter took control of the team on June 28, in Oakland, and he would lead the Rangers' swashbuckling gang of veteran players assembled from all over baseball to a 60–33 record and a second-place finish in the American League West division behind the pennant-winning Kansas City Royals.

Sparky Anderson was in no danger of being fired, but he probably felt like shedding tears of frustration after the third-place San Francisco Giants strolled into town and battered his pitching staff on Monday, June 27, for a 14–9 win in the opener of a four-game series. Starter Jack Billingham blew an 8–1 lead; the Giants putting the game away with a ten-run sixth-inning rally mounted against him and relievers Joe Henderson, another recent call-up from Indy, and Joe Hoerner. The Giants sent 13 men to the plate in that inning; and old man Willie McCovey, bad knees and all, hit two home runs in the inning. The first came against Billingham. The second came against Hoerner: a grand slam that came with odd and unfortunate aspects attached to it. Hoerner came into the game with the bases loaded, after Henderson had surrendered a run-scoring single, struck out Jack Clark, walked Rob Andrews, and issued another, run-scoring walk to Derrel Thomas. Hoener hit Darrell Evans with a pitch to force in a run, and then hit Gary Thomasson to force in another run. When Hoerner finally found the strike zone with a pitch, McCovey lost it; sending it deep into the night for the 17th grand slam of his distinguished career. Before he joined the Reds' bullpen in 1977, Hoerner had made 485 major league appearances, all in relief, without ever giving up a grand slam. In three appearances with Cincinnati, he had now given up two. Joe Morgan got four hits, Pete Rose went 3–5, Johnny Bench drove in four runs with two doubles, Dan Driessen collected a pair of doubles, and George Foster went 2-5 with a pair of RBI, but it was all for naught given how the Giants manhandled Reds pitching.

From afar, the Reds received another black eye in the form of a story about a bitter Gary Nolan, now a California Angel, who implied that the Reds had never taken the time or trouble to help him recuperate properly from injury and illness. "This is the first time I can see people are really concerned for me and doing all they can to help me," he said. "Everyone is working for me. Nobody against me."

After two lopsided, discouraging losses, the Reds got what they needed to turn things around: some decent, if not great, pitching from their starters and relievers both. With the offense still in high gear, it was enough to enable them to take the remaining three games of the series against San Francisco, 11-4, 5-4, and 11-5.

On Tuesday night rookie Doug Capilla got his first start in a Reds uniform and turned in a creditable performance, allowing three earned runs in seven innings. After his first-inning shellacking in the second game of Sunday's doubleheader against the Dodgers, Paul Moskau had quickly showered and left the ballpark. Doing that is a baseball taboo, a selfish move that shows a lack of support for one's teammates; but Sparky Anderson took it easy on the young man after the game, while still referring to the unacceptable stunt he'd pulled. "I just hope it was nerves," he said. "He will start again ... if he hasn't run off." Before starting Moskau again, Anderson gave him a chance to regain his confidence in a relief stint; and in relief of Capilla, Moskau did just that, pitching a hitless-scoreless eighth and ninth innings. Johnny Bench, now the hottest hitter on the team, led the way on offense. He went 3-4 with a home run, a pair of doubles, and a sac fly that produced five RBI. In his past seven games he'd hit five homers and driven in 13 runs.

Tom Seaver started Wednesday night and got a no-decision; leaving after eight innings with the game tied 4-4. Borbon held the Giants in check the next two innings, and by pitching a scoreless 11th Dale Murray picked up the win when the Reds scored in the bottom of the inning. The winning run came off left-hander John Curtis, who'd started the first game of the series and also relieved in the second game. He was available for relief because his start had been such a short one, of four outs duration. Curtis loaded the bases by walking Pete Rose, giving up a single to Ken Griffey, and walking Joe Morgan. With Dan Driessen at the plate, he threw a wild pitch that ricocheted off the backstop right to catcher Mike Sadek. Curtis raced in to cover home plate, and Sadek's throw to him was on target and in time to nail Rose running in from third base. With Driessen still batting, Curtis then threw another wild pitch, and this time Sadek's throw to home plate was not in time to prevent Griffey from scoring the winning run. In his three appearances against the Reds, Curtis gave up eight hits, seven walks, and ten earned runs in a total of two innings.

Ironically, just as the pitching was improving, a Jim Borgman cartoon appeared on the *Enquirer's* editorial page Thursday morning, alluding to the Reds' pitching problems, as well as problems with the Stadium itself. The cartoon depicted Riverfront Stadium with a multitude of home runs flying out of it and posed a pertinent question: "The scoreboard's busted, the stadium's mismanaged, it's millions of dollars in debt ... isn't there some way to solve this huge financial mess?" The joke was in the answer provided to the question: "Sure ... put a tax on the runs the Reds' pitchers give up."

That same morning cartoonist Jerry Dowling published one of his classics in the sports pages. His cartoon, showing Bench about to face a batting practice pitching machine instead of a real pitcher, alluded to Johnny Bench's recent hot streak. The timing of Dowling's cartoon was ironic as well, as Bench had sprained his right foot the game before, and he entered Wednesday night's contest only in the tenth inning as a pinch-hitter. Asked after the game about the statement he'd made a week earlier about catching Ron Cey in RBI, Bench said, "I really believed I'd catch Cey, but George [Foster], he's a different story. He hits in front of me. If he gets hot like he can, he'll pick up all the RBI."

The largest crowd ever (36,901) at Riverfront Stadium for a "Businessman Special," a weekday game with a 12:30 pm start, showed up on Thursday, June 30, to watch the Reds win the getaway game against the Giants, 11–5. George Foster, a bit quiet of late, went 2–5 and picked up two more RBI on a fourth-inning double to run his season total to 69. Dan Driessen did even better, knocking in four runs on a 3–4 day. Joe Morgan didn't get any hits, but amazingly did as much as either Foster or Driessen to secure the victory. He walked three times, also got on base via a fielder's choice and an error, stole two bases, and scored five runs. It was the equivalent of a pitcher winning without his best stuff, and it was one more demonstration of the various reasons he'd won back-to-back NL MVP Awards.

For once, Woodie Fryman had his best stuff, and he earned the win, allowing only two hits over six innings. While Joe Henderson had another rough outing in middle relief, Dale Murray successfully closed the game out, holding San Francisco hitless over the final one and a third innings. Bill Plummer, playing to allow Bench to rest his sprained foot, got tossed in the eighth inning for arguing balls and strikes with plate umpire Jerry Crawford. Fryman applauded him for doing so, saying, "I told him I'd pay his fine. I like a catcher to argue with an umpire, a guy who battles for you. It showed me he had a lot of guts. They're [the umpires] as human as anybody else. You've got to get your point across once in a while."

The Reds ended the month seven games over .500 at 40–33, matching their best previous winning percentage of the season. But they remained 8½ games behind Los Angeles. They had a long way to go, and every player on the team knew it.

6

July 1977

Spreading the Souvenirs Around

Hal King. A name little recognized by the world at large or even by baseball fans in general. But a name that resonates with a nostalgic sense of glory and exhilaration for fans of the Cincinnati Reds.

Harold "Hal" King of tiny Oviedo, Florida, was a backup catcher with four different major league teams, and he is remembered today for one swing of the bat; a swing which saved the Reds from certain defeat in a mid-season game against the Los Angeles Dodgers and, in the process, turned around the 1973 pennant race in the National League West Division.

King didn't play much at all in 1973, and before the July 1 game during which he made his mark most Cincinnati fans didn't even know he was on the team. It was once said about imperious New York Yankees owner George Steinbrenner that "there's nothing more limited than being a limited partner of George Steinbrenner." In a similar way, you couldn't be more of a backup than when you were the backup catcher to Johnny Bench. For King, it was even worse than that, for he was actually the backup to Bench's first-line backup, Bill Plummer. Being the third-string catcher meant that King spent the vast majority of his time in uniform in the Reds' bullpen; watching the games like a fan or warming up relievers who needed to get their arms loose.

Obscure players like Hal King did not win the devotion of large numbers of fans, but King did have a one-man fan club as rabid as any devoted to Babe Ruth or Mickey Mantle. The one "man" in the club was an eight-year-old lad named Scott Hannig, who today is a Miamisburg, Ohio, jewelry salesman and a baseball artist so devoted to the Cincinnati Reds and his art that he executed more than 800 different miniature paintings to illustrate a graphic novel about a former Reds manager, entitled *Hutch: Baseball's Fred Hutchinson and a Legacy of Courage*. Hannig followed the Reds religiously from his home in Anderson Township, a neighborhood on the east side of Cincinnati; and like almost every boy born in Cincinnati and its environs, he grew up playing

Little League-level baseball, known locally as "Knot Hole" baseball. But he didn't play it very well. Hannig was a catcher, and he began to become aware of his deficiencies one day when an umpire said to him, "Son, if you're not going to use that mitt, do you mind if I borrow it." Because of the kindness of his coach, a man named Bud Linville, Hannig continued to catch for Jerry's Restaurant despite all the passed balls; and he recognized in Hal King, the backup to the backup catcher of the Reds, a kindred spirit.

King's big day came on Sunday, July 1, 1973, in the first game of a doubleheader between the high-flying Dodgers and the struggling Reds. The day before, the Reds had blown a 5–1 lead and lost 8–7 in 13 innings to drop into fourth place, 11 games behind first-place Los Angeles. They were losing 3–1 in the bottom of the ninth inning and in danger of falling 12 games behind when, with two outs and a runner on second base, Johnny Bench pinch-hit for Dave Concepcion. The Dodgers intentionally walked Bench to set up a force at second and third and also to get to the next batter, Bill Plummer, who'd started the game at catcher to give Bench a day off. Sparky Anderson sent the left-handed batting King up to pinch-hit for Plummer. Dodgers starting pitcher Don Sutton quickly got ahead 0–2 in the count, but King hit the next pitch, a screwball, over the right field wall for a stunning three-run walk-off home run and 4–3 Reds win. A photographer perfectly captured the essence of the moment in a photo familiar to Reds fans: King approaching the end of his home run trot around the bases, a welcoming committee of ecstatic teammates—Tony Perez, Pete Rose, Joe Morgan, Darrel Chaney, and Bobby Tolan—standing shoulder-to-shoulder in a half circle around home plate, their palms upturned ready to be slapped by King, with more teammates racing up to join them. The victory over the Dodgers and their ace when he needed only one more strike to finish the game set the Reds afire and made them almost unbeatable going forward. They won the nightcap 3–2 in ten innings on a double by Tony Perez, beat the Dodgers the next day in the series finale 4–2 when Perez hit a two-run homer in the bottom of the ninth, and went on to overtake L.A. and win the division by 5½ games, going 60–26 from that July 1 game to the end of the season. The home run also inspired a starry-eyed Knot Hole catcher with a big hole in his catcher's mitt. "The home run vindicated me," says Scott Hannig, "and it made an indelible mark on me. I knew then that a person doesn't have to be a superstar to be a hero … at least for a game or two or a few moments."

The July 1 contest became known as "The Hal King Game" to Reds fans like Hannig, but King had a few other moments to remember; including a Reds win on July 9, in Montreal that he helped bring about with a sixth-inning pinch-hit grand slam against Pat Jarvis. Since April of 1975, King had been playing for Coahuilla in the Mexican League, which he told Bob Hertzel was comparable to Double A ball in the United States. Of course, the 33-year-old King felt that he was still good enough to help a major league club.

In retrospect, the odd thing about Hal King is that based strictly on the numbers, he appears to have been a legitimate slugger. In 1973, for instance, he batted only 43 times and hit a dismal .186; however, four of his eight hits were home runs, giving him a home run percentage of 9.3, a Ruthian figure! (Home run percentage indicates how many home runs a player averages per 100 at bats.) King's best year in the majors came in 1970 with Atlanta when, perhaps not coincidentally, he got to play the most. He appeared in 89 games, had 204 at bats, and hit .260 with 30 RBI and 11 homers; producing a very good home run percentage of 5.4. Over his career, King appeared in 322 games, recorded 683 at bats, and homered 24 times. His lifetime home run percentage of 3.5 would not cause a member of SABR (Society for American Baseball Research) to have an analytics malfunction, but it is interesting to note that it is higher than the percentage achieved by any Reds player for the 1977 season, other than Johnny Bench, George Foster, and Champ Summers.

The Reds opened July with a road trip to San Diego, Atlanta, and Houston. The ten-game, 11-day sojourn was their longest of the season so far. And while the Reds had no Hal King on the bench waiting to pinch-hit a home run that would turn the season around, they did have the National League Player of the Month for June in their lineup: George Foster, whose nine home runs, 30 runs, 38 RBI, and .333 batting average in 28 games earned him the honor.

As if the season were a book he was reading, Foster picked up in July right where he'd left off the month before. On Friday, July 1, in the third inning against starter Bob Shirley, he blasted a two-run home run over the right-center field fence at San Diego Stadium (later renamed Jack Murphy Stadium) to provide all the runs the Reds would need, as Fred Norman pitched a superb five-hitter to win 2–1. Norman struck out eight and only lost his shutout with two outs in the ninth when Gene Tenace touched him for a solo home run. The win upped Norman's record to a team-best 9–3. Foster's homer was his 21st of the season, and it tied him with Mike Schmidt for the league lead. It was also the 100th home run of his career. Anybody but George Foster would have toasted the achievement in the clubhouse after the game with at least a glass or two of champagne. Asked about his penchant for hitting his home runs to all fields, Foster joked, "Abner Doubleday said he didn't want any discrimination between left field, right field and center field, so I'm just doing my part." Cincinnati's fourth win in a row was enough to re-energize Sparky Anderson's optimism. "We're making our move," he said. "We're ready to win 40 of 50, to go on a red hot streak."

The Reds made it five in a row with a 6–3 victory Saturday night, and the hero of the game was 24-year-old rookie Ray Knight, playing third base in place of Pete Rose. Plagued by bone chips in his right elbow, Rose was in an 0–13 slump, and so Anderson thought it best to rest him. Rose's consecutive games played streak of 564 games did not end though, as he pinch-hit, unsuccessfully, in the eighth inning. Knight salted the game away for Cincinnati with his first major league home run. With the score tied 2–2 in the top of the seventh inning, he went yard against starter Bob Owchinko with two runners on base. The left-handed Owchinko had gotten Knight out in his previous at bat, jamming him with an inside slider; so the heady Knight was looking for the same pitch in the seventh. "It was a matter of coming inside once too often," he said afterwards. Paul Moskau started on the mound for the Reds but left with one out in the fourth due to a strained groin muscle. He was followed by Dale Murray, who got the win to go 5–2, and Pedro Borbon, who picked up his sixth save.

George Foster hit his second home run of the series on Sunday afternoon, a solo shot to left field in the first inning against Padres starting pitcher Dave Freisleben, and the Reds jumped out to a 5–0 lead after two and a half innings. But, once again, Jack Billingham couldn't stand prosperity. He blew the lead, gave up a total of eight runs, and was saddled with the 8–7 loss. It wasn't entirely his fault as an error by Pete Rose on a grounder hit by Mike Ivie led to three unearned runs in the third inning. The player who sealed the deal for San Diego was 6'6" outfielder Dave Kingman, a boyhood friend of Foster's. Kingman and Foster had played on the same Little League All-Star team in 1961 in Hawthorne, California. Here, 16 years later, they both homered in the same major league game; Kingman's three-run blast coming off Billingham in the sixth inning. Kingman, who like Foster had begun his career as a San Francisco Giant, was in the middle of a crazy season. He'd started 1977 with the New York Mets, but they'd traded him to San Diego on June 15. The Padres would later sell him to the California Angels, and before the season was over the Angels would sell him to the New York Yankees. This rolling stone activity was due in part to Kingman's personality which tended to rub people the wrong way, but the main reason he was treated in 1977 as a "rent-a-player" is that he was playing out his option. After the season he signed a free agent contract for 1978 with the Chicago Cubs. The stiff-looking Kingman was a liability on defense and he struck out a lot, but with a long, sweeping swing he generated a lot of power and many of his home runs were lengthy "no-doubters." In the mid–1980s, Kingman would surprisingly rank fifth in career home run percentage; at the end of 2017 he had fallen to 13th, which is still a respectable ranking.

The Reds rallied in the ninth against San Diego's great closer Rollie Fingers, scoring twice on a Dan Driessen home run, but Fingers got Foster to fly out to left field to end it. A stoic Billingham who described himself as "consistently inconsistent" had now blown leads of 6–0, 6–0, 8–1, and 5–0. Something had to be done, and Sparky Anderson did it; the next day demoting Billingham to the bullpen, and promoting rookie Doug Capilla to the starting rotation. While Anderson was not crazy about playing young players, he felt that circumstances had forced his hand. Referring to the 25-year-old Capilla and 23-year-old Paul Moskau, he said, "I'm going to have to bring two kids along. If it's not a wasted year. If the staff ERA is going to be 4.45, then it's going to be 4.45 with kids." (Actually, as Hertzel pointed out, the staff ERA at the time was 4.55.) Obviously having been briefed by Anderson, the veteran Billingham accepted the demotion resignedly, saying, "I've never been on a staff where all five starters were going good. There's always one in the outhouse, and right now I own that piece of real estate. But I intend to sell it soon. What can Sparky do but put me in the bullpen. This way he can see what the kids can do. I've been there before. I'll be out there again, too. I don't know how long it will be but I'll be back starting."

If there was a National League team with a pitching staff in greater disarray than that of the Cincinnati Reds it was the Atlanta Braves, and the three-game series the Reds played next against them bore that out. The Reds won the final two games, averaging 12 runs per win. They lost the opener 5–4 on July 4, leaving 11 runners on base and going 1–13 with runners in scoring position against Phil Niekro and Rick Camp. Tom Seaver pitched just poorly enough to lose, dropping his overall season record to 8–5. In addition to a rare win (coming as it did against the Reds and against Seaver), the crowd of 50,595 was also treated to a post-game fireworks show celebrating the nation's birthday at Atlanta-Fulton County Stadium.

The next night a more typical Braves crowd of 14,344 were on hand for game number two and a pre-game home run hitting contest won by, no surprise, George Foster, who in his ten allotted swings knocked five batting practice-speed pitches over the outfield wall. Remaining in home run-derby mode once the main event started, Foster hit one that counted while leading off the fifth inning against Buzz Capra; Atlanta's second of six pitchers on the day. The shot into the bleachers beyond the left-center field power alley was Foster's 23rd of the season, and it upped his RBI total to 74. Dan Driessen, Ed Armbrister, and Dave Concepcion also homered to contribute to the Reds' 9–4 thumping of the Braves. Woodie Fryman held Atlanta to two runs in six innings while striking out nine to even his record at 5–5. Apparently, Fryman had been doing some soul searching, the fruitful results of which he shared with the media after the game. "My problem was that I was trying to be too much of a pitcher," he said. "I'm a power pitcher. Always. I get people out with a fastball inside or outside or a hard slider inside or outside. Early this year I was throwing changeups and curveballs, just too much off-speed stuff. I'm not sure why I was doing it. I think maybe I realized I was getting older and thought I'd lost something off my fastball. Then a couple of weeks ago I realized that if I lose my fastball, I'm gone anyway."

Wednesday's get-away game was a 15–13 slug-and-mistake fest, which the Braves couldn't win despite the Reds handing them ten unearned runs produced by four costly Cincinnati errors. Two of the errors were made by Fred Norman in an ugly fourth inning. Enjoying a 6–0 cushion, Norman got himself into trouble by throwing a double-play ball into center field to put runners on the corners with no outs. After walking Jeff Burroughs to load the bases, he allowed two runs to score on a force out and a sac fly. He threw a wild pitch to let in another run, and then fielded a bunt so close to the first base line that he had to race the batter-runner Roland Office to the bag. When rookie umpire Eric Gregg called Office safe, a fourth run scored, and Norman went ballistic. Joe Morgan had to get and stay between Norman and Gregg in order to keep his enraged teammate from doing something he'd later regret. After Norman calmed down enough for the game to continue, Cito Gaston pinch-hit for pitcher Dick Ruthven and hit Norman's first pitch to him over the left field wall for a two-run home run. Sparky Anderson finally sent Norman to the showers, and Dale Murray came on to get the third out. All six runs the Braves scored to tie the game were unearned. After an error by Rich Auerbach, a defensive replacement at second for Morgan, the Braves scored three more unearned runs in the bottom of the ninth before Jack Billingham could get the 27th out to end the game. What saved the Reds was more bad pitching by Atlanta. Once again, it took six Braves hurlers to get through nine innings, and for the second day in a row four different Reds players (Johnny Bench, Ken Griffey, Pete Rose, and Dave Concepcion) sent gopher balls sailing out of "the launching pad," as Atlanta-Fulton County Stadium had come to be known. Afterwards a drained Anderson seemed to be as incredulous about the un-artistic victory as anyone else. "Anyone can win 2–1," he said facetiously. "A game like that just shows what a genius I really am. Someday we're going to play a 50–49 game with 22 homers. I don't know who will win, but it has to happen."

From Atlanta, Georgia, the Reds backtracked to Texas to play a four-game series against the Houston Astros, former patsies who in 1977 were no longer rolling over and playing dead for their supposed betters from Cincinnati. True to form, the Astros pulled off a split after dropping the first two games.

Clearly now in a power groove, George Foster helped Cincinnati win the opener 8–5 on Friday, July 8, by driving in four runs on two long drives: a fourth-inning double off the center-field wall and a three-run home run that broke a 3–3 tie and knocked Astros starter Floyd Bannister out of the game with one out in the seventh inning. The homer, a shot deep into the left field seats, was Foster's 24th of the season. Coming as it did in the team's 80th game of the season, it put Foster on a pace to hit 50 homers in the season, something no player had ever done in the long history of the Cincinnati Reds' franchise.

Wasting no time, Sparky Anderson gave the ball to the newest member of his starting rotation, Doug Capilla, who managed to pick up the win with help from the bullpen and from Anderson himself. In the second inning with no score, Capilla walked weak-hitting Roger Metzger to load the bases with no outs. Anderson trotted out to the mound to calm Capilla down and boost his confidence. "You're pitching like it's a one-run game right now," he said, "and it's only the second inning. Forget about that guy on third. He's not going to beat you.... And you're pitching from the stretch."

"Well, the infield's in," Capilla said, referring to a forward shift that teams employ to cut off a run at home plate.

"You dumb so-and-so. They're back," pointed out Sparky.

The little pep talk worked as Capilla, using a full windup, struck out Bannister and then induced Wilbur Howard to ground into an inning-ending 5–2–3 double play. Capilla went six innings, giving up three runs, before Anderson turned the game over to Dale Murray who finished it.

With the annual All-Star Game scheduled for July 19, right around the corner, current voting totals were in America's newspapers again, and it was reported that George Foster had the third highest number of votes among National League outfielders behind the Phillies' Greg Luzinski and the Pirates' Dave Parker. The three outfielders with the most votes would start the game. Starting the game was an important distinction because in addition to being an honor, it would provide the players with more face time on television and more name recognition; both of which presumably would result in increased endorsement opportunities and possibly bonus payments stipulated by incentive clauses in their contracts.

Foster had made the All-Star team for the first time in 1976, and he'd made his debut in the Mid-Summer Classic one to remember. He not only started the game, played in Philadelphia, in center field, but he was named the Game's Most Valuable Player for hitting a two-run homer and collecting three RBI in the National League's 7–1 victory. The NL roster for that game was littered with Cincinnati Reds. Along with Foster, Pete Rose (3B), Joe

Morgan (2B), Johnny Bench (C), and Dave Concepcion (SS) were voted into the starting lineup, and Sparky Anderson added Ken Griffey and Tony Perez to the squad as reserves. As manager of the league's defending champs, Anderson was obliged to pick the NL's pitchers and reserves, and he didn't hesitate to reward his own players. "I feel you owe the players on your own club," he said. "These are the guys who got you there." Nobody argued with him afterwards, as every Reds player other than Perez, who walked in his only at bat, got at least one hit in the game.

Anderson would be managing the 1977 All-Star Game as well, and it was evident that player selections were on his mind as the Reds and Astros went at it in game two of the series on Saturday night. Tom Seaver started for the Reds and drew the Astrodome's largest crowd of the season so far, 40,718, which was still below the average for a Seaver game of 41,524. The Astros countered Seaver with Joaquin Andujar, and the two aces treated the fans to a pitcher's duel won by Seaver and the Reds 3–1. Andujar's big mistake came in the second inning when he served up a home run to Johnny Bench with George Foster, who'd singled, aboard. The loss dropped Andujar's record to 9–5, the same as Seaver's, and prompted Anderson to make a frank assessment about Andujar's chances of making the NL All-Star team. "If he [Andujar] had won, it would have forced me to put him on the team," he said. "Not really forced me. He would have earned it."

On Sunday afternoon Paul Moskau did a great impression of Tom Seaver, holding Houston scoreless on four hits for five innings before his nagging groin injury forced him from the game. Unfortunately, the Reds' bullpen did not follow the script and once again blew a big lead, this time a 5–0 cushion, to hand the Astros a 6–5 comeback win. The big blow in Houston's four-run eighth inning was the bases-loaded triple hit off Pedro Borbon by slumping center fielder Cesar Cedeno, who entered the game batting .213. "It was a fastball down and in," said Borbon. "He get lucky, you know. I throw him like that all the time, you know." The Astros didn't need any luck to finish off Borbon in the eighth; as they tied the game on a leadoff homer by Jose Cruz and scored the go-ahead and eventual winning run on a single, sacrifice bunt, ground out, and pinch-hit single by Joe Ferguson. While the Reds fumbled away this game, the Dodgers lost a doubleheader to San Diego yet remained eight games in front of Cincinnati. Exasperated, Sparky Anderson admitted, "I don't know what to do. We have got nothing solved. It is amazing. We get five runs and we lose. It isn't supposed to be like that. I don't feel we have any game anymore. We should be 30 [games] over .500. We've given 10 games away, easy."

The Reds didn't have to give away the series finale on Monday, July 11;

J. R. Richard took it away from them, firing a complete-game five-hit 2–0 shutout at the Cincinnatians. Richard was exactly the kind of pitcher Reggie Jackson once referred to while trying to explain to a clueless sportswriter why a "fastball hitter" like Jackson did not relish batting against a "fastball pitcher" like Richard. "Everybody likes ice cream," said Jackson, "but nobody likes to have it jammed down their throat." Bob Watson, the Astros' burly first baseman who'd called out the Big Bad Wolf Reds earlier in the season, gave Richard all the support he needed; hitting a two-run double off loser Fred Norman in the sixth inning. With the loss the Reds headed home having pulled off a 6–4 record on the road trip and achieving what would normally have been considered a pretty good outcome. But they were in too deep a hole for "pretty good" to gain them any advantage.

Back home in the Queen City, the Reds stayed within the Division for their last two series before the All-Star Game break, facing in Atlanta and Houston two of the same teams they'd just played on the road. The six-game home stand was a big disappointment; the impressive power-hitting display put on by George Foster in the middle of it being about the only thing to happen to excite the fan base.

Cartoonist Jerry Dowling was at it again in the *Enquirer*'s edition for Tuesday, July 12; this time mocking the Reds' bullpen. The cartoon showed a totally freaked-out Reds relief pitcher leaping into the air and onto a kitchen chair over a rat labeled "Big Leads" while involuntarily emitting a girlish "EEEK!" The implication was clear to anyone who'd been following the team's fortunes.

While the bullpen did not lose a lead in Tuesday's opener against Atlanta, it did in the person of Joe Henderson give up the winning run, as the Braves edged the Reds 4–3 behind the pitching of Phil Niekro and Rick Camp. Reds starting pitcher Doug Capilla turned in a good outing (three runs in seven innings), and George Foster tied the game 3–3 with a sac fly in the eighth; but the Braves scored the winner against Henderson in the top of the ninth on a walk, a balk, a single, and a sacrifice fly. Reds homers by Joe Morgan and Champ Summers went for naught in the loss.

An unexpected no-show for Tuesday's game was pitcher Woodie Fryman, who suddenly quit the team and went back to his tobacco farm in Ewing, Kentucky. Officially, Fryman requested to be placed on the "voluntary retirement list." In reporting the development in Wednesday's paper Bob Hertzel stated that Johnny Bench felt he understood Fryman's desire to quit. "All he wanted to do was pitch," said Bench. "He didn't care if it was with the Cincinnati Reds or not. He just wanted to pitch." From Hertzel's perspective, if Bench's interpretation of Fryman's point of view was correct, it was a troubling indication of the difference between the current Reds team and the squads which had won back-to-back World Championships. "The statement, though, unveils one of the major faults with the Reds of 1977," wrote Hertzel. "The pride that once went into being a Red, the comradery that once was a unique thing with the team, no longer seems to exist. There are too many new faces, and many different backgrounds. The feeling of oneness is not the same as it was."

On Wednesday night the Braves beat the Reds again, by the same 4–3 score as the night before. And again, the Braves scored the winner in the top of the ninth inning; however, this time it was the starting pitcher, Jack Billingham, who was nicked for the game winner on a walk, a sacrifice, and a double by Braves second baseman Rod Gilbreath; who got three of Atlanta's seven hits on the night. The Reds' bullpen was just too worn out for Anderson to turn to. Buzz Capra, 1–7 coming into the game, picked up the win for the Braves. His only mistake was grooving a pitch to George Foster who lost it over the center-field wall with one on and two outs in the sixth inning. It was Foster's 25th homer and 82nd and 83rd RBI of the year. The National League ERA champ in 1974, Capra had hurt his shoulder in 1975 and barely pitched in 1976. Pitching well against the Reds vindicated his comeback efforts, and he was gracious towards his vanquished opponents. "It is always nice to do it against this club," he said. "In my book they are tops."

The Reds scored a run in the bottom of the ninth on Mike Lum's home run to right to cut the lead to one, and they had the bases loaded when Dave Concepcion fouled out to the first baseman to end the game; but the comeback attempt did nothing to prevent the team's fourth loss in a row.

The best pitcher on a baseball team is commonly known as its "ace," a reference of course to the one card in the deck with the highest value. Another name for a team's best pitcher is "stopper" because one of the main things such a man is counted on to do is "stop" a team's losing streak. And that is exactly what Tom Seaver did for the Cincinnati Reds on Thursday, July 14, 1977; defeating the Atlanta Braves 7–1 and ending the Reds' four-game slide.

At this point in Seaver's distinguished career, about the only thing he hadn't done was throw a no-hitter. He came close in this game. With one out in the seventh inning, left-handed hitting first baseman Willie Montanez hit a fly ball against the right-center field wall for a double to break up Seaver's bid for his first no-hit game. The ball just eluded right fielder Ken Griffey who was still recovering from a sore right ankle which he'd injured a couple of weeks before in Los Angeles on a chopped foul ball. The only other hit Seaver allowed in the game was a ninth-inning leadoff double hit down the right field line by Rowland Office. Tom Terrific lost his shutout when Office scored on a throwing error by Dave Concepcion, attempting to complete a double play on a grounder to first by Jeff Burroughs. The victory was Seaver's first in Riverfront Stadium since 1972, as well as his first ever as a Cincinnati Red in the Stadium. "We needed a win today, a big win, and that's what we got," he said.

As big a day as it was for Seaver, it was an even more momentous game for George Foster, who went deep three times in four at bats. A player hitting four home runs in one game is a rare accomplishment, something that's occurred only 18 times in major league baseball history (as of the beginning of the 2018 season); however, contrary to public assumption, even hitting three homers in one game is a rare feat, one that occurs less frequently than the pitching of a no-hitter.

In his first at bat Foster grounded out to short against Braves starter Dick Ruthven. Leading off the fourth inning he blasted a Ruthven pitch into the left-field bleachers. The next inning he hit a three-run homer to center to knock Ruthven out of the game. Then, leading off the eighth inning against reliever Ron Kline, he hit number 28 on the season over the wall in left-center field. It was an impressive performance which uplifted teammates and left Braves pitchers shaking their heads with rueful respect. It was the 14th such performance in Reds history and the first occurrence since Johnny Bench did it in 1973. The slugger's explanation to the media for the show he'd just put on was typical Foster positive thinking. "If you just go out and apply yourself, you will be amazed at what you can do," he said. "I have my ups and downs. I just try to have more ups than downs. If you go out and do your best every day, you can accomplish anything within reason." Asked about his penchant for hitting his homers to all fields, he joked, "Just trying to spread the souvenirs around." When one reporter noted that since his three homers had come in his final three at bats, while he wouldn't get credit for four homers in one game, he would be able to tie the record for most consecutive home runs, four, if he homered in his first at bat in Friday night's game against the incoming Houston Astros. "I will be trying to hit that fourth homer to tie the record," he said. "What if Sparky Anderson gives you the bunt sign?" somebody teased. "I would have to get fined," Foster replied.

After Houston starter Gene Pence retired the Reds in order in the first inning on Friday night, he faced the torrid George Foster leading off the bottom of the second. Aware of what Foster had done the night before, the home crowd came alive and buzzed with anticipation; however, Pence worked Foster carefully and managed to hold the National League's hottest hitter to a single to left field. Foster later said, "It wasn't the type of pitch I could hit out. I guess he didn't want to be the guy who gave up the fourth straight home run."

Foster grounded out to short in the fourth, but then in the sixth with one on and one out he lifted a fly ball into left field. Astros left fielder Wilbur Howard drifted back on the ball until he reached the wall, leaped towards the descending ball, but failed to catch it. The "scraper," as ballplayers call a home run that barely gets over the wall, was Foster's 29th of the season. It tied his career high set the year before and gave him five homers in three games. After the game Sparky Anderson said what most any Reds observer might have said: "That's the first one I ever remember him hitting that just made it over the wall." Foster himself was so used to hitting howitzer shots that this one didn't feel like a homer to him. "I didn't think it was going out," he said. "I saw the outfielder going back, back and then jump."

Foster's modest clout put the Reds up 4–1 and they went on to win 8–3, but the Astros stormed back to take the remaining two games of the series.

It had been a frustrating season and tempers were fraying. Mired in a batting slump and fighting a bad hand, Dave Concepcion had slung his bat during Friday night's game and almost decapitated the Reds' bat boy. Johnny Bench called him out, and Joe Morgan had to step between the two players to prevent the exchange from escalating. Bench said later, "I don't care if he's mad. I just don't want him to hurt someone." On Saturday, July 16, before the fifth largest regular season crowd in Riverfront Stadium history on hand to celebrate "Farmers' Night," Sparky Anderson got himself ejected from the game. J. R. Richard and Joe Sambito held the Reds to five hits while Wilbur Howard and Jose Cruz went deep and light-hitting Julio Gonzalez collected four hits for the Astros. Towards the end of the embarrassing 8–0 spanking, Reds reliever Dale Murray threw a couple of high and tight message pitches to Reds-killer Bob Watson. After home plate umpire Art Williams issued a warning to Murray, which meant fines for the pitcher and his manager, Anderson went crazy, appealed to the other umpires, and eventually was invited to leave the premises.

Good pitching by Doug Capilla (three hits/two runs in six innings) was wasted on Sunday afternoon in the first half finale, a 3–1 loss. Twenty-one-year-old Mark Lemongello, saddled with a 1–11 record coming into the contest, and Joe Niekro throttled Reds hitters; and Watson and Enos Cabel homered for Houston. In the two losses to Houston the Reds scored one run, left 20 runners on base, and went 1–23 with runners in scoring position. In the 20 previous games against Atlanta, Houston, and San Diego, teams Cincinnati was accustomed to thrashing, the Reds had gone 11–9. Playing that schedule they should have gained ground on the Dodgers, especially as the Dodgers had just lost five of six; but they did not. Heading into the All-Star Game break, the Dodgers had the best record in baseball (59–33) and the biggest lead of the four Division leaders (9½ games). With such a comfortable cushion, the ever-optimistic Tommy Lasorda wasn't worried at all about his team's minor losing streak. "We'll snap out of it," he said. "We're just not hitting the ball like we have been—that's how simple it is. But the guys who aren't hitting are the same ones who got us where we are today." Lasorda wasn't the only one confident about the Dodgers' chances. Alvin Dark, San Diego's third manager for 1977, opined that Los Angeles had no weaknesses and predicted that with their pitching staff "They're never going to have a long losing streak." The Reds weren't quite ready to throw in the towel, and this time Tom Seaver functioned as their spokesman. Dave Anderson of the *New York Times* wanted to check up on New York's former Golden Boy, and during a wide-ranging interview Seaver said, "We've got a long way to go to catch the Dodgers. But everybody here thinks we can. And that's the most important thing."

Once upon a time, major league baseball's All-Star Game was not primarily an honorary, ritualized social event; the goal of which is mostly the injury-free participation of as many players as possible and the maximized revenue enhancement of MLB from advertising, adjunct event admission fees, and sponsorship payments. In the old days, the goal of the players and managers was quite simply to win the game, and in the process to prove which league was better. Nothing else much mattered. But, as is so often the case, big money changed things and winning the game began to take a back seat to other considerations. When winning no longer took precedence, inane things began to happen; and it became possible to interrupt the game one year for 15 minutes to hand out a couple of cheesy trophies for some made-up award; to end another game in a tie because all the pitchers had been used up; and for a player trying to score to suddenly pull up and politely invite the opposing team's catcher to tag him out. These latter embarrassments would never have occurred in the old days, and the 1977 All-Star Game definitely took place in the good old days. As the managers of the previous year's World Series, Sparky Anderson and the Yankees' Billy Martin faced off once again, and there was no question that both men regarded the game as a continuation of their personal competition to prove himself the better man. Before the game Anderson told his assembled charges, "The only reason we are here is to kick the living hell out of those guys." Martin certainly felt the same way, but before turning his attention to the National League, he became involved in an intra-league controversy.

Martin had chosen the California Angels' Frank Tanana as one of his pitchers. When Tanana dropped out of the game because of injury, Martin chose Tanana's teammate Nolan Ryan to replace him. However, Ryan declined the invitation, which infuriated Martin, who said the pitcher should be fined and suspended. Furthermore, Martin said he would not pick Ryan, who had 13 wins at the time of the 1977 game, for a future All-Star Game even if Ryan had 40 wins. The media depicted Ryan's absence as a case of Achilles-like sulking, but years later he had a different explanation. "I was having a good year, and I was planning on going to New York for the game at Yankee Stadium and seeing old friends. But then I wasn't picked, and I made plans to take my family away during the All-Star break. Then, when I was picked as a replacement for Tanana, I decided to take my family away anyway. Some people thought I was mad but I wasn't. I just made other plans and stuck to my guns. I have no regrets." In the end, reliever Dave LaRoche was added to the AL team as the Angels' required representative.

If Tanana had been the AL's only injured player, the Senior Circuit might have had a better chance of prevailing. As it was, Vida Blue, Mark Fidrych, and Don Money also stayed home; while several other key American Leaguers participated but played hurt: Rod Carew, Fred Lynn, Thurman Munson, Carl Yastrezemski, and Richie Zisk. In contrast, the National League lost only Cubs' relief pitcher Bruce Sutter to injury.

The National League, which had won five All-Star Games in a row and 13 of the previous 14, was primed to win again. The NL squad was loaded with Cincinnati Reds and Los Angeles Dodgers: 12 all together with seven in the starting lineup. The Phillies' Greg Luzinski and the Pirates' Dave Parker, flanking George Foster in the outfield, were the only non–Reds/Dodgers to start the game for the National League.

The Baltimore Orioles' Jim Palmer started the game on the mound for the Americans, and he quickly put his one-game teammates into a hole they couldn't dig out of. Joe Morgan led off for the NL and homered to deep right field on a 3–2 pitch. After Steve Garvey was called out on strikes, Parker singled and George Foster knocked him in with a double to left-center. Palmer wild-pitched Foster to third and then gave up a homer to Luzinski to put the NL ahead 4–0 before most fans had had a chance to order their first beer. Palmer pitched a scoreless second but gave up another long home run, this time to Garvey leading off the third inning. When Martin got to the mound to relieve the battered pitcher, Palmer said, "What took you so long?"

During the pre-game introductions, Tom Seaver received the loudest and longest ovation of anyone else, including the game's two honorary captains, Joe DiMaggio and Willie Mays. He received another huge ovation when he entered the game in the bottom of the sixth inning. The American League started a comeback by scoring three times against Seaver, but the National League scored a couple of runs against the Yankees' Sparky Lyle in the eighth

6. July 1977

inning and held on to take the 48th Mid-Summer Classic 7–5. The Dodgers' Don Sutton who started for the NL and pitched three scoreless innings was named the game's MVP. In addition to his run-scoring double, Foster aided the NL cause by making a great leaping catch against the outfield wall to rob Rod Carew of a home run in the third inning. A photo of the catch appeared in the Cincinnati *Enquirer* on Wednesday, July 20, the day after the game, with the caption "He Can Field Too!" appended to it.

The Cincinnati Reds began the second half of the 1977 season in Pittsburgh, Pennsylvania, on Thursday, July 21; playing what was their 90th game of the year. Eager to start fresh and begin the serious comeback that would enable them to overtake the front-running Los Angeles Dodgers, they sprang out of the gate ... and fell flat on their faces, losing all three games of the series with their intra-division rivals, the Pirates. Before Thursday's game Sparky Anderson admitted that "it's gonna be tough, no doubt about it. We can't lose no more than 23 games the rest of the way." After the Pirates' 6–2 win behind Jerry Reuss' complete-game six-hitter, Sparky lamented, "This can't go on forever." *Enquirer* beat reporter Bob Hertzel, published a sarcastic reply to that remark, saying, "It doesn't have to. About another week will do. Then the only things the Reds will have to look forward to is next year, and that is not a pleasant prospect for the defending, but not-so-well, world champs."

Thursday night's game took only two hours and 14 minutes to play, despite being interrupted by a 31-minute rain delay. The rain affected play in the fifth inning, when Pirates shortstop Frank Taveras lofted a foul pop-up against Fred Norman, just inside the first-base box seats. The ball hit a blue umbrella on the way down, preventing Dan Driessen from getting a glove on it. Umpire Jerry Crawford refused to call interference, after which Taveras tripled into the left-field corner. He scored on a single by Dave Parker, and the Pirates wound up getting three runs altogether in the frame. Taveras, batting .230 coming in, hit a second triple later in the game. George Foster, with a pair of singles, was the only Cincinnati player to garner more than one hit against Reuss, who raised his record to 5–10 and notched his 100th major league victory. The hits boosted Foster's batting average to .318, second on the team to Ken Griffey's .330. Over the All-Star break, the Reds had brought up Indianapolis pitchers Manny Sarmiento and Mario Soto, and Soto was immediately cast into the fire. He pitched the sixth and seventh innings in relief of the losing Norman, giving up two earned runs in the sixth.

On Friday, July 22, a story by Allen Lewis of Knight News Wire on the home run situation appeared in newspapers around the country. Entitled "Homer Increase Staggering," the story was somewhat self-contradictory;

presenting anecdotes and data about the increased number of home runs being hit throughout the majors but then concluding that the increase didn't actually amount to all that much. For instance, while noting that only two teams (the Cubs and Mets) were behind their pace of the previous year and that several clubs were on their way to breaking their own season record for homers; the total number of homers hit in 1977, even if it surpassed the record of 3,429 set in 1970, would probably not be recognized by major league baseball as a significant new landmark. There were 26 teams in 1977 as opposed to 24 in 1970, explained Lewis, and more important than the total number of homers hit was the frequency with which they were being hit. The record for home run frequency by all teams was 1.86 home runs per game set in 1956, and in 1977 baseball was on a pace of 1.76 homers per game. Interestingly, Lewis did not mention the one player who was on a record-setting home run pace, the Reds' George Foster. Two days earlier though Bob Hertzel had done so. In his "Reds Notes" for Monday, the day before the All-Star Game in New York, Hertzel had pointed out that "George Foster is hitting homers at a record pace. In 1930, when Chicago's Hack Wilson set the National League record with 56 home runs he had only 28 homers in his first 89 games. Foster has 29 and Foster will play eight more games, the season now being 162 games."

The Reds' losses on Friday and Saturday were damaging and also discouraging for the ways they came about. The Pirates knocked Reds ace Tom Seaver out of Friday night's contest after only four innings and won the game with a run off Jack Billingham in the bottom of the 12th; after Joe Morgan's clutch two-out three-run home run had tied the game in the top of the ninth. The staggering Reds lost their fifth in a row and ninth out of their last 11 games on Saturday afternoon when starting pitcher Doug Capilla blew a 4–0 lead. The rookie Capilla was sailing along, having given up only three hits and one run in six innings when the Pirates staged a four-run rally against him in the bottom of the seventh which caused his exit and enabled the Bucs to pull out a 5–4 win and the three-game sweep. Foster, who went 0–4 in the game, was held at bay and kept in the ballpark by Pirates pitchers for the third straight day. More of a factor, although not enough to make a difference in the games' outcomes, was Pete Rose, who went 3–5 in the finale while being booed all day. Rose went 6–15 in the series and homered in each of the first two games. His seventh-inning single off Jim Rooker was the 2,880th hit of his career, and it tied him with Frankie Frisch for the all-time record for hits by a switch-hitter. The hit was not only historically significant, but it also gave Hertzel something positive to write about in the *Enquirer*. In an article entitled "Rose, Morgan Look Ahead to Hall of Fame Days," Rose revealed his feelings about his accomplishment, saying, "The one thing in this world, the only thing in baseball that I can be No. 1 at, is this thing, the thing I have worked hardest to get. I can't be the all-time home run king. No one can be the hit leader, not with the hits Cobb got. For me, I had to work to become the all-time switch hitting leader." From our perspective, knowing that Rose eventually passed Cobb and did become, in fact, baseball's all-time hits leader, this insight into Rose's thinking is startling; as Pete Rose seems to have been a man who never sold himself short. Furthermore, in another statement in the article, Rose disclosed that he envisioned a career hit total for himself that would have left him well behind Cobb. In speaking about his presumed-to-be definite future election to the National Baseball Hall of Fame, Rose said, "If I have 3200 or so hits when I retire and I'm not voted into the Hall of Fame on the first ballot, then I don't want to go in." Ironically, while Rose surpassed Cobb to position himself not only as an unquestionable first-ballot Hall of Famer but also as perhaps the player to receive the highest percentage of votes ever cast, he never even appeared on the Hall of Fame ballot. As manager of the Reds, he was caught in a gambling scandal and placed permanently, it appears, on baseball's "Ineligible List." Baseball then double-downed on the punishment by retroactively passing a rule that anyone on the Ineligible List would not be allowed to even appear on the Hall of Fame ballot.

The Reds couldn't get out of Pittsburgh fast enough, but things got no better in St. Louis where once again the NL schedule makers had arranged an odd series for them: a two-game set on a Sunday and Monday. The Reds lost both games. In the Sunday afternoon opener on July 24, a third-year right-hander named Eric Rasmussen shut them out 3–0 on four hits, all singles. The loss was a mental turning point of sorts, and it was Pete Rose who best summarized the psychic depths to which the team had sunk. "We get four singles off a guy who is 6–10 going into the game," he said. "I don't mean to belittle the guy, but the records don't lie. He has not been a winning pitcher. I wish it were one phase. Then you could hold a real butt-chewing meeting with the guys involved. But this involves everyone. It is amazing, seven All-Stars and lose six in a row. This has changed us. We're not used to losing. This is the Cincinnati Reds. We've been the winningest team in the world since 1970. The Dodgers aren't worried about us anymore."

On Monday night the sleeping bats came alive, but the Reds still lost 9–8, despite a pair of home runs by George Foster; his first homers of the second half of the season. Cincinnati led only once in the game, in the top of the third after Foster and Johnny Bench hit back-to-back homers to put the Reds up 3–2. The third-inning homer to right off Cards starter Pete Falcone was

Foster's 30th of the season and represented a new one-season high for him. Sparky Anderson used four pitchers and the Cardinals scored off three of them (starter Jack Billingham who took the loss and relievers Joe Hoerner and Pedro Borbon). Bob Bailey's two-run pinch-hit homer in the eighth and Foster's solo shot to left in the ninth off former teammate Rawley Eastwick, his 31st of the year, brought the Reds to within two of St. Louis. Dan Driessen doubled in the eighth run with two outs, but then representing the tying run he died at third to end the game when pinch-hitter Mike Lum grounded out to short. The dazed Reds, only two games over .500, dropped 11 games behind Los Angeles. After the game it was announced that Sparky Anderson had been given a two-year contract extension. The vote of confidence did little to boost the 43-year-old Anderson's current spirits or reassure him about his future. "You can't wash away the disappointment with a contract," he said. "Oh, is this game humbling. I'd better win next year. If for no other reason than for myself. The people will allow you to fail once, not twice." Given the admission implicit in Sparky's remarks that the cause was over for 1977, there was nothing much for Hertzel to add about the situation in his game story.

Remaining in the mid-west and the East Division, the Reds made the short jump to Chicago where their woes continued; losing three of four to the front-running Cubs. They suffered their eighth consecutive loss in the opener on Tuesday, July 26, getting shut out 3–0 in the process for the second time in three days. It was no disgrace being bested by Rick Reuschel, as the mammoth right-hander was the hottest pitcher in baseball; but the mighty Cincinnati Reds, as Rose would have pointed out, were not used to being shut out. Not used to it at all. Reuschel's five-hitter improved his record to 14–3 and ran his record at Wrigley Field for 1977 to 9–0. Reuschel extended his scoreless innings streak at Wrigley to $34\frac{2}{3}$ innings and his streak of allowing no earned runs at the venerable ballpark to 50. The big boy's ERA dropped to 2.15 after the victory. A crowd of 38,113 witnessed the Cubs' win which enabled them to maintain their lead over the Phillies at 1½ games. Before the game Sparky Anderson had held a clubhouse meeting, and when asked what he'd expected to accomplish, he said "Nothing." "I've held more pow wows than in all the other years I've been here combined," he elaborated. "I used to think meetings don't help. Now I'm totally convinced they don't. I've tried everything I can think of. I've ranted and I've raved." Fred Norman turned in a quality start (three runs in seven innings) but took the loss nonetheless and saw his record drop to 9–7.

To make up the game postponed by bad weather earlier in the season, the two clubs played a double header the next day, and the Reds took the first game 6–2 to finally halt their losing streak at eight. Rookie Mario Soto got his first major league start and went all the way, striking out nine Cubbies and prompting Sparky Anderson to compare the youngster to his hero and countryman, Juan Marichal. Predicting that Soto would get even better once he put on ten pounds or so, just as a young Marichal had done, Anderson said, "Marichal had exactly the same body when he came to the big leagues. It is like they made a duplicate of Marichal. If he [Soto] reaches 75 percent of what Marichal did, he can go back to the Dominican Republic proudly." George Foster led the Reds' attack, going 3–4 and slugging his 32nd home run through a stiff wind that blew in all day. The solo homer, which came in the top of the sixth against Pete Broberg, gave the Reds a 3–1 lead and proved to be the game-winning RBI. If not for the wind, Foster might have also homered in the first inning. As it was, his deep drive off starter Mike Krukow was held down and caught by center fielder Joe Wallis.

As for the losing streak which erased all the ground the Reds had worked so hard to make up, a proud Joe Morgan disdained it as the Reds' just desserts. "It wasn't the losing streak that bothered me as much as that we weren't playing good ball," he said. "I didn't even know how many we had lost, but I knew how poorly we were playing."

The glow of victory didn't last long, as the Cubs won the nightcap 5–1, starter Steve Renko and closer Willie Hernandez combining on a three-hitter. The wind cheated Foster out of another homer in the first inning, yet George's drive off the center-field wall still netted him a double and drove in Cincinnati's only run of the contest. Doug Capilla had a shutout going until the eighth inning when the Cubs mounted a five-run rally against him and reliever Manny Sarmiento.

For the fourth game of the series, played on Thursday afternoon, July 28, the fickle Great Lakes winds shifted and blew out all day long; resulting in a crazy 13-inning, five-hour game and a 16–15 win for Chicago. A combined 11 homers were smashed on the day, five by the Reds and six by the Cubs. The 11 homers tied the Reds' club record, set in 1966 when the Reds hit five homers and the Pittsburgh Pirates six. Ironically, the game was not decided on a homer but by three consecutive two-out singles, allowed by Jack Billingham in the bottom of the 13th. Equally ironic, none of the 11 home runs were hit by George Foster, who nevertheless enjoyed a 3–6 day at the plate. The state of the Reds' worn-out pitching staff had as much to do with the slugfest as the billowing wind. Dale Murray got the start for the Reds, and it was the first of his career after 215 relief appearances. He lasted exactly one inning, giving up two homers, five hits, and six runs. The night before the game Sparky Anderson had apparently had a premonition of the slaughter to come, telling infielder Ray Knight in the hotel elevator that he might be the game's "lancerdor" at some point.

Anderson had meant to say "lanceur," the French word for pitcher; on his mind no doubt because Murray, the Reds' acquisition from Montreal, was slated to start the game. Editors in the *Enquirer* sports department mocked the effort with the headline "The Wind Blew and the Balls Flew, the Reds Lose, So What Else Is New?" and the Reds concluded the sorry road trip with a 1–8 record, leaving them 12½ games behind the Dodgers.

The beleaguered Reds returned to the Queen City to start a nine-game home stand, the longest of the season. They would face the same three East Division teams they'd just encountered on the forgettable road trip: the Cardinals, the Cubs, and the Pirates. As if the schedule makers were mocking them too, Sparky Anderson's charges began with a twi-night double header on Friday night, July 29, at possibly the worst time. The problem of the pitching staff's exhaustion was compounded by Tom Seaver's suffering from the flu. Anderson called Seaver's ailment "the old zippity-do or something"; in any case, it was bad enough that Seaver's turn in the rotation was skipped. The situation was so dire that Anderson handed the ball to Jack Billingham to start the nightcap, even though Billingham had started on Monday and relieved the day before. "It's unfair that I gotta use him," said Anderson, "but what can I do?"

A crowd of 50,366 showed up for the twin bill; not because they were excited about a pennant race but because residual excitement over the Reds' recent championship play had spurred them to make plans and purchase tickets for the games well in advance. What they got for their money was exactly what the 1977 Reds had been delivering all season: the inconsistency and frustration of a split of the two games.

The Reds pulled out a 6–5 squeaker in the first game behind the decent starting pitching of Paul Moskau and Pedro Borbon's shutdown relief effort (no runs over the final two and two thirds) and got trounced in the second game, 10–3. The Cardinals racked Billingham for a nine-run second inning, the big blow being a grand slam off the bat of first baseman Keith Hernandez.

Eric Rasmussen, the pitcher Rose had politely disrespected, beat the Reds again with a complete-game effort. The two games combined lasted four hours and 54 minutes, four minutes more than the single game the day before in Chicago. The *Enquirer* was no longer pulling its punches in its coverage of the season. The mini headline over the two box scores in Saturday's paper read: "Wait Til Last Year." At least the editors were trying to retain a sense of humor about the unfolding disaster of a season. Judging by his lead, it was clear that Hertzel also saw no point in trying to sugar coat the situation. "The split left the Reds in nowheresville, at even .500, and still dead in the West," he wrote.

6. July 1977

Another big summertime crowd (50,023) showed up at Riverfront Stadium on Saturday night, for the same reasons as the night before, as the Reds and Cardinals played game three of the four-game set. The Cardinals started right-hander John Denny, making his first start since June 21, when a pulled hamstring injury had put him on the shelf. Denny kept the Cardinals in the game early, giving up one run in four innings on back-to-back doubles by Johnny Bench and Cesar Geronimo, before turning the game over to the St. Louis bullpen. Reds starter Fred Norman did even better, holding St. Louis to a single run scored, on another Keith Hernandez homer, for eight innings. The 1–1 game turned on the ninth inning when St. Louis scored three times to win by a final of 4–1. Norman, turning into the hard-luck pitcher of the Cincinnati staff, thought he'd gotten out of the inning unscathed, when he induced Mike Tyson to hit a double play ball to Joe Morgan with one out. The Reds got the force at second for out number two, but as shortstop Dave Concepcion took the ball out of his glove to throw to first he dropped the ball, allowing Tyson to reach first safely. No error was scored on the play as a double play cannot be assumed, but it kept the Cards alive. Afterwards Norman said, "I had started for the dugout. You count those when Morgan and Concepcion are going for a double play." Pinch-hitting for pitcher Butch Metzger, Tony Scott blooped a pop fly double down the right-field line to score Hernandez from third with the go-ahead run, and then moments later center fielder Jerry Mumphrey hit another double which plated the final two St. Louis runs. The Reds got two on in the bottom of the inning against Al Hrabosky but couldn't score, so Norman absorbed his fifth straight loss to drop his record to 9–8. Meanwhile, the Los Angeles Dodgers, who probably weren't even paying attention to the Reds any longer as Pete Rose had suggested, coasted to a 7–4 over Montreal after exploding for all seven runs in the first inning.

The Reds closed out the series and the month of July with a 6–2 win over the Cardinals on Sunday afternoon. Six strong innings by starter Doug Capilla and three shutout frames by Pedro Borbon did the trick for Cincinnati from the mound, and Reds hitters knocked around Cardinals ace Bob Forsch and reliever Rawley Eastwick for 13 hits and all six runs scored by the home team. George Foster, rebounding somewhat from 0-fers in the two previous contests, went 1-4, knocking in the eventual winning run with a third-inning single. Foster was also part of an interesting cat-and-mouse game-within-the-game involving St. Louis' dramatic reliever Al Hrabosky, whose pre-pitch psych-up/psych-out antics tended to wear thin on the opposing batters.

With one run in, two on, and two out, Foster came to bat against Hrabosky in the sixth inning. After Hrabosky did his usual routine behind the mound and then stepped on the rubber ready to pitch, Foster stepped out of the batter's box. Asking for time, Foster began smoothing the dirt in the batter's box. Finished with his grounds keeping, Foster stepped out of the box again. Having seen enough, plate umpire Jerry Dale ordered Foster to get into the batter's box and Hrabosky to pitch. Hrabosky delivered a pitch and Dale called it a ball. Afterwards, Hrabosky admitted that he thought the pitch would be an automatic strike, a penalty for Foster having caused a delay of game. Hrabosky wound up walking Foster to load the bases, but he got out of the inning undamaged by popping Dan Driessen up to short. The dueling delays had no outcome on the game, but it was still the hot post-game topic of conversation with the media. Asked to explain his role in the mini-drama, Foster said, "I realize he was getting himself ready. Thusly, I have to get myself ready, and I'm not going to let him break my concentration. It isn't fair for them to restrict me and not restrict the pitcher." Asked if the at bat against Hrabosky was a victory, Foster said, "No, he won. He walked me. If he had thrown me a strike, they might have had to change balls." The remark represented the kind of confidence bordering on arrogance that Foster's more famous teammates had been displaying for years and being admired for, and Sparky Anderson might have been pleased to see it had he not been raving mad about the incident. Sparky was so ticked off that he formulated a bizarre plan to counter Hrabosky's antics and the umpires' countenance of them. Next season, Anderson claimed, he would have his batter claim that his jock strap had broken and then head to the clubhouse for a replacement. "They'll have to wait a good five, ten minutes for him to get back," he said. Demonstrating that he'd thought through the objections to his little revenge scheme, he continued, "You can't call a guy a liar if he says he broke his jock strap. You can't frisk him! If you fine him, he goes to court." The absurd fantasy was a fitting end to a disappointing month.

Sparky Anderson had never had such troubles as manager of the Cincinnati Reds, but if he needed anything to give him a little perspective on the relative importance of his woes, the headlines out of New York about a serial killer terrorizing the entire city would have done nicely. It was the summer of the "Son of Sam" and the toll was already five dead and six others wounded in seven incidents over the past year. The same night Hrabosky only acted a little crazy at Riverfront Stadium, setting off Anderson, a truly deranged person had shot and critically wounded a young couple as they sat in a car parked on the Brooklyn waterfront. Yes, the Reds were struggling mightily, but it was baseball. And, as Sparky knew better than most, in baseball there's thankfully always another game tomorrow.

7

August 1977
"Doctor Foster's no imposter"

The Reds began August, the fifth month of the six-month baseball season, hosting the hot Chicago Cubs. The first-place Cubs came into the three-game set holding a two-game lead over Philadelphia, while the Reds lingered in second place; 14 games behind Los Angeles and 4½ games ahead of third-place Houston. The Reds were so far behind the Dodgers that winning two of the three games against Chicago did nothing to improve their standing; however, George Foster put on a show that increased his lead in the NL home run and RBI races and that greatly raised his profile as one of the game's most feared sluggers.

The August 1, game on Monday night was ABC-TV's "Game of the Week," and the national exposure apparently agreed with Foster, who hit two tremendous home runs his first two times up to lead Cincinnati to a 7–6 victory. Both homers came off Cubs starter Steve Renko; both were hit to left field (the second traveling even farther than the first); and each one followed a base on balls to Joe Morgan. The pair of homers, numbers 33 and 34 on the season, gave Foster a considerable cushion over Greg Luzinski; running second to George with 26 homers. The pair of blasts also raised Foster's RBI total for the season to 102. The power display put on by Foster not only impressed the national television audience; it also made Cubs pitchers wary. With one out in the bottom of the seventh inning and the game tied 5–5, Paul Reuschel, Rick's brother, walked Foster on four pitches. While understandable, the strategy went against the proverbial "Book" and promptly backfired. Dan Driessen tripled to drive in Foster with the go-ahead run, and then Bruce Sutter (in relief of Reuschel) gave up a single to Johnny Bench to drive in Driessen with what proved to be the eventual winning run, after the Cubs plated one run in the top of the ninth.

Foster homered again the next day, driving a Pete Broberg pitch into the left-field stands as the Reds' leadoff hitter in the ninth inning. The solo shot (number 35) was irrelevant to the game's outcome, as Dave Roberts came on to retire the side on a fly ball and a pair of ground outs to nail down the Cubs' 5–2 win. Indicative of their respect, the Cubs walked Foster twice prior to the ninth inning, in the sixth inning intentionally. Unfortunately, Foster's hitting was a sideshow to the rest of the game. Rookie Mario Soto pitched a shutout for seven innings but came unglued in the eighth, when a dustup between Dave Concepcion and the Cubs' Bill Buckner caused him to lose his concentration. The Concepcion-Buckner spat began in the sixth. Playing with a chronically bad ankle, Buckner took a big lead off second base, which naturally invited the Reds to attempt to pick him off. Apparently, Buckner resented the Reds' not taking his infirmity into consideration, and he let his displeasure at the attempted pickoff be known. Concepcion, who fielded the pickoff throw and applied a late tag, had no sympathy for that train of thought, saying later, "I play to win, not to feel sorry. He had a bad ankle and a lead from here to the f**king bathroom." With two outs in the eighth, and the Reds clinging to a 1–0 lead, Soto walked Buckner, who left the game for a pinch runner. After Jerry Morales singled, Buckner began riding Concepcion from the dugout. Infuriated, Concepcion ran over to the Cubs' dugout and began screaming back at Buckner. By the time the umps calmed Concepcion down enough to continue the game, Soto had lost all focus on the task at hand. He walked Bobby Murcer to load the bases and then walked in two runs to put the Cubs up 2–1. Dale Murray relived Soto and promptly gave up run-scoring singles to Manny Trillo and George Mitterwald, boosting the lead to 5–1. The inning ended when Johnny Bench threw out Mitterwald, 7-2-4, trying to advance to second on Foster's throw home. All five runs were charged to Soto.

Even the normally reserved and imperturbable Joe Morgan became involved in a dispute. With two outs in the bottom of the eighth, Morgan beat out a ground ball to short but was called out by umpire John Kibler. When Morgan told Kibler he'd blown the call, Kibler threw him out of the game. Of course, Mr. Anderson rushed onto the diamond and demanded to know why Mr. Kibler had ejected Mr. Morgan. "Because he said I blew the call," said Kibler. "Well, John, you DID," said Anderson. "You're gone too," said Kibler, saddling Anderson with this third ejection of the year.

When Anderson explained that all he did was say that Kibler had erred, Kibler replied, "I don't tolerate that." Sparky refused to leave, causing Kibler to threaten to call the police. "Be my guest," said Anderson. Of course, Anderson did eventually make his way off the field, but after the game he remained angry and defiant. "No way, I'll pay that fine," he told reporters. "No way, shape, or form. No, no, no, no." Morgan too remained bothered by the incident. "It doesn't pay to be a nice guy," he said. "From now on, they miss a call on me at the plate or on the bases, I'm gonna mess with them."

In the 33-year history of Riverfront Stadium, from 1970 through the 2002 season, only 22 batters ever reached the distant and highly elevated upper deck with a home run. As the hard plastic seats in that section which encircled the ballpark were all red in color, any home run landing among them was called a "Red Seat Home Run" or a "red-seater." Such prodigious blasts were spoken of reverently, breathlessly, as capable of being achieved only by the strongest and most gifted of hitters. Prior to the final game of the Reds-Cubs series on Wednesday, August 3, 1977, only three hitters had red-seat home runs under their belts: Bob Bailey; Tony Perez, who had deposited two long balls into the Everest-like reaches of Riverfront; and Foster himself who'd joined the exclusive club the year before.

Now the hottest hitter in baseball, Foster reached the red seats again in the finale against Chicago, capping a dominating series in style and serving notice that the most powerful and feared hitter in baseball was the slender Alabaman slotted in the middle of the Cincinnati Reds' batting order.

With the Reds trailing 3–1, Joe Morgan led off the bottom of the eighth inning with a single off of left-handed Cubs reliever Willie Hernandez. Foster jumped on the next pitch, as if he knew before Hernandez let it go exactly what the pitch would be and where it would be located. Players in both dugouts rose to their feet along with the crowd as the ball soared high and deep into the night down the left-field line. The ball landed 15 feet fair in the fourth row of the reds seats, tying the game 3–3. In his game report for Thursday morning's paper Bob Hertzel said the home run was hit "as hard as a baseball can be hit."

The Reds won the contest 5–3 on Dan Driessen's one-out, considerably shorter, walk-off tenth-inning homer that just dropped over the right-field wall. It drove in Foster, who'd singled for the second time in the game.

After the game, Foster, who'd hit a ball into the red seats in that day's BP, said, "When you hit one like that in batting practice, you want to hit one as far in the game so the people get to see it." When asked how he felt about being able to hit such tape measure home runs, he said, "You only get one time around the bases, but you do create a lot of talk." A lot of talk indeed. So much so that the name George Foster was no longer an afterthought when the Cincinnati Reds became the topic of discussion. In opponents' pre-series pitchers' meetings about how to pitch to Reds batters, Foster now received the most attention. The more people watched Foster bat, the more respect they began to have for him, including his own teammates. When asked to comment on Foster's virtuoso performance in the Cubs' series, Pete Rose himself gushed, "Awesome. When he walks up there he looks like he knows he's going to hit the ball out of sight. And, he's thrown himself into the Triple Crown picture." Rose's latter comment was a reference to the fact that with his 3–5 day Foster had raised his batting average to .322; putting himself into contention for the coveted, rarely-awarded honor, given to any player who ends the season leading his league in batting average, home runs, and runs batted in. Foster went to bed that night leading the National League in home runs with 36 and in RBI with 105 and trailing league-leading Dave Parker by 14 points in the batting average race.

Prior to Wednesday's finale against the Cubs, the Reds had assembled on the field of Riverfront Stadium for the taking of the annual team photo. They couldn't even pull that off flawlessly. Four players showed up late and were thus fined $25: Dave Concepcion, Dan Driessen, Pedro Borbon, and Ed Armbrister. Because it was the second time Concepcion had been tardy for a team function, his fine was doubled.

Thursday, the day before Pittsburgh came into town for four games, was a scheduled off-day, and the only Reds coverage in Friday morning's *Enquirer* was another delicious Jerry Dowling cartoon. This one was dedicated to the player who was clearly becoming the star of the season, not just of the Reds but of the entire National League: George Foster. The cartoon depicted a striding Foster, dressed like a doctor and sporting an Abe Lincoln–like beard and top hat, on his way to home plate. In the carton he is depicted carrying a medical bag bearing a sign saying, "Home Calls Are My Specialty"; and his long black bat protrudes out of each end of the bag. In the background, a pitcher stands on the mound, trembling and sweating. His shirt labels him as "Victims," and he mumbles "…I feel terrible!" Pointing to the pitcher, a grinning Foster says, "I'm going to do a little surgery to your E.R.A.! … and thusly also an operation on the record book!" Dowling capped off the tribute to Foster with a little poem, the words of which appear as if printed onto a piece of parchment hanging in the upper left-hand corner:

> Doctor Foster's no imposter,
> the pitchers pray for rain:
> the balls they hung,
> when Foster swung,
> were never seen again!

In addition to being a humorous commentary, the cartoon was the second published opinion by the media that Foster was likely in the midst of a record-setting season.

"Doctor Foster's No Imposter." Here Dowling turns around the normal medical relationship, as his practitioner, Doctor Foster, causes pain instead of relieving it. Dr. Foster has "victims" instead of patients, his type of surgery raises ERAs, and the operation he performs will be on the record book. Doc Foster does have a stethoscope hanging around his neck, but the fearful medical tool sticking out of both ends of his medical bag is his big black Louisville Slugger.

The Pittsburgh series opened with a twi-night doubleheader on Friday, August 5. The Pirates won both games by pounding the Reds' starting pitchers. Fred Norman lasted only one and a third innings in the first game, and Doug Capilla gave up nine runs, all earned, in five and two thirds innings in the second game. Dave Parker homered twice for Pittsburgh in the first game, but it was light-hitting shortstop Frank Taveras who riled the boys adorned with the red wishbone "C"s. In the third inning with Pittsburgh ahead 7–0, Taveras reached on a fielder's choice and then stole second base: a blatant violation of baseball's taboo against running while enjoying a big lead. Reds reliever Dale Murray threw at Taveras several times, without hitting him, during Taveras' next two at bats. In the ninth with two outs and the Reds trailing by 11, Joe Hoerner threw a couple of pitches at Taveras too and finally plunked him. Taveras threw his bat towards the mound and shouted "Come on!" at Hoerner. The angry Pirates shortstop didn't get far before catcher Bill Plummer wrapped his arms around his torso, pinning his arms to his side. This allowed Hoerner, rushing off the mound to meet Taveras, to sock the slender leadoff man with a "strong, glancing blow" to the cheek. Both benches emptied, and there was a lot of dancing around but no further punches were thrown. Both Taveras and Hoerner were ejected from the game, and the umpires cleared both benches of players not in the game. The Reds went quietly in the bottom of the inning, and the game ended 12–1. No one in the Reds' clubhouse was the least bit apologetic. "He should have been looking for it," said Plummer. "Running seven runs ahead. What do you expect?" "No one came out swinging," added Reds sub Champ Summers. "They knew they had it coming. It was between Joe and Taveras."

Taveras revenged himself against the Reds in the second game by hitting an inside-the park grand slam, the key blow in the Pirates' six-run second inning. The liner into the right-field corner which eluded Ken Griffey just long enough for Taveras to scamper around the bases was Taveras' first major league home run. The Pirates put the game away with another big inning, when they scored four runs in the sixth; three of them coming on Bill Robinson's 16th home run. It was something of a long shot that Robinson even played the second game. He'd been beaned by Norman in the first one, taken to the hospital, undergone x-rays, and been cleared to play the nightcap. The four-run inning broke a 6–6 tie and resulted in a 10–6 final score.

Had it not been for Johnny Bench and George Foster, the second game, as the first, would have provided nothing for Reds fans to get excited about. Bench's 25th homer in the fourth inning cut Pittsburgh's lead to 6–4. Foster had another big game, going 3–5 with a double, another pair of homers, and four more RBI. Foster doubled in a run in the second, hit a solo homer against starter Odell Jones in the third, and blasted a two-run homer against Grant Jackson in the fifth that tied the score 6–6. The multi-home run game was Foster's eighth of the season; two shy of the National League record. The pair of long balls gave him 38 on the season, moving him within spitting distance of 40; a milestone that only four other Reds sluggers had reached or surpassed in the ball club's long and glorious history: Ted Kluszewski (twice), Wally Post, Johnny Bench (twice), and Tony Perez. The two homers also gave Foster six homers in five games; a tear that clearly made him the most dangerous hitter in the National League.

The Reds regrouped and won the final two games of the Pittsburgh series. They won Saturday afternoon's contest 8–3, with no help from Foster who went 0–4 against Terry Forster and Larry Demery. The slack was picked up by Joe Morgan who hit his 16th homer of the year and by Johnny Bench who hit his 20th. Tom Seaver went all the way to run his record to 11–5, despite giving up three homers, which fortunately were all solo shots (by Al Oliver, Bobby Tolan, and Bill Robinson). Afterwards Seaver explained the way he looked at his performance, saying, "I'm very pleased with this game. It gives us some sense of stability and that is one thing I wanted to accomplish. In my recent games I've been giving up 5 runs, 4 runs, not holding the lead. I haven't been consistent and that bothers me. The one thing I pride myself on is being a consistent pitcher." When one reporter asked him if he was disappointed with the trade given how poorly the Reds' season was going, he replied,

> It has been anything but disappointing. Just as I don't want people judging me on a couple of months, I'm not going to judge this team like that. This club will be in a race three out of four years. I don't judge things over a short period of time, only over a long period of time.
>
> A Bench, a Rose, a Morgan, they have done it over a long period of time and will continue to do it. That is what you judge on.
>
> The way I've been pitching here so far is just short term. In the long run I'll do my job. Three homers are all right, as long as they are solos.

Shortly after the game around 7 p.m. a gruesome discovery was made in downtown Cincinnati not far from Riverfront Stadium: the body of a man found on the sixth-floor ledge of the Netherland Hilton Hotel. Police speculated that the unidentified man, who was not a guest at the hotel, had either jumped or been pushed from the 14th floor. Reds fans might have been forgiven if they had mused that the dead body was a fitting symbol for Cincinnati's pennant chances.

In Sunday's *Enquirer* another story about the season's plethora of home runs was published, and this time it was written by Reds beat man Bob Hertzel and it focused on George Foster. For the story entitled "Of Homers, Foster, and the 'Rabbit Ball,'" Hertzel relied on Reds hitting coach Ted Kluszewski, who said the fans loved the increased number of homers being hit. Apparently accepting the "rabbit ball" theory, Big Klu said that he'd heard "they [the fans] don't feel they have the ball juiced up enough." This meant that "we're going to have to re-evaluate what a good pitcher is." Hertzel was careful not to attribute Foster's home run binge strictly to a juiced-up baseball; citing instead Foster's dedication to developing his ability to the utmost, a process which had taken time. Kluszewski's reaction to this explanation was to say, "That's why Foster might even get better than he is now. He can't hit more homers, but he can time them better and hit for a higher average, challenge for the batting title." In the end the story did not resolve the questions swirling around the homer happy season. Instead, it gave credit to where the credit was due.

The Reds won again Sunday afternoon, taking the get-away game 6–0 behind rookie Mario Soto's complete-game seven-hitter. The first shutout of Soto's young career prompted Sparky Anderson to say, "He's so talented. Unless I'm crazy, the kid will be outstanding in a couple of years." Foster went homerless but hit two doubles and scored twice. The game was the last Reds-Pirates matchup of the year, and despite the win by Cincinnati Pittsburgh took the season series 9–3.

It was out to the west, or as the wags like to say, "left" coast for an eight-game road trip: four against the Dodgers and four against the Giants. The Reds' modest two-game win streak was coupled with a four-game losing streak by the Dodgers. It wasn't much to hang one's hopes on, but it was something. The four-game set would hardly decide anything no matter how it turned out, but Dodgers fans certainly thought it was important, or perhaps they were just smelling blood; in any case, 48,242 of them (including singer Frank Sinatra and his wife Barbara) turned out for the Monday night opener. Rookie Paul Moskau started for Cincinnati, and Los Angeles countered with Tommy John, a cagey veteran left-hander who'd already won 12 games and came in riding a six-game personal winning streak. Moskau pitched well but John pitched superbly. The Reds beat John's sinker into the dirt all night and collected a total of two hits: a single by George Foster and a double by Ken Griffey. Adding insult to the injury of the 4–0 shutout he threw, John put L.A.'s first run on the scoreboard with a third-inning home run, his first as a National Leaguer (he'd hit four while pitching in the American League). After the game, a frustrated Johnny Bench, who'd gone 0–3, said, "The man drives me crazy. I may never play against him again. I may just walk up to the plate with a 3-wood. The secret is he doesn't throw strikes. Why should he? You keep thinking he's going to throw you something to hit but it never comes." When a reporter pointed out that the Reds were 8–1 lifetime against John, Bench asked incredulously, "You mean we've beaten him?"

Before the next game on Tuesday night, the Reds became aware of an embarrassing story which had appeared that morning on the front page of the *Cincinnati Enquirer*. Accompanied by mug shot photos of Bench, Concepcion, Rose, and Foster plus a headline that read "World Champs Pout Over Reds Ink," the story by AP sportswriter Norm Clarke averred that the players were upset over a previously published newspaper article by Hal McCoy of the *Dayton Daily News* that had been posted on a clubhouse bulletin board. In his story in the Dayton paper McCoy had suggested that "the Reds' poor performance was due to a country club atmosphere during spring training." According to Clarke, "tempers are flaring in the clubhouse of the frustrated Cincinnati Reds" and "several players are feuding with the press." In various ways Clarke tied each of the four players pictured with the story to his premise. He asserted that Bench was "miffed at what he terms 'cheap shot artists.'" He depicted Concepcion as fuming for being singled out as a scapegoat (an error by the shortstop on a botched double play cost the team a game against St. Louis). He claimed that Foster was snubbing writers; quoting him as saying, "There are some writers who only ask negative things. I don't plan to talk to negative writers." And he reported that Rose both agreed with McCoy's assessment, defended the two writers, and issued his own personal complaint, saying, "The only thing this team leads the league in is sun tans. Five years ago, we had some rules. There was no golf, tennis, or swimming on game days. It's different now. The only rule we have says I'm not allowed to bring my boy into the clubhouse anymore." According to Clarke, even Sparky Anderson, the man whose leadership had supposedly became lax, had to admit that the team's troubles had begun before the start of the 1977 season. "We were all wined and dined," Anderson was quoted as saying. "The guys went to Hawaii [for ABC television's "Superteam" obstacle course competition] and made a lot of money." Rose refused to walk back his comments, saying that "I told the truth. I was honest." But Anderson and Bench rejected Clarke's interpretation of the situation, claiming that the clubhouse talk Clarke made such a big deal about was just that: a lot of meaningless talk.

A sell-out crowd of 53,385 showed up for Tuesday night's game and watched the Reds even the series behind the stellar pitching of Doug Capilla, who flirted with a no hitter. The Dodgers did not get a hit until there were two outs in the seventh inning. Ron Cey hit a smash off Capilla's glove which ricocheted to shortstop Concepcion who threw on to first. Umpire Lee Weyer took a long look at the play, started to call Cey out, and then signaled "safe." An infuriated Concepcion rushed towards Weyer but was intercepted and restrained by Capilla. Cey was stranded and Capilla was lifted to a standing ovation from the L.A. crowd after the first two Dodgers reached in the eighth inning, on an error and a walk. Borbon came on to pitch out of that jam and set down the Dodgers in the ninth; completing the Reds' 4–0 whitewashing.

Speaking to reporters after the game Capilla sounded the part of the stoic team player. "I'm not interested in a no-hitter," he said. "I could pitch and give up 12 hits and win the game. That is the important thing. If the Man upstairs is willing, I'll get that no-hitter. This time He wasn't willing."

True to form, Concepcion still saw the play his (and Capilla's) way. "To me, he was out. No doubt," he said. "Nobody will take from my mind that he was out."

Sparky Anderson's comments were also in character and reflective of the odd logic he sometimes expressed. "Holding Davey back like that showed me what we got is a man," he said. "You know, deep down, I'm kinda glad he didn't get the no-hitter. It's too early for something like that. You don't want too many good things to happen too early."

And, once again, it was Joe Morgan who expressed best the opinion most seasoned observers would have held about the controversial call. "Whether it was our guy or their guy, the guy [Cey] ought to be called out in that situation. We're all professionals and we're putting on a show for the fans. With two outs in the seventh inning, you have to give the kid a shot at the no-hitter."

Despite the win and the impressive performance by his young pitcher, Anderson knew nothing much had changed for his team. He said: "I'm not dead until they bury me but I have the terrible feeling that they're getting ready to. They're [the Dodgers] running us out of games and out of time."

Before the third game of the series on Wednesday, August 10, Morgan expressed similar sentiments, a mixture of defiance and resignation. "I don't know, maybe it's too late. Maybe not. I do know if I was in the Dodgers' position I wouldn't be laughing. I'll guarantee you one thing. This team won't quit. The Dodgers might beat us but we won't roll over and die for them. If we don't win these two games and cut it to 9½ games, we won't quit trying, but you can only fool yourself for so long."

That night the Dodgers' obvious advantage over the Reds, their starting pitching, came into play once again, as L.A.'s fifth starter, Rick Rhoden, pitched a complete-game, two-hit shutout before a second straight weekday sellout crowd. It was Rhoden's 13th win of the season and more than that owned by any Reds pitcher. The Dodgers' only run came in the third inning as a result of a botched pick-off play. Second baseman Dave Lopes led off the inning with a base on balls. Moments later, as Lopes broke for second, Fred Norman picked him off. Lopes applied the brakes and then stayed in a rundown for six throws, as the Reds made their throws to each other too early; until he was finally caught sliding into second base on a throw by Joe Morgan to Pete Rose, who'd joined the rundown from his third base position. Except that Rose dropped the throw for an error. After Bill Russell sacrificed Lopes to third, Reggie Smith knocked him in with a single to left field.

Postgame in the visiting manager's office, after grousing about the key play of the game, the usually upbeat Anderson sounded defeated.

> I'm writing it all down, keeping a book on mental mistakes. Then next spring we will correct it. All of it. But there is so much. Tonight, a rundown. It'll be in that book. R-U-N–in big letters. We pick a guy off base and he beats us. That can't happen.
>
> One throw, that's all there's supposed to be.
>
> We are totally ashamed of 1977. You want to hang your head somewhere and not let someone see you. I don't want to be out socially. That's how disgraced I feel. I just want to be in dark alleys.

That night former Reds ace Don Gullet was placed on the 21-day Disabled List by his new team, the New York Yankees. Writers traveling with the Reds knew better than to ask Anderson if the team missed Gullet and the 10–3 record he had compiled so far in the 1977 season.

In front of a third consecutive weekday sell-out crowd, the Reds salvaged a split of the series the next night behind the gutsy pitching of Tom Seaver. Despite allowing a pair of homers, Seaver went all the way in the 5–4 win, striking out seven and walking but one. Dan Driessen's three-run homer in the top of the first gave Seaver an early cushion, while Morgan's fifth-inning RBI single turned out to be the game-winner. George Foster, who singled ahead of Driessen's homer in the first, went 1–4 on the night. He left town having gone 2–15 in the series, and the Reds headed to San Francisco in the same position as when they'd arrived in L.A.: 11½ games behind the Dodgers. As the team's Western Airlines flight approached the San Francisco airport, the pilots had trouble getting the landing gear to descend. The players did not take the problem seriously until an alarmed flight attendant screamed for them to "Buckle Up, NOW!" Even then, the players masked their concern with jokes, the best of which came courtesy of Pete Rose. Charley Hustle had just reached another milestone in his career, getting his 2,900th hit in L.A.; and he later admitted to reporters that that had given him special cause for concern. "Yes, I was scared," he said. "I thought I can't go down yet. I still need another hundred hits!"

Playing in San Francisco was always a bit of a homecoming for George Foster, as he'd come up through the Giants' farm system and made his major league debut with the Giants; but a head cold, which left him feeling "drained, sapped," kept him out of the Reds' lineup for three of the four games from August 12 through the 14th. Mike Lum started Friday night's contest in place of the National League leader in home runs (38) and RBI (109), and he homered in his first at bat in the top of the second to tie the game 1–1. With the

Giants ahead 4–2, the Reds rallied with two outs in the ninth to pull within a run. That's as close as they got though after Ray Knight, pinch-hitting for the left-handed Lum, struck out against Randy Moffit with the tying run in scoring position.

The Reds found themselves in a similar situation the following afternoon, but this time the Giants handed the game to them on a silver platter. For eight innings Paul Moskau and Dale Murray held the Giants to one run. That lone run looked as if it would be enough when Giants starter Jim Barr, working on a three-hit shutout, got two quick outs in the top of the ninth. Ken Griffey kept Cincinnati's hopes alive by beating out a bunt for a base hit (third baseman Darrell Evans let the ball roll, hoping it would go foul). After Joe Morgan singled to right, Giants manager Joe Altobelli called to the bullpen for Gary Lavelle. Sparky Anderson sent the right-handed Bob Bailey up to pinch-hit for the left-handed Driessen, and Bailey walked to load the bases. Lavelle then induced Johnny Bench to lift a high pop fly into shallow right field that should have ended the game. However, right fielder Jack Clark lost the ball off Bench's bat. As he jogged forward, Clark looked at second baseman Rob Andrews and then looked back up into the sky trying to locate the descending baseball. He never found it, and the ball hit the turf 20 feet away from him. All three Reds base runners, moving on contact, scored easily, and Bench's gift triple enabled Cincinnati to pull out a 3–1 win, after Pedro Borbon held San Francisco scoreless in the bottom of the ninth despite allowing a hit and a walk. Clark accepted responsibility for the play, saying, "It was definitely my ball and I missed it."

On Sunday the Reds split a doubleheader; losing the first game 6–1 and winning the nightcap 9–3. The split of the twin bill gave them a split of the series with San Francisco and thus a split of the entire 8-game west coast road trip. In treading water like that they were never going to reach pennant shores. Foster returned to the lineup for the first game and went 1-4. He doubled in the fourth inning and then, making a bone head decision, was thrown out trying to advance to third on a grounder to shortstop. With Foster again on the bench, Joe Morgan single-handedly destroyed the Giants in the nightcap; blasting a pair of homers, the first of which was a grand slam. Freddie Norman went all the way in the 9–3 laugher, finally chalking up another win after having lost seven straight to even his record at 10–10. While the Reds had been running in place, the Philadelphia Phillies had been sprinting away from the rest of the teams in the East Division. On Sunday they completed a sweep of the Cubs in Chicago for their 12th win in a row. They now led the second-place Pirates by 3½ games and the fading Cubs by 7. They also sported at 71-44 the best overall record in the major leagues. If the Cincinnati ball club was to have any chance of catching the Dodgers and facing off against the Phillies (or whoever wound up winning the East), they had to get "Reds hot" immediately. With ten of their next 14 games at home and the four away games against the lowly New York Mets, they were facing a "now or never" part of the 1977 schedule.

Before traveling to the Big Apple for the four away games, the Reds hosted the San Diego Padres for three games beginning Monday, August 15. Jack Billingham (seven innings) and Pedro Borbon (two) combined to blank San Diego 3–0, and the Reds scored all their runs in four innings against Randy Jones (5–9), the curve-balling left-hander who'd won the NL Cy Young Award the previous year. Pete Rose, who went 2–4 to climb back over .300, had an exaggerated explanation for the struggling Jones: "He threw more pitches in the first inning than he used to do in a whole game." Billingham used a "new" slider to also end a long personal losing streak (of six games) and even his record at 9–9. After the game, Johnny Bench, who hit a triple and his 27th home run to drive in two of the three Reds runs, suggested a couple of new reasons for the Reds' predicament. "We are mentally exhausted," he said.

> It is all coming out this year as two games over .500. That is why we have played so poorly. It hasn't been the pressure of trying for a third straight championship. It has been the effect of all five years.
>
> Money has something to do with it. Finally you have some security. The money can make you sit back, take away your motivation. The trouble is you can be motivated just so long.
>
> You've seen us make plays that are not Cincinnati Reds plays this year. You shake your head over them. They are mental mistakes. Lapses. It is not a physical problem. It is a mental one.

When asked about the effect the Dodgers' fast start (winning 21 of their first 25 games) had on the team, Bench said, "That just magnified everything. We couldn't give Dale Murray a chance to be absorbed into the team, give him and the young pitchers a chance to blend in."

After a 50-minute rain delay, Cincinnati won again the next night, 5–1, behind another complete-game effort by Tom Seaver. The win boosted Seaver's record as a Red to 6–2 and 13–5 overall. Going for a desperately-needed sweep on Wednesday, August 17, the Reds were stymied by Bill Almon, a light-hitting shortstop who came into the game batting .248. *The Sporting News'* College Player of the Year and the overall number 1 pick of the 1974 June draft out of Brown University, Almon had earned a starting job in 1977 for the first time in his career. His three-run home run in the fourth inning and two-run single in the fifth almost single-handedly beat the Reds and pinned the 7–4 loss on Mario Soto. The Reds also, uncharacteristically, committed five errors. Almon's comment on his big, 5-RBI day was "I haven't driven in 5 runs in a month." Sparky Anderson's comment to reporters about the Cincinnati fielding fiasco was "If I comment on tonight's game I will be saying stuff you can't print and that will get the churches after me." The one glimmer of hope for the Reds was provided by George Foster, who hit his 39th home run of the season, a three-run shot over the right-center field wall, in the seventh inning. It was Foster's first homer and first runs batted in since August 5. The home run drought, of 11 days and 12 games, would be the longest of the season for George.

After an off day on Thursday, the Reds opened the series in New York with an unscheduled doubleheader on Friday, August 19, in order to make up the rainout of June 6. It was the team's seventh and final twin bill of the year, and their sweep of the two games (4–1 and 4–3) was only their second DHer sweep of the season.

Good pitching by young Reds starters and the play of George Foster, who homered in each contest, pretty much ruled the day. In the first game Doug Capilla threw his first major league complete game while giving up six hits and striking out six; while Foster went 2-4, hit his 40th home run of the year, and made a "spectacular running catch of [Mets center fielder] Lee Mazilli's leadoff line drive" in the ninth inning. Capilla tipped his cap in Foster's direction and later said, "A guy makes a catch like that, he deserves some credit."

Capilla's early innings performance was nothing less than a magic act. In the first three innings Capilla gave up four hits and three walks, hit a batter, and made two throwing errors himself, yet somehow held the Mets to the single run they wound up scoring all game. Getting out of a bases-loaded, one-out jam in the third was the key. "Getting out of that generated me," Capilla said. "I told myself to relax and bear down. 'Have yourself an easy inning or you're not going nine.' Going nine was on my mind."

In discussing the milestone homer at Foster's locker at the end of the night, one reporter pointed out that no NL hitter had put together a 40-homer year since 1973, when four players had done so: Willie Stargell, Hank Aaron, Dave Johnson, and Darrell Evans. Foster's comment was: "I'm not really concerned about the number of home runs I hit. If there was a big award for hitting 40, maybe I'd get excited. But now I'm just taking them home run by home run, trying to get my strength back from the flu I had." The reporter then wanted to know if Foster was aware of Ted Kluszewski's club record of 49 home runs in a season. "I know what's going on," said George. Foster also insisted that he was not aiming to break Klu's record, although he added a paraphrase of the old baseball saw about records: "Klu knows records are set and records are broken."

Foster was the hero of the nightcap win as well. He staked starting Reds pitcher Paul Moskau to a 2-0 first-inning lead by slamming his 41st home run of the year off Nino Espinosa, and in the eighth inning he hit a sacrifice fly to plate the eventual decisive run after the Mets scored two runs against Pedro Borbon to make the final score 4-3. The three RBI boosted Foster's total to 116, and the home run left him four behind Johnny Bench's second highest total in Reds history.

On Saturday afternoon at Shea Stadium the Reds won their third game in a row, 8-2, and the starting and winning pitcher was Freddie Norman, celebrating his 35th birthday. It was Norman's second consecutive win, after he'd lost seven in a row, and got him above .500 again at 11-10. During that nightmarish streak the Reds had scored a total of one run for Norman. After the game Norman admitted, "The streak was getting to me. I was beginning to wonder if my lack of confidence would affect me. I'd been through things like this before, lost my confidence, and had a terrible time of it. I was determined not to let it happen again. I looked at Don Sutton last year. He went more than a month without winning and still wound up with a good year. If a guy like that can go through a slump mentally, why can't I? I can still have a good year." Foster went 2-4 and picked up another RBI with a ground-rule double in the third inning.

On Sunday the Reds pulled off the four-game sweep, winning 5-1, as former Met Tom Seaver enjoyed a successful homecoming; pitching a complete-game six hitter with 11 strikeouts. The majority of the crowd of 46,265 was in Seaver's corner, or at least not rooting against him personally, and they gave him a rousing standing ovation when he jogged out to throw his first warm up pitch of the game. The organist played "Hello Dolly," certain that the line "It's so nice to have you back in town" was highly apropos. "It was awfully nice to come home, what was home for so long," said Tom Terrific when it was all over. "The toughest part was waiting for the game to start. I wanted to get started. Once it got going, I was all right."

Seaver's mound opponent was his old friend, lefthander Jerry Koosman, who moved up a day in the rotation just so he could face off against the Reds' ace. When they'd been teammates in New York, Seaver and Koosman had enjoyed a friendly competition of trying to outhit the other guy; a competition they renewed in the game. In their first confrontation in the top of the second inning Seaver hit into a 4-6-3 double play and took a ribbing from Koos as the two men left the field. In the bottom of the inning, Koosman hit a long fly ball to right field but it was caught by Ken Griffey. The game-within-the-

The Reds' acquisition of Hall of Fame pitcher Tom Seaver halfway through the 1977 season was one of the best trades in team history. The trade addressed the team's biggest need: better starting pitching. Seaver was spectacular, going 14–3 with a 2.35 ERA for Cincinnati, but he wasn't able to turn things around by himself. Seaver's steely competitiveness and powerful delivery are dramatically illustrated in this photograph.

game was decided in Seaver's favor in the fifth inning, when Seaver doubled to right-center and scored on a single by Pete Rose and then struck out Koosman to end the bottom of the frame. Seaver also reached on an error by Mets shortstop Bud Harrelson in the eighth inning and scored a second run following another Mets error and a pair of base hits. After the second hit of that inning, Koosman was removed for reliever Skip Lockwood. Only two of the five runs Koosman allowed in the game were earned, and the tough loss was typical of his 1977 season. The loss dropped his record to 8–15, but the Mets had scored only 21 runs in those 15 losses. Seaver improved his record to 14–5. The win also made Sparky Anderson the winningest manager in Cincinnati Reds history. Sparky's 748th victory gave him one more than Bill McKechnie. Foster went 1–4 on the day, his lone safety an RBI first-inning single. In the American League 40-year-old Brooks Robinson announced his retirement. The highly beloved Baltimore Oriole, widely regarded as the best fielding third baseman in the history of the game, was hitting .149 with one homer and four RBI in 47 plate appearances. Still fresh in the minds of Reds fans were bittersweet memories of the great plays he'd made in the 1970 World Series, won by Baltimore, to extinguish many a Cincinnati rally.

The Reds returned to Riverfront Stadium for seven games, having won seven of their previous eight games. Before the game of Monday, August 22, against Montreal, Sparky Anderson couldn't help but express some cautious optimism. "The next four days will tell," he said. "If we can win the next four days, we have a legitimate chance. If we can win 30 out of 38 we'll be right on their doorstep. By Labor Day we have to get it to five or six. We have to finish with 95 wins, at least. To have any chance of winning we have to win 95 and, to be honest, the chances of winning 95 are very slim." As usual, Cincinnati reporters gravitated with their notebooks and tape recorders to Tony Perez, who remained as popular with them as he did with his former Reds teammates. Perez entertained them with an anecdote about his long distance phone conversation earlier in the season with some Reds players after the Expos had beaten L.A. three straight, while the Reds lost three straight to Pittsburgh. "We trying to help you," Perez said he told his Cincinnati buddies, "and what you dummies do ... lose three straight." Asked about the Reds' chances of catching the Dodgers, he said, "Nine and a half games, it will be tough. Last time we here Morgan tell me they going to catch the Dodgers and that I will be home watching the World Series on television. Well, Morgan may be there watching with me. It is not impossible, it is just tough. I guess it is just a different year for the Reds. Certainly, it has surprised me." Always thinking about others, he added, "I just hope the fans no blame Danny Driessen." In fact, there was no reason to blame Driessen, as his year to date statistically was better than Perez's. Driessen held small leads in home runs (15 to 12) and RBI (70 to 68) and a bigger one in batting average (.296 to .268).

Because of a three-hour delay of their flight into Cincinnati, the Expos arrived at the ball park only an hour and 20 minutes before game time. It didn't matter. Wayne Twitchell held the Reds to four hits and one run over eighth innings, and rookie Warren Cromartie with a two-run homer in the fifth inning gave Twitchell all the support he needed. While George Foster went 0–4 in the 5–1 loss, Bob Hertzel thought it prudent to point out in the *Enquirer* that Foster was now three games behind the pace Hack Wilson had set in 1930 when he set the NL single season home run record with 56.

Perez and Co. beat the Reds again on Tuesday night, 4–2, in a frustrating game for both teams' offenses. Combined, they went 1–22 with runners in scoring position and left 27 runners on base. A fifth-inning solo home run by Montreal catcher Gary Carter that put the Expos up 3–1 was the difference in the game. Expos starter Steve Rogers (14–12) and two relievers kept George Foster in the ball park, but Foster did collect a pair of singles (in five at bats) and his 119th RBI. Since the All-Star break the Dodgers had faltered a bit, going 15–18; yet with their own record of 17–20 the Reds had not taken advantage of the opportunity. In a reminiscent mood, beat reporter Bob Hertzel tracked down former Reds catcher and pinch-hitter extraordinaire Hal King. Hertzel found King playing in the Mexican League. Sounding a little bitter at his baseball fate, King insisted that he was still good enough to be helping a major league team. With no offers forthcoming from the teams in the National or American Leagues, he was hoping to go to Japan and play there for more money than he was making in Mexico.

The home stand continued on Wednesday and Thursday with a pair of games against New York, and the accommodating Mets dropped them both to hand the season series to Cincinnati 10–2; the Reds' best ledger against any team for 1977. The Reds pounded Jon Matlack and two relievers for 15 hits and 11 runs in the first game, and Fred Norman (12–10) and Pedro Borbon combined on a six-hitter as the Reds pulled out a squeaker, 3–2, in the second game. George Foster also got back on track in the first game against the Mets, going 2–4 and blasting his 42nd home run against the facing of the left-field yellow-seat deck, right below the top, red-seat deck. The two-game sweep of the Mets was a modest achievement certainly; but it gave the Reds nine wins in their last 12 games, cut the Dodgers' lead to 8½ games, and occasioned some bravado from, of all people, beat reporter Bob Hertzel. "Don't look now, but we have a pennant race again," he wrote. "An honest-to-goodness pennant race, the kind where one team is chasing the other and where the team in front is looking back over its shoulder and stumbling and falling all over the joint. The chaser is the Cincinnati Reds. The target is the Los Angeles Dodgers."

Pete Rose lamented the two losses to the Expos on Monday and Tuesday, saying, "Those two games with Montreal loom very large now"; and Joe Morgan and Sparky Anderson embellished Hertzel's theme. "We have to get it to four or five games real quick," said Morgan. "We have to put some pressure on them. Do that and they'll start making errors, blowing plays. Right now they're not doing that. They're just not scoring runs and losing. But they aren't looking bad. They are capable of playing worse. The reason they are is because they're all rabbit ears over there. If the newspapermen start getting on them, that could do it."

"I think we are in a race. I really do," said Anderson. "They'll have a tough time winning. I know that. They haven't been able to win since the first 26 games of the season."

The Philadelphia Phillies came into town for the final three games of the home stand carrying the best overall record (78–47) in baseball with them. They had also widened their lead over second-place Pittsburgh to 6½ games. The first game on Friday night, August 26, was a matchup of staff aces, Steve Carlton vs. Tom Seaver, and drew a crowd of 46,079. It took Seaver 150 pitches to do it, but he outdueled "Lefty" and led Cincinnati to a 4–2 win. It was Seaver's fifth straight complete game and his seventh win in a row. Meanwhile, over in the American League the pennant race pictures had cleared up considerably, and the frontrunners in each division won on Friday night to lengthen their leads. In the East the Yankees came from behind to defeat Texas 6–5 for their 17th win in their last 19 games. The Bronx Bombers now led Boston by three games and Baltimore by four. In the West, behind Dave Leonard's six-hitter and Hal McRae's 17th home run, Kansas City beat the Orioles 4–3 to win their club record tenth game in a row. The Royals now enjoyed a three-game edge over both the Chicago White Sox and the Minnesota Twins.

Saturday afternoon's tilt was a good old-fashioned barn burner, won by the Reds 6–5 in a most unexpected way. Philly led 5–4 going into the bottom of the ninth inning and appeared to have the game wrapped up after they turned a double play: George Foster striking out and Ken Griffey getting nabbed on an attempted steal of second base on the same play. With the Reds down to their final out, Dan Driessen stepped in against Phillies closer Tug McGraw, who'd come into the game with one out in the seventh inning. Driessen drove a pitch deep into center field, and when it hit the wall and eluded center fielder Jerry Martin he just kept running around the bases.

Right fielder Jay Johnstone finally corralled the ball and threw it to cut-off man Mike Schmidt, who then relayed it home. Driessen and the ball arrived simultaneously at home plate, and when the dust cleared Driessen was sitting on home plate with Phillies catcher Barry Foote, minus the baseball, sprawled nearby on his back. The inside-the-park home run tied the game, causing Schmidt to throw down his cap and glove in disgust. Four pitches later Johnny Bench took a McGraw screwball over the left-field fence for a dramatic, walk-off home run. After the game Driessen described his thought process regarding his hurried round-tripper, saying, "I thought it had a chance to go out but I was running to make sure. I'm no Foster who can tell right away." Despite their better judgment, the Reds could not help but feel a little hopeful after the exciting, unlikely win. "It is still somewhat discouraging, being so far behind," said Bench. "But if we play like this over the next 30 games, maybe then we can look back on a game like this and say it was the turning point."

The Reds pulled off the three-game sweep the next day, jumping all over Barry Lerch and Warren Brusstar for seven runs in the first two innings. Foster punctuated the onslaught in the second inning, hitting his 43rd home run of the season, a three-run shot to left-center, off Brusstar. For the first time all season, Sparky Anderson revealed that he was aware of an important milestone that was now clearly within Foster's reach. "He'll hit his 50 now," he said. "If he just keeps on his average he'll hit eight or so more and that would be 51. He's capable of hitting ten more." A reporter asked Foster if he thought he'd reach 50. Without cracking a smile Foster said, "Well, I'm 28 now. If I keep my health, live a clean life, and take vitamins, I think I'll reach 50." The 9–0 victory represented the first complete game and first shutout of rookie Paul Moskau's career. Moskau, who'd been roughed up by Philadelphia in his major league debut, felt vindicated by his performance, which evened his record at 4–4. "I did have incentive to show them [the Phillies] I know how to pitch," he said. "I had something to prove. That first time, well, it was the first time. Now, I've been around. I know how to prepare for a game." The sweep against Philadelphia, an excellent team definitely headed for the post season, was encouraging on its face. The problem was that as the Reds were sweeping the Phillies, the Dodgers were sweeping the St. Louis Cardinals; which enabled Los Angeles to maintain their 8½ game lead over Cincinnati. There was nothing for the Reds to do but continue to grind it out and hope for the best.

The Reds ended the month of August with three games in Montreal, marking the start of their second-to-last road trip of the season. They lost the opener 7–2 but rebounded to take the final two games, 4–3 and 6–0. In the Monday opener Fred Holdsworth, picked up in a mid-season trade with

Baltimore, combined with Don Stanhouse to hold Cincinnati to five hits; while Tony Perez led the Expos' hitting attack. Perez went 2–4 with a home run and three RBI. Cognizant of the Reds' position, Perez joked afterwards, "I'd like for those guys to get the money. Pete, Johnny, Joe, Davey. But it is not my fault if they don't. I am on the other side now."

Perez almost donned the hero's mantel in the second game as well. Montreal went to bat in the bottom of the ninth inning trailing 4–1. They scored two runs against Pedro Borbon who then faced Perez with two outs and the tying run in the person of Warren Cromartie standing on first base. Perez drove a Pedro Borbon pitch deep into the right-center field alley, and Cromartie tore around the bases determined to score the tying run. After picking up the ball, Cesar Geronimo wheeled and fired the ball towards the infield. "I see no one," he said. "I just throw." Geronimo hit cut-off man Dave Concepcion who threw on to home plate; where Johnny Bench, the best ever at blocking the plate, applied the tag to Cromartie for the out. And the ball game. It was simple execution according to Concepcion, who said, "On that play I go to the spot and wait for the ball from Geronimo. I know I have to go home. I can go nowhere else. He is the tying run." Sparky Anderson called the play "As perfect a relay as you'll ever see." Cromartie disagreed with home plate umpire Doug Harvey's "Out!" call, saying, "I was safe. My foot got it [touched home] on the corner of the plate." In the Reds' clubhouse Bench was adamant, insisting, "He never touched the plate." While it was the execution of the so-called "fundamentals" that prevented Montreal from tying the game, it was the big bat of George Foster that put the Reds in a position to win it. Foster went 3–5 and knocked in three of the Reds' runs. His 44th home run gave the Reds a 2–0 lead in the first inning, and his seventh-inning single drove in the eventual winning run. The home run off right-hander Jackie Brown gave Foster 12 for the month of August; a total which matched his previous monthly high of 12 in the month of July.

In winning the final game in Montreal, 6–0, on Wednesday, August 31, the Reds finally beat Wayne Twitchell. Two of Twitchell's three wins on the season (against ten losses) had come against Cincinnati. The game was dominated by Twitchell's opponent, Tom Seaver, who held the Expos to three hits. It was the 44th shutout of Seaver's career and ran his record for 1977 to 16–5, 9–2 as a Cincinnati Red. Seaver also picked up his 2,500th strikeout which put him 11th on the all-time list and led reporters to ask the 32-year-old right-hander about his future prospects. "I'm looking forward to reaching 3,000," he said. "And two more wins and it's 200 for me. That's a big step towards 300. I don't think I'll be able to get there but you don't know if you don't try." Seaver's teammates, who were still pinching themselves to make sure they really were his teammates, certainly had plenty of confidence in him. Joe Morgan spoke for the whole team when he said, "It is something to watch him pitch. I always marveled at him when I was on another team. I mean, it was challenging to face him because he is such a great pitcher. But now, seeing him all the time, I say to myself, 'How did you ever get a hit off him?'"

Seaver wasn't the only ball player reaching personal milestones. Over in Japan Sadaharu Oh hit his 39th home run of the 1977 Central League season and the 755th home run of his career to tie the world home run record set by Hank Aaron. Oh took the achievement in stride, saying, "I tied Aaron's record step by step, so I have no special feeling now. Since my 753rd homer there has been a tense atmosphere in the ball parks. Some home runs come easily but others come more than 10 games apart."

George Foster knew exactly the way Oh felt. And so did *Enquirer* cartoonist Jerry Dowling, who posted another big-jawed Foster cartoon in the Thursday, September 1, edition of the paper. With bat and ball in hand, Foster is depicted as taking aim at a shooting gallery of heads of single-season home run targets ... Johnny Bench (representing the Reds' right-handed batter record, 45), Ted Kluszewski (Reds team record, 49), Hack Wilson (the National League record, 56), Babe Ruth (the major league record, 60), and Roger Maris (the asterisk-hampered record, 61). Rally Rat quips, "A few ducks on the pond, George!" A calm and composed Foster mutters, "...one at a time!"

"Foster's Shooting Gallery." This is the Dowling cartoon directly concerned with Foster's home run chase. George's targets are arranged in order and embodied, as Dirty Rat points out, like "ducks on the pond." Fellow Reds sluggers Bench and Ted Kluszewski were almost certainly going down, and NL home run record holder Hack Wilson was within reach. Babe Ruth, sitting on 60 long balls, and Roger Maris, 61, were going to be much harder to hit.

8

September–October 1977
Getting Over the Hump

Heading into the last month of the season, the Reds were playing good baseball, having won 14 of their previous 18 games. Nevertheless, the players and most of their fans as well knew that it would take a historic, late-season collapse by the Los Angeles Dodgers for the Reds to win the West Division pennant. Such collapses had happened before—the Phillies' collapse of 1964 which almost led to a pennant for Cincinnati came readily to mind—but no one in Cincinnati was counting on the Dodgers of 1977 to succumb to a similar unraveling. Furthermore, in that era before the playoffs were expanded, there were no Wild Card "second chances." If you didn't win the pennant in your division, your season was over.

The schedule was also not favorable for Cincinnati. Counting the two October games on their slate, the Reds had 28 games left: 12 at home and 16 away. The most important games left on the schedule were the five games the Reds would play against the Dodgers: three at home and two in Los Angeles. If the Reds were to have any chance at the pennant, they had to win all five of those games because beating the Dodgers head-to-head was the fastest and surest way to reduce the lead. When playing teams other than the Dodgers, the Reds had to rely on other teams to beat Los Angeles; and when other teams did not beat Los Angeles, the Reds gained no ground even when their won their own games. The Reds would get their shot at the Dodgers in Riverfront Stadium September 9–11, in the middle of the next-to-last home stand of the year. First, they had to finish the current road trip, which after a travel day on Thursday continued Friday, September 2, in Philadelphia.

The Reds felt that they carried a psychological edge into the series. After all, they'd just swept the Phillies in Cincinnati, and the Reds knew that the Phillies were still lugging around the mental baggage of having been swept by the Reds in the NLCS the year before. The problem was that 1977 was not 1976. In 1977 the Phillies were practically unbeatable at home. After losing five straight at home to start the season, the Phillies had won 51 of 60 games at Veterans Stadium, including their previous 14 in a row. Right-hander Jim Lonborg (10-3) kept the streak going, throwing a complete-game five-hitter at the Reds; and outfielder Bake McBride gave Lonborg all the support he needed with a 3-4 day at the plate. With two doubles and a home run, McBride drove in all three runs in Philadelphia's 3-0 victory. After the game, the Reds announced they were calling up four players from their Triple-A farm team in Indianapolis: Tom Hume, Angel Torres, Dan Dumoulin, and Don Werner. All of them were pitchers except for Werner, a light-hitting catcher. This was somewhat surprising, given the .185 batting average sported by Reds pinch-hitters. For whatever reason, the Reds failed to promote Dave Revering, Indy's slugging first baseman batting .300 with 29 home runs and 110 RBI. Revering was both mystified and angry at the snub.

The Saturday night game matched Paul Moskau (4-4) against Larry Christenson (12-6), and Christenson and the Phillies came out on top 9-3. Christenson, who would finish the year 19-6, gave up the Reds' three runs in seven innings and then turned the game over to Philadelphia's closer Tug McGraw. Moskau didn't get out of the third inning, when the Phillies batted around, scoring six runs. Bake McBride had another 3-5 day, including a two-run homer in that deciding third frame. George Foster went 2-4 and drove in a run, but it hardly mattered as the Reds dropped ten games behind Los Angeles again. Fred Norman went all the way the next afternoon, pitching a seven-hitter, to help the Reds win 5-2 and avoid a three-game sweep. With his fifth win in a row, Norman improved his record to 14-10. George Foster and Pete Rose led the Reds on offense. Foster banged out four hits (in five at bats), including his 45th home run of the year, which he hit off starter Jim Kaat into the right-field seats in the fifth inning. With that homer Foster crossed Johnny Bench off his list of targets

Rose went 3-5 on the day, getting as many as three hits in a game for the first time since July 29. Ever conscious of personal milestones, Rose was intent on getting 200 hits in the season. He needed 33 more hits in the final 25 games to do so, which would then tie him with Ty Cobb for the most 200-hit seasons in a career with nine. In reference to his facing an uphill climb to reach the 200-hit plateau, Rose described his season as "an unlucky year." Bob Hertzel sagely pointed out that "most of the Reds could say the same thing."

For once, not even the great Tom Seaver could halt Cincinnati's most recent slide, as the Astros beat the Reds 5-1 in the Astrodome on Monday night, September 5. Ignoring his poor record (6-14), Mark Lemongello put it to the Reds; pitching a complete-game six-hitter and stroking a triple himself off Seaver in the third inning. Lemongello even scored Houston's eventual winning run when Bench, trying to pick him off, threw wildly past third base. A mixture of bad luck and bad base running cost the Reds on offense. Pete Rose tripled to open the game but then got trapped off third base and tagged out on a Morgan ground ball to short. A second rally was snuffed out in the second inning when Cesar Geronimo was picked off first base. And in the fourth Astros center fielder Cesar Cedeno leaped against the wall to corral a Morgan blast and rob him of a home run. Cedeno hit his head on the wall and slumped to the ground momentarily, but he held onto the baseball for the out.

Tuesday night's game started eerily like Monday's, with Pete Rose again getting trapped off third base on a grounder by Joe Morgan, being put out, and the Reds failing to score in the first inning. The game, an 8–3 Houston victory, went downhill from there.

Cincinnati starter Doug Capilla pulled a muscle in his back and left after the second inning. Houston scored two runs in the third inning, helped most uncharacteristically by throwing errors by Johnny Bench on steals of second base by Enos Cabell and Ceasar Cedeno. They salted the game away in the sixth inning, scoring three runs while batting around against Dan Dumoulin, making his second major league appearance. Still exhibiting the "red ass" for "the team that gave up on him [the Reds]," Joaquin Andujar went the first sixth innings for the Astros and got credit for his first win since the All-Star break, after reliever Joe Sambito baffled Cincinnati over the final three innings: allowing one hit and no runs.

The two losses in the Astrodome emboldened the Houston players, who now began making noises about catching Cincinnati and finishing in second place themselves. The losses gave the Reds a 3–5 record for the road trip: a disaster given the circumstances. The Big Red Machine lurched coughing and sputtering back to Cincinnati 11½ games out of first place; their worst position since August 17. For a two-week stretch they'd played like defending champions but hadn't been able to keep it up. Now they were facing the inevitable probability that the remaining portion of the season would not involve a pennant race but would devolve into a series of individual players racing to achieve personal goals and milestones. At the head of that list of players was George Foster, who went 2-4 but homerless in the final game of the road trip. Nevertheless, in Wednesday morning's paper it was announced that Foster had been named National League Player of the Month for August, based on his .293 average, 12 home runs, and 28 RBI.

The Reds opened their next-to-last home stand of the year on Wednesday, September 7. They would play the Giants twice, the Dodgers three times, and the Astros twice, before hitting the road for the final and longest (11 games) road trip of the year. As if to celebrate the latest Player of the Month announcement, Foster found his home run stroke again in the fifth inning of Wednesday night's game, driving an Ed Halicki pitch high into the red seats for his 46th homer of 1977. It was Foster's third red-seater and the eighth in ballpark history. Hertzel said of the gargantuan blast: "The homer was probably the hardest ever seen in Riverfront Stadium and would have been the longest had it not struck the foul screen and dropped into the first row of the red seats." After the game San Francisco second baseman Rob Andrews couldn't resist teasing his teammate, telling Halicki, "You may have given up the longest homer ever!"

"Maybe so," said Halicki, "but he had to look at one of mine too."

That was true enough, as the gangly right-hander had also homered (a solo shot) in the top of the sixth to provide an insurance run in San Fran's 6–3 win. Halicki pitched just long enough (five and two thirds innings) and just well enough (seven hits, three runs) to get the win, end a personal seven-game losing streak, and improve his record to 13–10. He had reliever Gary Lavelle, who held the Reds to one hit over the final three and a third innings, to thank for saving his win.

The Giants' winning runs were provided by veteran first baseman Willie McCovey; having, near the end of his long and distinguished career, his best season since 1970. McCovey's two-run homer off Mario Soto in the third inning was the 489th of his career and gave the Giants a 5–2 lead. McCovey, who also picked up hit number 2,000 in the game, later engaged in some interesting self-evaluation with reporters, describing himself as "the type of hitter who gets the maximum out of the minimum number of hits. I never got good pitches to hit when the bases were empty. Therefore I didn't have that many opportunities to hit."

Regardless of the respect accorded to the venerable and well-liked McCovey, the post-game buzz was all about Foster's gigantic homer and how far it might have traveled unimpeded. Unfortunately for Foster, the Reds did not have a publicist like Red Patterson, the New York Yankees' employee who back in the 1950s had had the moxie to turn one of Mickey Mantle's long home runs (against Washington's Chuck Stobbs) into a captivating myth of super-human strength and skill … through nothing but guesstimate and sheer sensationalism. Instead of becoming a foundation for legend, Foster's homer was treated as just another cipher in the statistics of all National and American League players that appeared in the Sunday morning sports sections of the nation's newspapers. In other words, it was forgotten about by the time the teams took batting practice the next afternoon.

If a media machine had existed in Cincinnati as it did in New York, it would have made as much of Foster's performance the next day as the day before, even though Foster did not send any pitch deep into the night during the Reds' 6 to 5 win over San Francisco. What he did do was win the game with a walk-off sacrifice fly and then say exactly the right things, the kind of selfless, team-first things the sporting public likes to hear from its heroes.

With one out and the game tied 5–5 in the bottom of the ninth, Pete Rose bounced a little dribbler back to the mound and reached on an error when Giants first baseman McCovey (who'd hit two homers in the game) bobbled the throw from pitcher Randy Moffit. Rose helped first base umpire Jim Quick make the right call by yelling "SAFE!" as he ran across the bag. According to Rose, "Soon as I saw him juggle the throw I yelled. I knew the umpire seen it, but sometimes they don't call it. I'm glad I ran hard. Your first reaction is not to, you're so mad you topped the ball." With Ken Griffey at bat, Rose stole second and raced to third when Griffey beat out a bouncer to second. The Giants intentionally walked Joe Morgan to load the bases, and moments later Foster hit a high fly ball to center field, which allowed Rose to tag up and score easily with the winning run.

Foster's comment about the play said it all. "The sacrifice fly was more satisfying than the home run last night. It's always more satisfying when you win. If the team loses it doesn't seem like you've done enough." Reds beat man Bob Hertzel got Foster's words into the paper, but the sentiment expressed in them did not blossom into a widely-disseminated and -admired quote representative of the man's character. Not that Foster cared. All that mattered to him was the respect of his teammates, and he was assured of that now. In fact, the superstars of the team … Rose, Bench, and Morgan … all expressed their support of Foster as the hands-down most deserving candidate for the National League Most Valuable Player Award; an honor they had all previously won. Strangely, Reds manager Sparky Anderson was not in Foster's corner. He refused to discuss Foster's chances for winning the award, and Hertzel reported that he was "leaning" towards Dodgers outfielder Reggie Smith. "He [Smith] kept them up there when they were going down," he said. "Everything he has done has been in the clutch. I'd just like to go back and check his home runs and see when they came." For any manager not to support his own player would be a puzzling thing. In this case it was especially so, given Anderson's reputation as a manager who routinely went overboard in rating and praising his players; and given the fact that Smith simply could not touch the year that Foster was putting together. At the conclusion of the season Smith's .307 batting average, 32 home runs, and 87 RBI looked like a very nice year, but those numbers paled in comparison to the ones posted by Foster. Perhaps Anderson harbored a subconscious grudge over the implications of prejudice that had arisen out of Foster's old complaint about not getting to bat cleanup because of his race. That's possible but unlikely; especially since the matter had long ceased to be an issue. Once Foster got untracked in 1977 he regularly batted fourth in the lineup no matter who was pitching, and he always batted fourth against left-handed pitchers (overall, only 15 of the 52 homers Foster would hit in 1977 came when he was slotted anywhere in the batting order other than fourth). Eliminating a personal animus of some kind, the only plausible explanation for Anderson's stance and comments is human nature. At one time or another, everybody says something stupid, and in regard to his opinion about the most qualified candidates for the 1977 NL MVP award Sparky Anderson definitely needed a mulligan.

The Dodgers came into town for a weekend series and immediately took a Reds sweep off the table with a 4–1 win on Friday night in front of a crowd of 39,518. Once again Tommy John stymied the Reds, going all the way to win his 18th game of the season; and Dusty Baker provided all the runs John needed with a three-run homer off Fred Norman in the sixth inning. Foster drove in the Reds' only run with a single to right in the fourth inning. The RBI was his 131st of the season.

The Reds bounced back to win the next two games 7–4 and 6–2. Stopper Tom Seaver was the Cincinnati hero of Saturday night's game. He held L.A. to two runs in his eight-inning stint, picking up his 17th win of the season; and he helped his own cause by hitting a home run into the left-field green seats off Dodgers starter Doug Rau in the second inning. Seaver rounded first base clapping his hands like an ecstatic Little Leaguer as he saw the ball land in the green seats. Seaver's continued, consistent brilliance filled Sparky Anderson with hope for the future and a determination to right the ship in 1978. "We'll take the lead next year and we'll take it right from the start," he said. "We won't get behind immediately next year, I promise that. We'll have the big honcho [Seaver] and we'll stop that. He wouldn't have mattered this year. One guy couldn't turn this around. But there's no question in my mind, with a few corrections and a whole new spring training, he'll turn it around next year."

Sunday's win was the result of a brilliant performance from an unexpected source and provided more hope for the future in the person of reliever Tom Hume, who picked up his first major league win. Jack Billingham started for Cincinnati and ran into trouble in the third inning. Billingham loaded the bases with no outs, and when he complained of "tightening in his shoulder" Sparky Anderson decided to replace him with a reliever. As young right-hander Tom Hume trotted in from the bullpen, Anderson told catcher Johnny

Bench, "We've got to find out if he can pitch and we'll find out right now. We can't wait until next March." Earlier in the season after his ERA had ballooned to 12.50 and his record had dropped to 0–3, Hume had been demoted to Indianapolis. It wasn't much of a stretch to say that this appearance was going to be his last chance with the Reds.

When Hume was ready, he stood facing Reggie Smith with Ron Cey and Steve Garvey to follow: the very heart of L.A.'s potent batting order. Hume popped Smith up to short for the first out. He induced Cey to fly out to left for the second out, although Rick Rhoden tagged at third and came in to score. Garvey drove in a second run with a single, but Hume retired the side on a ground out force play (6–4) by Rick Monday. Hume then held the Dodgers to four hits and no more runs over the final six innings to earn his first major league victory. For the first time there was a bevy of reporters around his locker after the game, and Hume told them, "It got so I was scared to go out there. When you are in the minor leagues you think these guys [major league players] are immortals. You think they're all superstars. But they're not. They're just like me. I finally just relaxed." Across the clubhouse a reporter congratulated Johnny Bench on having reached a milestone with his two-run double in the first inning. With that hit Bench reached the 100 RBI mark for the sixth time in his career, and as the reporter pointed out, Tony Perez was the only other active player with as many seasons. "So what when you are 11½ games out," Bench said. "If you get 130 like George Foster and lose, it doesn't matter."

With such a big lead over the Reds and the Reds' opportunities to make up ground dwindling fast, the Dodgers displayed a certain insouciance towards Cincinnati. Not so the Houston Astros who came into town on a mission to deliver a message. The Reds didn't like the message but they got it ... loud and clear, as the Astros won the final two games between the West Division rivals, 7–2 and 13–4. On Monday night Houston pummeled Mario Soto (2–6), Angel Torres, and Dale Murray for five home runs; while the Reds were silenced by the intimidating J. R. Richard, who struck out 11 and held them to two hits over eight innings. In Tuesday's fiasco, started at 5:00, the Astros scored six runs in the second inning against starter Paul Moskau and Murray and five runs in the ninth against Dan Dumoulin. Bob Watson homered for the second night in a row, as did one-man Reds wrecking crew Cesar Cedeno who went 8–10 in the two games with three homers, two triples, five RBI, eight runs, and a stolen base. For the second night in a row George Foster collected a pair of hits, including, in Tuesday's game, a home run, which came in the fourth inning against Houston starter Floyd Bannister. Foster would certainly have agreed with Hertzel's low-key mention of the round tripper: "It was his 47th of the season and probably the least meaningful." The two losses left the Reds 13 games behind Los Angeles. Houston's two wins were their fifth and sixth straight over the Reds and gave them a final advantage of 13–5 in the season series between the two teams. When the 1977 season was over, the Reds' inability to beat the Astros would look like one of the reasons they were unable to repeat as West Division pennant winners.

After the 13–4 beat down, the Reds flew out to Los Angeles to start their final, long road trip during which they'd visit all the teams in the Division except for Houston. Waiting for them on the Dodger Stadium mound was their nemesis, Tommy John and his 18–5 record. John had beaten Cincinnati four straight times while compiling a 1.05 ERA, and he had a 9–1 lifetime record against the Reds. George Foster injected some new life into the exhausted Reds when he took John deep in the very first inning with two outs. The shot to right scored Dave Concepcion who'd doubled and put Cincinnati up 2–0. The lead was short-lived though and after Steve Yeager homered in the bottom of the seventh to extend the Dodgers' lead to 8–3, the contest appeared to be over. Amazingly, the Reds rallied to score four times in the eighth and twice more in the ninth to pull the game out, 9–8 after Dale Murray held Los Angeles scoreless in the bottom of the ninth; and all nine runs came against John. It was a bit of an insult that Dodgers manager Tommy Lasorda even left John in the game to start the ninth inning after the Reds had racked him for four runs in the eighth to make it a one-run game. But the move (or lack of one to be more precise) was an indication of how unimportant the game was to the Dodgers as a team ... and conversely, how important it was to John as an individual, a veteran pitcher who was trying to win 20 games for the first time in his career. Joe Morgan led off the ninth against John with a walk but was caught stealing. After Pete Rose singled to left, left-handed Ken Griffey hit one of John's many mistakes of the day out of the park to give the Reds the lead, 9–8. The home run visibly stunned John who walked towards the Dodgers' dugout as if he momentarily thought the game was over. In the Reds' dugout Sparky Anderson couldn't help smirking, "There goes the Cy Young Award, I'm afraid." The win meant nothing in the league standings but that's not to say it was meaningless. As Fred Norman, whom the Dodgers had knocked out after pitching three and a third innings, said: "As much as we've been involved in this thing, we don't want to be here when they clinch it. We've won the thing two years in a row. We don't want to watch someone else drink champagne. They're gonna win it, sure. Great for them. But so what."

With his 48th big fly of the year Foster was now one home run away from tying the Reds' all-time record for home runs in a single season. With 15 games left to play, it was clear that unless the world came to an end first, Foster was going to break the club record established back in 1954 by Ted Kluszewski. As Kluszewski was the Reds' batting coach, beat reporter Bob Hertzel did not have to go far or to much trouble to interview the man whose 24-year-old record Foster was about to break. When asked how he felt about his record being broken, Kluszewski said, "Somebody's going to break it. I'd rather it be someone I had something to do with than some stranger." When asked for an explanation for Foster's rapid development into the League's most dangerous power hitter, Klu said, "He's not guessing anymore. He's hitting." As for his own role as hitting coach Kluszewski said his biggest contribution was getting Foster not to change his swing depending on whether the pitch was inside or outside.

Forty-nine home runs is a lot of home runs to hit in one baseball season, yet the number lacks by a lot the prestige accorded the "rounder" number of 50, a simple fact that had been impressed on Kluszewski over the years since his retirement as a player. In fact, not hitting one more home run in 1954 had been suggested more than once as one reason for Klu's inability to garner enough support to gain election to the Baseball Hall of Fame. Looking back on the 1954 season, the former Reds slugger, he of the bulging biceps and cut-off sleeves, said, "I really didn't put any importance on it. In fact, I didn't even think about hitting 50 homers, even though I had about a week left in the season when I got to No. 49. Back then, hitting 50 homers was a frequent thing. Mantle, Mays, Kiner, they all were doing it. I didn't really care about 50 but now I wish I had. Very few guys have actually done it." Klu's references to his heyday naturally invited Hertzel to ask which player faced the greater difficulty in reaching the magic 50 home run level. Kluszewski didn't hesitate to say (as if Foster's achievement was already a fait accompli), "I think it was tougher for George. You can judge that by noticing that there just haven't been any great amount of home runs in recent years. Mike Schmidt has won [the NL home run title] the last three years with less than 40. The ballparks are bigger too. Today's pitchers are better. The pitchers have more variety. It used to be fastball, curveball. You could count on one hand the pitchers who threw sliders. But those days are gone and the more variety the pitcher has, the more the hitter is thrown off balance."

Ken Griffey, whose 11th home run of the season proved to be the game-winning hit against the Dodgers and Tommy John that day, also made a comment that showed Foster's teammates were highly cognizant of the spectacular year he was having. "Tell Babe Ruth to move over," he said. "Me and my roomie gonna hit 60 home runs!"

Tom Seaver was one of the Reds' players trying to make the most, personally, of what was left of a most disappointing season from a team perspective; and on Thursday, September 15, he took the ball in search of the 200th win of his illustrious career. Seaver shut the Dodgers down on six hits and would have recorded a shutout if not for a strange and embarrassing play. Seaver opened the fourth inning by striking out Ron Cey and Steve Garvey. He got two quick strikes on Dusty Baker but lost him. With Baker on first base via the base on balls, outfielder Rick Monday ran the count to three-and-one and then lifted a fly ball to deep left field. Sub Bob Bailey, getting the start in left, settled under the ball on the warning track; but then after the ball landed "right square in the pocket" of Bailey's glove, as Bailey attempted to close his glove, the ball kind of flipped upwards ... and over the wall for a two-run home run. The Bailey-aided homer gave L.A. a 2–0 lead, but the Dodgers never scored again and the Reds scored three times to win it, 3–2. The winning Reds run came in the seventh inning against Dodgers starter Dour Rau on consecutive singles by George Foster, Johnny Bench, and Dave Concepcion.

Seaver had trouble keeping his fastball down all day, and it took him 150 pitches to vanquish the Dodgers. With the tying run in scoring position, Dave Lopes hit a two-hopper back to the mound for the last out of the game, and Seaver's relief was obvious. He partially ran the ball to first base, and he and Reds first baseman Dan Driessen both lit up with huge smiles on their faces as Driessen caught the short soft toss and stepped on first base for the final out. Afterwards the classy Seaver refused to criticize Bailey, describing the play as "frustration, that's what it had to be. The ball gone. You can't even pick it up or see where it went."

Everybody else was not so genteel and, in fact, had a field day making fun of Bailey and the mishap, which had looked absurdly funny. On the bus to the hotel in San Francisco where the Reds played next, a score of "Reds 3, Bailey 2" circulated through the aisles as a running joke. "Let's see, that was your first three-RBI night of the year," said broadcaster Marty Brennaman. "One for the Reds, two for the Dodgers." Brennaman's jest referred to the fact that Bailey, while having gone 0–2 at bat in the game, had driven in a run with a ground out. Bailey also was saddled with a new nickname: "Flipper." Even Seaver couldn't resist getting in one barb, light-hearted as it was: "You'll hear from the Commissioner tomorrow. Something about the integrity of the game."

Hertzel's coverage of the Thursday night game did not appear in the *Cincinnati Enquirer* until Saturday, and his headline for the story was "Seaver 200, Reds 3, Bailey 2 and a Million Laughs." The first number was a reference, of course, to the great pitcher's milestone win, which made him a member of a pretty exclusive club. As Hertzel pointed out, only four other active pitchers had 200 wins or more to their credit: Jimmy Hunter, Fergie Jenkins, Jim Kaat, and Gaylord Perry.

Suddenly playing like contenders, if not dominating World Champions, the Reds went into San Francisco, always a Death Valley for the team, and almost swept the three-game series; losing the finale by one run in the late innings. On Friday night, September 16, Doug Capilla outpitched Greg Minton to lead Cincinnati to a 5–3 win. Dealing with a bad back which had caused him to miss a start, Capilla threw 100 pitches in six innings and he walked six, but he kept the Giants off the scoreboard. "I was terrible," he said. "I pitched like a minor leaguer. I was scared, holding back, trying not to hurt the back again." The next afternoon the Reds won again in more dramatic fashion, sub Mike Lum blasting a three-run homer in the top of the tenth inning to give the Reds the win 8–6, after the Giants scored only one run in the bottom of the inning. Lum, batting .156 on the season, had entered the game in the bottom of the eighth in a complicated series of moves by Sparky Anderson. Johnny Bench had been given the day off but was called on to pinch-hit in the sixth inning. To keep his bat in the game, Anderson sent Bench to left field and shifted George Foster from left to center. When Lum entered the game in the eighth, he replaced Bench in left field, Bench replaced Plummer behind the plate, and Lum took Plummer's spot in the batting order. The game-winning homer was clearly the highlight of Lum's season. "That one really felt good," he said afterwards. "This year has been frustrating, frustrating. I just didn't do the job. I started thinking, 'Am I getting too old? Can I still hit?' I mean I was messed up mentally and I know I couldn't do anything right until I got myself straightened out. Really, that's all I can say about it."

Before Lum's big blow, George Foster and the hot Pete Rose carried the offensive load for Cincinnati. Foster went 3–5, with two doubles, and three RBI, while Rose went 3–6; extending his hitting streak to 18 games and pulling within 11 hits of 200 with 13 games left to play. The game was marred by a conflict between Anderson and second baseman Joe Morgan. After Morgan hit a ball off his shin and subsequently grounded out in the third inning, Anderson inserted utility infielder Rick Auerbach into the game to replace him. This highly irritated Morgan, who left the clubhouse in a huff for x-rays and then went home to Oakland. Anderson's comment was: "He'll get over it."

On Sunday afternoon the Reds came close to pulling off a sweep on "Willie McCovey Day" at Candlestick Park. They led 2–0 heading into the bottom of the eighth inning, but the Giants came back to tie the game in the eighth and win it with a run in the ninth. Appropriately, Big Mac, who'd been showered earlier with gifts and an outpouring of love, got the game-winning hit, an opposite-field single to left with two outs. It was a tough loss for starter Paul Moskau, who gave up only one earned run in his seven-and-a-third-inning stint. Prior to the game a sulking Joe Morgan had sat in the training room, nonchalantly reading the newspaper. "I feel just like I felt yesterday so I guess I can't play," he'd said. "I've learned something the past week. I just don't care anymore." Reds coaches tried to mediate the dispute, but Morgan refused to talk to them and Sparky Anderson wasn't in much of a conciliatory mood either. "I see no reason why we should talk," he said. "I didn't do anything wrong." To cap off a bad day at the office, the loss meant that the Dodgers clinched a tie for the West Division crown, even though they lost to Atlanta 9–8 in Los Angeles.

Monday, September 19, was a travel day. The news out of Cincinnati was that Bob Bailey was no longer with the team. The former $175K "Bonus Baby" with the Pittsburgh Pirates was traded to the Boston Red Sox for 23-year-old minor league pitcher Frank Newcomer. In 49 games Bailey had hit .253 with two home runs and 11 RBI. He left town still stigmatized by the home run he'd gifted to the Dodgers' Rick Monday. As a parting shot, Pete Rose found a way to poke additional fun at Bailey, comparing his suspect fielding to his penchant for being the first player to attack the post-game spread in the clubhouse. "If it [Monday's fly ball] had been a sandwich he would have caught it," said Rose.

As they had against the Giants, the Reds took two of three from the home-standing Padres September 20–22. Homerless the past four games, George Foster wasted no time in San Diego victimizing game one starter Bob Owchinko … and in tying Ted Kluszewski's single-season home run club record. With two outs and roommate Ken Griffey on first base in the opening frame, Foster took an Owchinko offering "far into the left-field seats" at Jack Murphy Stadium. Hertzel wrote "No. 49, like so many other Foster homers, was a no-doubter." Kluszewski was as happy for Foster as anybody associated with the team, and he graciously posed for photos with Foster for days afterwards.

The other Cincinnati Reds player having a spectacular year, Tom Seaver, turned in another brilliant performance. Seaver pitched a complete-game two-hitter to win his 19th game of the season overall and run his record with the Reds to 12-3. He also almost hit a home run himself in the second inning. As it was, his drive to left hit the top of the fence and scored Dan Driessen from first base when Padre shortstop Bill Almon made an error on his relay throw to the plate. Catcher Don Werner hit a solo homer in the fourth inning to make it 4-0, which is how it ended after Seaver set the Padres down 1-2-

Former Cincinnati slugger and the team's batting coach in 1977, Ted Kluszewski, poses with the player who broke his single-season home run record for the Reds. Big Klu, who hit 49 homers for the Reds in 1954, could not have been more gracious about seeing his record surpassed. He was one of the most popular players in franchise history, and the Reds erected a bronze statue of him outside Great American Ballpark.

3 in the bottom of the ninth on two fly balls and a pop to short. Joe Morgan, back in the starting lineup, hit a triple in three at bats and downplayed his spat with the manager after the ballgame. "I was not mad at Sparky, only about being taken out of last Saturday's game," he said. All in all it was great night for the Redlegs and their fans, except for the fact that in San Francisco the Los Angeles Dodgers clinched the 1977 National League West Division pennant with a 3–1 victory over the Giants. Anderson sent a telegram to Tommy Lasorda, which said: "Congratulations on the job done by you and your coaches."

If baseball fans in San Diego were excited about the possibility of watching George Foster become the first player since 1954 to hit as many as 50 home runs in one major league season, they had a funny way of showing it. Attendance for the game on Wednesday, September 21, was 11,669, and on Thursday afternoon, a 1:00 start, only 6,370 fans walked through the turnstiles. In all fairness, Foster's pursuit of the milestone was about the only thing the two games had to recommend themselves; as the woeful Padres with their 65–87 record languished in fifth place, 27½ games out of first.

In the end San Diego fans did not miss a record-setting homer, as Padres pitchers managed to keep Foster in the ballpark. On Wednesday Randy Jones and Rollie Fingers combined to hang an 0-4 collar around Foster's neck, yet George's teammates got the job done without his help and pulled out a 3-2 win. The game-winning hit came in the eighth inning, when Joe Morgan tripled against Fingers and then was driven home by Johnny Bench with two outs. Fingers threw two fastballs for called strikes to get ahead of Bench 0-2 but then delivered a "changeup curve." When Bench reached out and punched the ball into right field for a soft single, allowing Morgan to scamper home, a disgusted Fingers threw his glove 20 feet into the air. The Padres may have had reason to feel that the Fates were against them in that game, as the Reds had scored their first run in the seventh inning when Cesar Geronimo's ground ball down the right-field line hit the first-base bag and bounced over the head of first baseman Gene Tenace. In any event, Dale Murray got the win for turning in his best outing of the year (three scoreless innings in relief of Fred Norman), and the victory assured Cincinnati at 82–71 of finishing the season with a winning record

No one is more fickle than the Fates, as the Thursday afternoon Padres-Reds affair illustrated. The game was decided in the fifth inning when a Dave Concepcion error on a questionable scoring decision broke a 1–1 tie. With runners on first and third and two out, San Diego's All-Star outfielder Dave Winfield hit a slow dribbler towards short against Reds starting pitcher Dave Capilla. Concepcion charged the ball and attempted to short-hop it, but it kicked away from his glove. Winfield, who ran well for a big man, was safe at first and the tie-breaking run scored on the play. Gene Tenace then dumped an RBI-single into right field to give the Padres their final margin of victory of 3-1. The Reds losing the game on an error, described by Hertzel as "the toughest of chances," was ironic, given that the team was on a pace to set a new team and National League record for fewest errors in a season. Cincinnati already owned the current NL record of 102, set in 1975 and tied by the Reds in 1976. The current Major League record of 95 had been set by the Baltimore Orioles in 1964. Counting Concepcion's tough error in Thursday's game, the 1977 Reds had 87 errors with eight games to go in the season. While Foster did not homer in the finale in San Diego, he did "have a day," as the players say. He went 4-4 with a double and raised his average to .321, which prompted reporters to ask Pete Rose about him. Recalling his voluntary move from the outfield to third base which allowed the Reds to get a young Foster into the lineup on a regular basis, Rose admitted that "to this day" he preferred the outfield. "But I saw this kid was going to be a star," he said. "He worked so hard and was so strong."

The Reds could feel the long season rushing to a close as they flew from San Diego to Atlanta for their final three road games of the year. They were now playing on residual energy ... and pride. Atlanta remained a Cincinnati patsy, and the Reds swept the series; only the middle game on Saturday even being competitive. On Friday night, September 23, the game belonged to one George Foster. The Cincinnati Reds' slugger with the "V-shaped" upper body, thick forearms, and heavy black bat went 4–5 and etched his name into the record books by hitting his 50th home run of the season. It came in his last chance of the night. With Cincinnati ahead 4–1, Foster came to bat with two outs and nobody on in the top of the ninth inning. Right-handed Braves reliever Buzz Capra, who'd already served up two Foster home runs in 1977, gave the Reds' left fielder too good of a pitch once again; and Foster deposited it into the left-field bleachers of Atlanta-Fulton County Stadium. As he stood at the plate, watching another of his no-doubter home runs leave the ballpark, Foster thought "It's over. I'm over the hump."

After the game Foster told the media crowded around his locker, "I wanted to get it as quick as I could. The games are getting fewer and fewer. I was swinging for it from the start. The lefty was pitching, and I knew that it's easier to hit balls out of this park than at home. I remembered, too, that last year I hit 29 and thought it would be easy to get No. 30. I never got it."

Asked if he thought he could hit another six homers to tie Hack Wilson for the National League single-season home run record, Foster said, "It's not out of the question. It depends a lot on what I get to hit. I just have to relax and try to hit the ball hard."

Could he catch the Pirates' Dave Parker in the race for the NL batting title and thus win the Triple Crown? "I'll try to get my hits and add 'em up later," Foster said. "I have to get torrid to catch him [Parker]. But if I get close, maybe I'll go for it." With the 4–5 night, Foster raised his average to .325, but Parker was hitting .341.

The big night by Foster also re-engendered talk around the Reds' clubhouse about Foster being a cinch to win the NL MVP Award. And this time even the previously dubious Sparky Anderson was on board. "They can't take that away from him now," he said. "Not now." Despite the confidence shared by Reds players and coaches, it was, in fact, not a settled matter. A trenchant question often reared its head in discussions about the MVP Award: Can the Most Valuable Player in the league be on a team that doesn't win the pennant? There were always some who answered that question in the negative, and the

Reds were not going to be pennant winners in 1977. The leading candidate for the honor, besides Foster, seemed to be the Phillies' Greg Luzinski. He was having a fine year (.309, 39, 130) and his team was going to win a pennant. The winner of the NL MVP Award would be determined later, after the season, by a vote of the sportswriters around the league. That night something important had already been determined, and the headline to Hertzel's game report in the next morning's *Enquirer* made it clear what that was: "50th IS JEWEL FOR HR KING FOSTER." It was the first time George Foster had ever been referred to by the title his spectacular 1977 season had now earned him.

On Saturday night the Reds picked up an ugly 8–7 win. Atlanta outhit Cincinnati 14–11 but came up a run short, despite a three-run rally in the bottom of the ninth inning. Foster had a quiet 1–4 evening and he was held in check partially because Atlanta took the bat out of his hands in the eighth inning; issuing him an intentional walk in the midst of the rally that put the Reds ahead 8–4. It was the ninth intentional walk issued to Foster on the year. Atlanta starting pitcher Phil Niekro should have used the same strategy the next day. Instead, with the game tied 0–0, Niekro pitched to Foster, leading off the seventh inning. Foster jacked a Niekro knuckleball into the front row of the left-field seats for his 51st homer of the year and, as it turned out, the only run needed by the brilliant Tom Seaver. As Hertzel put it, "Backed by George Foster's 51st home run [yawn] and a two-run double by Dan Driessen, Seaver shut out the Braves on three hits, 3–0." The final score was actually 4–0, the Reds scoring another insurance run in the top of the ninth, but the mistake hardly mattered. What mattered, now that there was no pennant race to worry about, were the milestones being reached and the records being set. In addition, to padding his team home run record, Foster set a new Reds record for Total Bases in a season; bettering Frank Robinson's old mark of 380 by two. The 31 homers he'd hit on the road also set a new NL record. The win was Seaver's 20th of the year, and 1977 became the fifth time in his career he'd reached that magic number. The shutout was also the 46th of his career. Finally, with a 3–4 day Pete Rose creep to within two hits of 200, insuring that he would reach that coveted milestone once again. The three-game sweep of Atlanta gave the Reds a 9–2 record for the final road trip of the year, but it was a case of too little-too late. Cincinnati finished with an overall losing record of 40–41 on the road for 1977.

On the off day of Monday, September 26, it was announced that the National League Player of the Week for the week just ended was George Foster, who'd hit .458 with five extra-base hits, five runs, and five RBI.

The Reds hosted San Diego on Tuesday and Wednesday; and Tuesday night's crowd of 13,651 was the smallest paid attendance at Riverfront Stadium since September 17, 1975. The Padres prevailed 3–1 in Tuesday night's game, as Johnny Bench's fourth-inning homer (his 30th of the season) accounted for the only run the Reds could score against Bob Shirley and Rollie Fingers. The *Enquirer's* coverage of the game showed that the media's focus was finally on George Foster, who unfortunately went 0–4 on the night. Three photos of Foster appeared above the fold of the front page of the paper's sports section and were explained by the following caption: "Most things have gone well for the Reds' slugger this season, which makes Tuesday night an exception. The Padres stopped him on four trips to the plate. Foster spent an idle pregame moment tossing a baseball to himself, then those unproductive appearances, and finally a lonely walk down the locker room tunnel." The headline on Hertzel's game story read: "Foster Held Homerless, Rose Gets One Hit in 3–1 Setback." Asked once again at the end of the night about his chances of catching Hack Wilson, Foster said, "There's still a chance. I figure I've got about 16 at bats left and I will be looking for my pitch." Foster added that he got his pitch about once every at bat. In Chicago, the Phillies beat the Cubs 15–9 to clinch the East Division pennant. By the time they left Riverfront Stadium that night, the Reds knew who they'd be home watching face off in the NL playoffs. It would be the Los Angeles Dodgers vs. the Philadelphia Phillies.

Foster hit a home run the next night, his 52nd of the year; but just that quickly the focus veered away from him and onto the Reds' abiding cynosure: Pete Rose. The headline to Hertzel's game story said it all: "Rose Star of Stars with Hit No. 200." In the same edition Hertzel also published a story entitled "Pete Cast in Cobb's Mold" which outlined similarities between Rose and the immortal Ty Cobb: they were both extremely aggressive but not dirty players; the both detested cheating pitchers; they both made boasting predictions and then backed them up; and they both fought for their money.

Thanks largely to a first-inning grand slam by Johnny Bench and a complete-game, five-hit effort by Paul Moskau, the Reds coasted to an 8–0 win. As historic as Foster's home run was, it was overshadowed by all the attention directed at Rose. Foster hit No. 52 off Padres starter John D'Aquisto with nobody on and two outs in the fifth inning. According to Hertzel, he "scorched one over the wall in deepest center for home run No. 52."

Rose picked up hit No. 200 in the seventh inning off reliever Dave Tomlin. The hit came on a smash that bounced off the plate and then the glove of S.D. third baseman Tucker Ashford. When the Riverfront Stadium scoreboards flashed the decision by official scorer Earl Lawson, the crowd of 13,010 began to chant "Pete! Pete! Pete!" It was the ninth time in his career that Rose had collected 200 or more hits in a season. No one knew it at the time, but it would also be the last time he had a 200-hit season for the Cincinnati Reds. With his son Petey at his side in the clubhouse following the game, Rose explained why the milestone was so important to him. "It's a symbol of consistency, something I've always tried to do," he said. "I didn't mean to wait this long. There are a lot more guys with 30 home runs and 100 RBI than there are guys with 200 hits." As usual, Rose knew what he was talking about when the subject was baseball records and statistics, especially when they involved him. Other than himself, only three other major leaguers would finish the 1977 season with 200 or more hits: Rod Carew, Dave Parker, and Jim Rice. In comparison, four players on the Los Angeles Dodgers alone would enjoy 30-home run seasons in 1977: Steve Garvey (33), Reggie Smith (32), Dusty Baker (30), and Ron Cey (30).

On the other hand, there was only player in all of major league baseball who hit as many as 50 home runs in 1977, and that player was George Foster; the newly crowned Home Run King of the Cincinnati Reds. And as previously mentioned, the only player to hit as many as 50 homers in a season during the entire 1970s and 1980s was George Foster.

The Reds closed out the 1977 campaign with a three-game series against the Atlanta Braves at Riverfront Stadium over the weekend of September 30–October 2. Atlanta's workhorse and staff ace Phil Niekro gamely took the ball for Friday night's opener, despite the fact that a defeat would saddle him with a 20-loss season. Niekro was practically guaranteed a loss, as the Reds started Tom Seaver. Working almost on auto-pilot, Seaver went the route to lead Cincinnati to an easy 7–1 win. Seaver finished the season with an overall record of 21–6 and 14–3 as a Cincinnati Red. His overall ERA came in at 2.59 and for the Reds at 2.35. His only personal disappointment was coming up four strikeouts short of 200, after having reached that milestone for a record nine consecutive seasons. After the game a weary but contented Seaver reflected on the 1977 season for reporters. "I don't want this season to end," he said. "I am tired. It has been a terrible emotional strain. But doing as well as I've done has made it all completely worthwhile." When asked if he would pitch out of the bullpen in the remaining two games in an effort to reach 200 strikeouts, he said, "Look, I'm 21–6. I'm more ecstatic about winning. The record [most consecutive seasons with 200 or more strikeouts] is mine, not like I was going after someone else's record. I mean, if it had been a Walter Johnson record, maybe. But even at that, Nolan Ryan is probably going to break the record anyway.... It isn't worth it. The only regret I have is that we're in second place ... and second place is anywhere from second to sixth. There is first place and then everyone else is second."

While Niekro lost his 20th game of the year, at least he didn't give up another home run to George Foster. Niekro retired Foster twice and walked him once. Reliever Duane Theiss also walked Foster but his was an intentional base on balls and drew the ire of Reds fans. The Reds were ahead 6–1 in the seventh inning with one out and a runner (Driessen) on second base when Theiss issued his free pass. Technically, it was the correct move ... setting up the double play or at least a force out ... and Reds fans understood that. Yet, taking the bat out of Foster's hands in such a meaningless game while he was in the final stage of a historic season did not seem very sporting, and they didn't like it. The one positive that came out of Foster's 0–2 day was that he picked up his 148th RBI of the year on a third inning ground out. The run batted in tied the Reds' single-season record established in 1970 by Johnny Bench. While Foster did not homer in the game, his best friend on the team did. Ken Griffey went 3–4 and all his hits went for extra bases: a double, a triple, and a fifth-inning home run. In the Reds' clubhouse after the game he jokingly boasted, "Our room's 64th homer! More than Ruth, Mantle, Maris!"

In addition to Hertzel's game report, Saturday morning's *Enquirer* included a story by Ross Newhan of the *LA Times* called "Lasorda's Sunshine Right Tonic for LA." The story quoted Dodgers players extensively, and they all praised Lasorda's inspirational leadership. "It's the little things," said outfielder Reggie Smith. "Like remembering the names of every member of your family. He's the only manager I've ever seen who took a personal interest in every individual player. The man has compassion and understanding. Instead of going on my alleged reputation, he took time to get to know me. He came to my house for dinner and he invited me to his. He found out I wasn't the man the reputation made me out to be. He believed in me from the start."

"The important thing about Tommy is that he is not just a guy who makes out the lineup and decides strategy," said shortstop Bill Russell. "He makes everyone feel a part of it. The lineup that will open the playoffs is the same one that opened the exhibition season—the same eight that has run together since the first day of spring training. If we have played harder for Tommy it's because he is also sticking his neck out on our behalf, bragging about us, saying we're the greatest, pumping us up in a way that every player loves to hear."

Pitcher Tommy John said: "We're all mirrors of the manager and he's made us cocky, confident, and convinced we can win by pounding it into our heads from the very start. He's loosened the reins, allowed us to attain our full potential."

Second baseman Davey Lopes: "Coming from someone else, it might not work. But you either accept Tommy for what he is or you don't. And the more you're around him, the more you realize he's sincere and genuine, that what he says makes sense. When you have been around him for as long as we have it's hard not to adopt his personality, his enthusiasm. He settles for nothing less than the best and there are simply some people who have the ability to draw it out. He has given us a cockiness and an esprit de corps. He has given us aggressiveness. He has given us the belief that we could beat Cincinnati. All of that we had lost to some extent over the last couple of years."

Even members of the team that had been supportive of Lasorda's predecessor, Walter Alston, gave Lasorda his due. "The chances are very good that this team would have won with Alston," said pitcher Doug Rau. "But it was easier with Tommy." Pitcher Don Sutton echoed Rau's comments, saying, "This is the best club I've ever been on. It possibly would have won anyway [with Alston at the helm]. That it won with the ease it did is a tribute to Tommy. He is a master psychologist who preached from opening day that we could go all the way and convinced us of it. It is a club that thrives on encouragement and Lasorda was the right man at the right time."

Of course, Lasorda deflected the credit from himself and steered it towards his players. "All I am is the traffic cop," he said. "Maybe I helped them believe in themselves, but nothing more. They made it happen. As I told them so often ... 'In the minors you needed me for instruction and advice and now I need you.' They didn't let me down. I have to be the luckiest guy in the world. I'm thankful and grateful. Every time I hugged one of them it was to show them that. I feel like a father sitting at the dinner table, feeling the pride and love of his family."

Perhaps it was Lasorda's mention of the dinner table that inspired the succinct way first baseman Steve Garvey framed his facetious commendation. "The only thing he hasn't handled is his weight," said Garvey.

On Saturday, October 1, the Reds defeated Atlanta 6–2 behind Tom Hume and Manny Sarmiento, who combined to hold the Braves to four hits. Hume, who evened his record at 3–3, had a no-hitter going until it was broken up with one out in the fifth inning. Interestingly, it was another rookie, catcher Dale Murphy, who spoiled Hume's attempt at baseball immortality by singling to left. Playing in his 17th game of the season, Murphy was at the start of an outstanding career, during which he would twice win the NL MVP Award while playing center field. Speaking once again about the turn-around he made after being demoted to Indianapolis earlier in the season, Hume said, "I was so messed up I didn't know what I was doing. I decided to change my attitude. I just wanted to blank everything out of my mind that had happened before and start all over again." Preston Hanna (2–6) took the loss for the

Braves, but he retired George Foster, who went 0–4 on the day, three times. In the American League the New York Yankees lost to the Detroit Tigers 10–7, yet they backed into the playoffs by virtue of Baltimore's victory over Boston. The Yankees had a two-game lead over both Baltimore and Boston with one game to play. They would meet the West Division champion Kansas City Royals in the American League Championship Series.

On Sunday, October 2, the Cincinnati Reds suited up for the last time in the 1977 major league baseball season. A crowd of 40,204 showed up for Fan Appreciation Day, boosting total home attendance at Riverfront Stadium for the year to 2,519,670. It was the second time in club history that the team had drawn over two a half million fans. Prizes were awarded to the fans throughout the game, but a victory over the Atlanta Braves was not one of them. Rookie Mickey Mahler and Dave Campbell combined to limit the Reds to five hits and three runs; while four of the Braves' six runs were unearned, the result of sloppy Reds defense. Despite four errors, committed by starting pitcher Fred Norman, Pete Rose, and Dave Concepcion (2), the Reds set a new team record for fewest errors in a season with 95. Joe Morgan also set a record for the fewest errors by a second baseman (6), playing in 150 games or more. Rose tied the team record held by Frank McCormick for most consecutive games played (652), and with 31 steals Dan Driessen became the first first baseman in more than 60 years to pilfer 30 or more bases in a season. (Hap Myers of the Boston Braves was the last to do it in 1914.) By playing, Driessen put his .300 season batting average on the line. He maintained his average at exactly .300, when he tripled in his final at bat after having grounded out his first two times to the plate. "If you back into it, it's not the same," he said after the game. "I mean, I wasn't uptight about it. Even if I didn't get .300, I would have had a good year." Indeed, he would have. His numbers (.300/17/91) for the season turned out to be almost identical to those put up by the man he'd replaced in the Reds' lineup, Tony Perez; who batted .283 for the Montreal Expos with 19 home runs and 91 RBI. And finally, there was George Foster, who would have had to homer four times in the season finale to catch the ghostly Hack Wilson. Foster did not go yard even once; however, he set another Reds team record, and it was an important one. With his only hit of the day, a single to right in the seventh inning, he drove home Rick Auerbach, who'd led off the inning with a walk. The RBI was Foster's 149th of the season, giving him one more than Johnny Bench had accumulated in 1970 to establish the team record. With 388 he also set a new team record for total bases in a season. While it wasn't a record, Foster's batting average for the season, .320, was the highest on the team. He also led the league in slugging percentage (.631) and OPS (1.017).

Foster's last chance of the season to add to his amazing totals came in the bottom of the ninth inning, with one out. As he walked to the plate, he heard a smattering of applause that grew and grew and grew until it erupted into a standing ovation. "When I first went up, there wasn't that much applause," he said later. "Then, it started growing and I was wondering what was going on, if Morgana had run on to the field. All those people cheering, I thought, 'The last thing I want to do now is strikeout.'" Against Dave Campbell he lined out to right field. When Don Werner flew out to left, the 1977 season for the Cincinnati Reds was over. They finished with a record of 88–74; the team's fewest wins since 1971 when their 79–83 record landed them in fourth place.

With players gathering their belongings into travel bags and saying their goodbyes for the off-season, Foster reflected on what his great season meant. "It would have been nicer if my numbers helped the ball club win a pennant, but they didn't. I'm confident next year will end up like it should, meaning the Reds on top."

Asked one final time about his chances of winning the NL MVP Award, he said, "I have the stats to qualify as the MVP. I just don't know what they [the writers] consider. If you have to be on a winner, I'm already out. But I think it will be close, me and Greg Luzinski. If I make it, I will be elated. If not, I will come back and try to have a better year next year." Only an uber-optimist like Foster would have even conceived at that point of having a better year in 1978.

9

Fall 1977 and Beyond
The Rest of the Story

On October 8, 1977, the Los Angeles Dodgers beat the Philadelphia Phillies in Veterans Stadium 4–1 behind their ace Tommy John to win the National League Championship Series (NLCS) three games to one. A few days later the Dodgers then met the New York Yankees, who needed five games to vanquish the Kansas City Royals in the ALCS, in the 74th World Series. The Yankees redeemed their loss to the Cincinnati Reds the previous year by winning the Series four games to two. With five home runs, eight RBI, and a batting average of .450, Reggie Jackson almost single-handedly destroyed L.A.'s vaunted pitching staff. In the deciding sixth game Jackson put on the most dramatic display in World Series history, homering three straight times, against three different pitchers (Burt Hooten, Elias Sosa, and Charlie Hough), all three times on the first pitch of the at bat. The spectacular performance made Jackson's legend and earned him the nickname "Mr. October."

On November 9, 1977, the news Reds' fans had been waiting to hear since the end of the baseball season became official when major league baseball announced that the winner of the 1977 National League Most Valuable Player Award was George Foster of the Cincinnati Reds. Foster received 15 of the 24 first place votes cast, and he outdistanced runner-up Greg Luzinski overall 291 points to 255. Rounding out the Top Five vote getters were: Dave Parker, 156; Reggie Smith, 112; and Steve Carlton, 100. The results proved that the voters recognized the significance of Foster's performance and that they did not hold the Reds' second-place finish against him; as well they shouldn't have. After all, Foster had turned in a year that few players in the history of the game had ever matched. As Greg Rhodes and John Erardi point out in *Redleg Journal*, "The only players in baseball history to match or exceed Foster's 1977 numbers in batting average, home runs, RBI's, runs scored, hits, and total bases in a single season are Babe Ruth (1921), Hack Wilson (1930), and Jimmie Foxx (1932).

When the moment that Foster had yearned for arrived, he was very happy but also a bit overwhelmed. According to his early biographer Malka Drucker, Foster recalled that "I was warned ahead I was a candidate. The judges said they would call Monday at 3:30 if I'd gotten it. I had to take a friend to the hospital that day, so I gave them the hospital number. As soon as the phone rang I knew what it was, because no one else had the number. Jack Lang told me and I was thrilled. He asked how I felt, but I couldn't tell him—a million things went through my mind, but I couldn't say anything." Predictably, Foster also viewed the honor more in terms of how it represented his development as a person rather than as a celebrity and a high earner. "What felt best," he said, "was my spiritual growth over the year. It was more important than the material gain." As proof of the validity of that sentiment, Drucker described how Foster celebrated the big honor. While the typical ballplayer would have rented a spacious room in a fancy hotel and invited celebrities and the media to a big party, replete with liquor and beautiful women, Foster retired to his mother's modest home in Hawthorn, California, where he entertained family friends from the neighborhood. A week later, he showed up at the nearby True Vine Baptist Church which was holding "George Foster Day." There he repeated his mantra of encouragement, urging the ordinary folks in the crowd to work hard, believe in themselves, and never give up. The people there knew that Foster's concern for them was genuine, and their love and respect for him was equally apparent. "I knew him before he became a superstar," said one True Vine member, "and he hasn't changed any. As good an athlete as George is—and he's the best—he's a better man." The pastor of the church, the Reverend Austin Williams, expressed similar praise, saying, "The only change in George now is in his confidence. George won the MVP Award. To me that stands for the Most Valuable Person, because that's what he is."

As the Reds rested and tried to reenergize themselves over the winter, the question remained: Why had they failed to defend their crown as two-time World Champions? More specifically, what had been the difference between 1976 and 1977? ... besides the potent dose of "Lasorda's Miracle Confidence Elixir" that each player on the Dodgers' roster had swallowed in spring training. One answer was presented while the season was still unwinding and came from the mind and pen of cartoonist Jerry Dowling. In his contribution to the September 24th edition of the *Enquirer*, Dowling depicted manager Sparky Anderson as the Riverfront Stadium janitor, sweeping up the trash left behind once the party of the "Summer of '77" was over. The empty soft drink and beer cans in front of Anderson's broom carry various labels referring to the problems that ruined the party for the Reds and left them with such terrible hangovers: trades, bullpen, missed signs, depth, base running, clutch hitting, and fielding lapses. All of these factors surely did negatively impact the team at one time or another, but the Reds' biggest problem was their lack of consistently good starting pitching. In 1976 seven different Reds' pitchers won in double figures: Gary Nolan (15), Pat Zachry (14), Jack Billingham (12) Fred Norman (12), Santo Alcala (11), Rawley Eastwick (11), and Don Gullet (11). With the exception of Eastwick, all of these pitchers were starters. They won a total of 75 games in 1976. That same group won 32 games for Cincinnati in 1977. Their replacements, journeymen acquired in trades and inexperienced rookies, simply were not able to pick up the slack. A quick look at the Reds' and Dodgers' run differentials for 1976 and 1977 bears out this explanation. In 1976 the Reds scored 857 runs, while allowing 633. The Dodgers only allowed 543 runs but they also only scored 608. The Reds' differential of 224 runs was nearly four times that of the Dodgers' 63. In 1977 the edge in run differential flipped. The Reds scored 802 runs but gave up 725, a difference of only 77 runs. The Dodgers meanwhile scored 764 and gave up 582, a difference of 187. Those 725 runs allowed are as good a shorthand explanation as we're likely to get for the Cincinnati Reds' disappointing season in 1977.

"Summer of '77." The Reds' bid for a third straight World Championship was officially over, as the Dodgers clinched the 1977 NL West Division pennant on September 20 in game #151. It remains the earliest such date in L.A. Dodgers history. The Reds' heralded leader, Sparky Anderson, is reduced to a janitor having to sweep up after a party that clearly got out of hand. Anderson's glum expression signifies the painful hangover felt by everyone involved, including Reds fans.

Much to the chagrin of Reds' fans, the Dodgers' 1977 season turned out to be no fluke, and they won again in 1978; this time by two and a half games over the Reds. Cincinnati was in the race, along with the surprising San Francisco Giants, until they lost six in a row in late August to drop out of contention. Once again, pitching was a problem for Cincinnati, as the Reds compiled the second worst staff ERA in the division. Only Atlanta's pitchers posted a higher team ERA. The Reds' stellar defensive abilities suddenly deserted them too. After making a record-low 95 errors in 1977, they made 134 a year later. In *Redleg Journal* Greg Rhodes and John Erardi attributed this defensive decline to "an overall breakdown in team discipline." They laid that breakdown at the feet of manager Sparky Anderson, who despite his earlier promises to crack the whip in 1978, apparently was just too nice a guy to actually do so. After the Reds lost their sixth straight to the Pirates on August 29, Johnny Bench said, "Our manager is too low key. It's time many of us got a good (ass) chewing." Finally, injuries to Bench and Morgan hurt the team considerably. Both players were lost for a significant number of games, and when they did play they weren't as effective as usual. Bench hit only 17 home runs, and Morgan's batting average dropped to .236. As usual, Pete Rose was the one to best put the loss of the two key players into perspective. "All clubs have injuries, but these are special cases," he said. "With Morgan hurt we lose our running game and with Bench hurt we can't control the opponent's running game." As for George Foster, now widely recognized as the top power hitter in the National League, he was unable to duplicate, much less surpass, the year he had in 1977; yet, he made the NL All-Star team starting lineup again, for the third year in a row, and defended both his home run and RBI crowns. Foster hit 40 homers on the season to beat runner-up Greg Luzinski by five. He hit No. 40 on the last day of the season, a dramatic walk-off home run in his final at bat, coming in the bottom of the fourteenth inning of the Reds' 10–8 victory over the Atlanta Braves. Foster's 120 RBI were also tops in the National League; making it the third year in a row he'd led the league in that department. He became only the sixth player in the history of the game to accomplish that feat, joining an exclusive club made up of Honus Wagner, Ty Cobb, Babe Ruth, Rogers Hornsby, and Joe Medwick: Hall of Famers all.

After the Yankees again beat the Dodgers in the World Series, the Reds toured Japan, playing 17 games against Japanese teams. Japanese media had a field day posing the Babe Ruth of Japanese baseball, Sadaharu Oh, with the American home run champion, George Foster. On November 28, Reds' management shocked the team and its fans by firing manager Sparky Anderson and replacing him with John McNamara, who'd had two previous mediocre big league managerial stints with the Oakland Athletics and San Diego Padres.

In nine years with Cincinnati Anderson had compiled a record of 836–586 for a winning percentage of .596, both team records which stand to this day. He'd won five divisional titles, four National League pennants, and two World Championships. It wasn't enough. A week later, the bad news continued when it was announced that Pete Rose had signed a free-agent contract with the Philadelphia Phillies.

In 1979 the Reds won 90 games under McNamara, two fewer than the year before; yet their 90–71 record was good enough to edge out the Houston Astros by a game and a half. Foster, now 30 years old, had another outstanding season, despite ankle and thigh injuries which limited him to 121 games. He was voted onto the All-Star team starting lineup for the fourth consecutive year and led Cincinnati in homers with 30 and RBI with 98. Unfortunately, the latter number was not sufficient for him to lead the league for a record-setting fourth year in a row. The season also ended in disappointment, as the Reds were swept in the NLCS by their old nemesis, the Pittsburgh Pirates, three games to none. The highlight of the series for Foster was the two-run homer he hit in the first game off Pirates' lefty John Candelaria. It was his third and final post-season home run. The division title, Cincinnati's sixth of the decade, was the last gasp of the Big Red Machine.

In January of 1980, Joe Morgan left the Reds, signing a free-agent contract with the team he'd started his career with: the Houston Astros. With "Little Joe's" departure, Johnny Bench was the lone member of the Big Red Machine's so-called "Big Four" to remain with the Reds. The Houston Astros finally caught Cincinnati and won the division; finishing one game ahead of the Dodgers and 3½ games ahead of the Reds. While Foster did not post gaudy numbers, he led the team again in homers (25), RBI (93), and OPS (.835).

The following year Foster's power numbers apparently dropped off even further, but that appearance was highly misleading and due entirely to the player's mid-season strike which resulted in a loss of a third of the 1981 schedule. In 108 games Foster hit 22 homers, which tied him for third place among the league leaders; and he drove in 90 runs, good enough for second place in the league. Foster also placed in the Top Ten in almost every meaningful offensive category. He was third in slugging percentage, total bases, and offensive WAR; fourth in OPS; sixth in hits; seventh in doubles; and ninth in on-base percentage. Any way one cared to look at it, the numbers indicated that George Foster was still one of the very best and most productive hitters in the National League. At least the sportswriters recognized this, as Foster received the third most votes for the NL MVP Award that year. As for the Cincinnati Reds, the team was royally gypped out of the pennant. They fin-

After the mid-season player strike of 1981 was settled, the Reds trained for several days on the University of Michigan campus in Ray Fisher Stadium, named after the college's long-time baseball coach. Fisher, who'd pitched for Cincinnati in the 1919 Black Sox World Series, was in '81 the oldest living player to have appeared in a World Series. Foster, who had an outstanding season in 1981, looks delighted to be getting back to work.

ished the year with the best overall record in the National League (66–42) yet were excluded from the playoffs because they came in second in both halves of the goofy split-season format adopted by major league baseball in an attempt to re-interest the fans in the interrupted 1981 pennant races.

The final dismantling of the Reds' once-great roster continued in the off-season. In November Cincinnati traded Ken Griffey to the New York Yankees (for Fred Toliver and Brian Ryder); and in February of 1982, they sent George Foster packing to the New York Mets for Alex Trevino, Greg Harris, and Jim Kern. Why were the Reds willing to part with the slugger who'd led the team the previous six years in home runs and RBI (and led the team the previous five years in OPS)? Simply because Reds' management was unwilling to pay the going rate for a player of Foster's caliber or to give him the long-term contract he wanted. Foster, who'd once said he wanted to end his career with the Cincinnati Reds, received a handsome consolation prize for leaving the team he'd come to identify with: a five-year contract worth, with all its bonuses and incentive clauses, $10 million. It was the richest contract ever awarded by the Mets and the second-richest contract ever awarded to any player (Dave Winfield's complicated contract with the Yankees was worth a bit more).

In retrospect, the news conference in New York at which Foster's historic signing was announced and the reporting about it contained ominous signs that things would not work out as hoped for. James Tuite of the *New York Times* reported that Foster "promised to earn his money;" an indication that Foster was fully aware of the high expectations under which he would labor. According to Tuite, the thirty-three year old Foster boasted, "You're going to see a lot of fireworks and a lot of excitement;" he surprisingly claimed that "I have not yet reached my potential;" and he jokingly issued a warning to low-flying planes from LaGuardia airport that might enter the flight path of his home runs at Shea Stadium. Tuite also described Foster as harboring some lingering hard feelings about his stay in Cincinnati. "Despite his hitting prowess, Foster was never able to generate the kind of popularity in Cincinnati that was accorded Pete Rose and Johnny Bench," Tuite wrote. "Foster, who acknowledged yesterday that he has grown 'disillusioned' with the Reds, alluded to some criticism in Cincinnati that he had not been sufficiently aggressive in the outfield. 'I'm an average outfielder,' he said, 'and I'm working on it. It's just my hitting overshadowed my defense.'" When Foster was asked if the big money would make him complacent, Tuite records his reply as "No matter how much money I make, or how many years I play, I'll still go out every day and give my best. Though I have experienced the thrill of winning pennants and World Championships, I want to experience another thrill by helping the Mets win a championship. That's what I came here for, and that's what I hope to do."

Wise Mets' manager George Bamberger, who knew the challenge which still lay before the Mets' organization, cautioned, "A miracle is not going to happen overnight." That's not what anyone in New York wanted to hear in reference to a team which had not had a winning season since 1976.

Foster's career with the Mets got off to a terrible start in 1982. In 151 games he batted .247 with 13 home runs and 70 RBI. It was the worst he'd ever done in a full season of play. Disappointed Mets' fans booed him, and the tough New York media exhibited little empathy towards him. As far as most of them were concerned, if a player was getting big money, he needed to produce big numbers or face the consequences. What made Foster's slow start in New York even worse was the outcome for the team, a 65–97 record and another dismal last-place finish. It was certainly little consolation to Foster that the depleted Reds did even worse in 1982, also finishing in last place and losing 100 games (actually 101) for the first time in franchise history.

Foster rebounded in 1983 and led the Mets in home runs (28) and RBI (90), but the team finished in last place again; and Foster began to be regarded as the face of the team's failure to improve. Mets' fans were close to despair, despite the fact that two key players (Keith Hernandez and Darryl Strawberry) who would soon help lead the team to a World Championship were added to the roster that summer. The Mets' turn-around began the next year (1984). Former Orioles' and Braves' second baseman Davey Johnson took over as manager, and the team responded well to his savvy leadership. More importantly, Hernandez and Strawberry played full seasons, and the pitching staff received a major upgrade with the addition of young studs Ron Darling and, especially, Dwight Gooden. The nineteen-year-old Gooden, armed with a blazing fastball and knee-buckling curveball, was a godsend. He went 17–9 with a 2.60 ERA and struck out a league-leading 276 batters in 218 innings to win the NL Rookie of the Year Award. Foster contributed 24 homers (second on the team) and 86 RBI (third on the team), and the Mets finished in second place in the East Division with a 90–72 record; winning 22 more games in 1984 than the year before. In the fourth year of Foster's big contract (1985), the Mets further strengthened their roster by adding gamers, such as third baseman Howard Johnson and catcher Gary Carter. Now a force to reckon with, they won 98 games; yet the St. Louis Cardinals won 101 games to take the division by three games. With reserves Danny Heep and Lenny Dykstra cutting into his playing time, Foster appeared in only 129 games; batting .263 with 24 homers and 77 RBI.

It was in the middle of the next season, 1986, when Foster's career as a

New York Met came to a sudden and unfortunate end. As the Mets ran away with the division, Foster was benched during the last week of July. With Strawberry a fixture in right field and Lenny Dykstra having replaced Mookie Wilson as the center fielder and the team's leadoff batter, the Mets found themselves with a log jam in left field. Wilson, Danny Heep, Foster, and budding young power hitter Kevin Mitchell were all competing for playing time in left; a nearly impossible situation for manager Davey Johnson to deal with. On Wednesday, August 6, with the Mets in Chicago for a doubleheader with the Cubs, an interview Foster had done with beat reporter Jim Corbett was published in Gannett's Westchester-Rockland newspaper. In the interview Foster made some comments about racism in baseball, in general. "I'm not saying it's a racial thing, but that seems to be the case in sports today," said Foster. "When a ball club can, they replace a George Foster or a Mookie Wilson with a more popular player. I think the Mets would rather promote a Gary Carter or a Keith Hernandez to the fans, so parents who want to can point to them as role models for their child, rather than a Darryl Strawberry, a Dwight Gooden, or a George Foster." The reporter also asked what Foster thought about the Mets having signed Lee Mazzilli, who was assigned to the team's Triple A farm club in Tidewater, Virginia. Mazzilli, a white outfielder, had just been released by the Pittsburgh Pirates. "I know something is brewing," said Foster. "I don't think a guy would go to Triple A if he had no major league offers and something wasn't promised."

The interview caused a firestorm; Davey Johnson interpreting Foster's remarks as an accusation that he was a racist, that he favored white players over black ones. Johnson immediately suspended Foster, and Mets' GM Frank Cashen went a step further by releasing him before the day was over. The next day the Mets replaced Foster on the roster by calling up Mazzilli from Triple A. Foster attempted repeatedly to explain that his words had been taken out of context. "I never said race had anything to do with who plays," said Foster. "I was talking from a business standpoint about promoting players, marketing players. You can take it from a business or economic standpoint: What product will sell to the public? What section of people will it attract to the ball park?" The following day, August 7, in a story in the *New York Times* by Joseph Durso, Johnson explained his position. "Normally, I wouldn't comment on something a player is quoted as saying, but this is an affront to me. He was alluding to my integrity as a baseball manager. I cannot have anybody on the club who questions my motives. George is a fine man, a good man, and he's been a great ball player. But it hurts me. He put me in a corner. The only thing I can think of is he's had a great career and I've had the unfortunate task of sitting him down near the end of his career. In the four years he's been here, he's been streaky. This year with the emergence of Kevin Mitchell, I couldn't afford the luxury of waiting for George. My job is to put the best nine players out there."

Johnson found Foster's remarks not only offensive but puzzling as well, as the players he was mostly platooning in left field in place of George, Kevin Mitchell and Mookie Wilson, were both black. Foster pointed out the same incongruity, arguing that it proved he hadn't been blaming his benching on the manager's racism; but this reasoning did nothing to defuse the controversy or get the Mets to change their minds about releasing him. (In his 2018 autobiography, *Davey Johnson: My Wild Ride in Baseball and Beyond*, Johnson surmises that Foster perhaps saw Dykstra's replacement of Wilson as an indirect, racist way to relegate him to the bench.) Some of the black players on the team came to Foster's defense, but again the remarks did nothing to change the outcome. Mookie Wilson said, "I would have to say he was misquoted. George was one of the great ones." And Darryl Strawberry, the leader of the team, said, "I'm disappointed with the way the organization handled it. A guy who had a career like that deserved to wait till the end of the season. Who knows, maybe I'm next."

While there is no doubt that Johnson was truly upset and put, at least in his mind, in an untenable position by Foster's comments, in the end the controversy gave the Mets an excuse to get rid of a player who had become expendable. At 37 years of age, Foster was the oldest player on the team, and he had definitely slowed down ... at bat, in the field, and on the bases. As Cashen pointed out in Durso's story, since July 11, when he'd been benched, Foster had gone 2–28 with ten strikeouts and one RBI; and that performance was what gave the Mets cover for issuing the statement that Foster was being released because he had been "ineffective as a part-time player."

On August 11, Foster called a press conference at Shea Stadium to clear the air and to try, one more time, to set the record straight. He explained that while there was definitely racism in baseball just as there was in society, he did not believe that the Mets were a racist organization or that playing decisions had been made on the basis of race. Cashen also spoke at the news conference, and in contradiction to what Johnson would later claim in his 2018 autobiography, he said that he'd decided to release Foster so promptly only because Johnson insisted on his doing so. In an attempt to soften the team's harsh manner of severing ties with Foster, the bow-tied GM said, "When we signed George in February 1982 he brought instant credibility to an otherwise pretty poor team. He was maybe the only legitimate major leaguer we had, and I've always appreciated his contributions." In an August 12, column about the unusual press conference, the *Times*' Ira Berkow made it clear that he thought Foster had been intentionally misinterpreted and ill-treated. He concluded the column by saying, "Cashen said that in 20 years in baseball he has never found an easy way to say goodbye to a ballplayer who has outlived his usefulness. The Mets, and Davey Johnson, found a most unfortunate way this time. It wasn't necessary to use race as the broom to sweep out George Foster. They could have waited another week or so, let this thing simmer down, and then done it. And with that, preserved to a degree the dignity of a ballplayer who has given them, as Cashen said, good and important service. The dignity that the overall record of George Foster merits."

Without George Foster, the 1986 Mets went on to finally win the National League East Division with a record of 108–54, beat the Houston Astros in a thrilling NLCS, and defeat the Boston Red Sox in an even more thrilling World Series. Cognizant of what Foster had meant to the franchise, the Mets' coaches and players voted to give Foster a World Series ring and a three-quarters share of their World Series loot. Still, getting "the bum's rush" out the door had hurt, and Foster's lingering sentiment echoed that of Strawberry's. "You would think after all the years I put into the game, I would deserve better than that. But it's over," he said.

Foster's career wasn't quite over though. He still had the itch to play, and at least two teams other than the Mets thought he could still play ... both of them in the American League. Foster spoke with the Detroit Tigers but signed a contract on August 15 with the Chicago White Sox. "I was looking at the future," said Foster in explaining his decision. "I felt I would have a better future with the White Sox because they are rebuilding. In Detroit, it felt like they would need my services with Lance Parrish out, but I felt it would only be a temporary period. I felt it is going to be a longer period with the White Sox." Asked if he thought he would have trouble facing unfamiliar American League pitchers, he said, "They are throwing a baseball up there same as they do in the National League. You have to go up there and be disciplined and at the same time be aggressive." The Chi-Sox signed Foster for the major league minimum salary of $19,000 with the Mets still on the hook for the million dollars-plus they owed him. White Sox general manager Ken "Hawk" Harrelson's comment about the signing evinced some of the empathy that had been sorely lacking in New York. "If he's happy, he'll hit," said the Hawk. "I don't believe he was ever completely happy in New York." Foster played that very night against the Milwaukee Brewers at Comiskey Park, went 2–4, and homered against right-hander Bill Wegman in his second at bat. Hopeful White Sox fans demanded he make a curtain call after the homer, and Foster happily obliged.

The home run on August 15, 1986, was the final long ball of Foster's career. Foster started nine straight games for Chicago, but he soon found himself pinch-hitting or riding the pines. His 15th White Sox and last overall appearance in a major league uniform came on September 6, when he drew a walk as a pinch-hitter against the Toronto Blue Jays. When the White Sox released him, he was 11–51 for a batting average of .216. Foster ended his major league career having batted .274 in 1,977 games. Over his 18-year career he compiled 1,925 hits, 348 home runs, and 1,239 RBI.

While playing for the Mets, Foster had made his home in Greenwich, Connecticut, and after he retired as a major league ball player he remained there for a number of years. As always, he supported numerous charitable causes and gave generously of his time, coaching and running clinics for young ballplayers on various levels and delivering motivational speeches. He tried his hand at a variety of projects and business ventures in and around New York City, and Mets' fans gradually warmed up to him as an autograph guest at baseball card and memorabilia shows; however, he was continually called back to Cincinnati for reunions, roasts, and ceremonies of all sorts, and he eventually moved to the Queen City to be near the epicenter of his past glories, as well as his on-going opportunities. After all, it was with the Cincinnati Reds that he achieved greatness and experienced the ultimate thrill for any professional athlete: winning it all. And it wasn't just that he played on a team that won the World Series. It was much more than that. George Foster was an integral part of a dynastic team, one of the greatest team's in the history of major league baseball, the Big Red Machine. He was, further, a member of the "Great Eight;" the eight men who took the field during the Reds' back-to-back championship years of 1975–76 when the very best players on the Cincinnati roster were available: Rose, Griffey, Morgan, Bench, Perez, Foster, Concepcion, and Geronimo. Those names are more than remembered in Cincinnati; they are revered, and those eight players have been memorialized by being depicted in a huge mosaic made of Italian marble which hangs on the wall inside Cincinnati's new riverfront stadium, Great American Ballpark. Yes, George Foster was born in Tuscaloosa, Alabama; he grew up in Hawthorne, California; and he played baseball for four major league teams, including the San Francisco Giants with his childhood idol Willie Mays and the New York Mets in the media capital of the world. But he belongs to Cincinnati.

Foster won some significant awards as a player—including a Silver Slugger Award, and an MVP Award which is highly coveted by any player—and he has enjoyed further recognitions in retirement. In 2002 he was inducted into the Alabama Sports Hall of Fame, and the next year he took his rightful place in the Cincinnati Reds Hall of Fame. But he did not gain election to the National Baseball Hall of Fame, as it once appeared he might. On the ballot for four years, he was dropped off of it after receiving only 4.1% of the vote in 1995. Which raises the question, Did his tenure in New York cost him a spot in Cooperstown?

While that question can't be answered with 100% certainty, the answer is probably "No," and the reason the answer is in the negative is the evolution of standards for admission to the Hall of Fame. A comparison of the records of Foster and Hack Wilson, the NL single-season home run record holder George did not catch in 1977, will illustrate this point. A lot of fans would be shocked to learn that Foster's career totals in hits, home runs, and RBI are significantly higher than Wilson's (Foster's career home run percentage of 5.0 is almost identical to Wilson's 5.1). True, Wilson had that one absolutely great year when he hit 56 home runs and knocked in a staggering 191 runs, but 1930 was the apex of an era of batting inflation. In his book entitled *'30: Major League Baseball's Year of the Batter*, Ray Zardetto points out that "Nine of the 16 teams hit over .300 and so did 60 percent of the regular players. Seven pairs of teammates hit .350 or better and 20 batters had over 200 hits. Hack Wilson had a record 191 RBIs and five others topped 150; both leagues' batting races came down to the last game of the season." Wilson was elected to the Hall of Fame in 1979, and the voters were so impressed with his 1930 season that they apparently ignored the context of his impressive 1930 season. They elected him to the Hall of Fame, despite the fact that he hit a total of only 244 home runs, collected only 1,461 hits, and drove in 1,062 runs. By the time Foster became eligible for the Hall of Fame in 1992, Sabermetrics had totally revolutionized the thinking about baseball statistics and the criteria for election to the Hall of Fame. With his 1,925 hits, 348 homers, and 1,239 RBI, Foster didn't stand a chance. Fair or not, Foster was also pretty much viewed as a one-dimensional player: a slugger, a power hitter, a run producer. His candidacy was going to hinge on the quality of that characteristic; and even had he hit more home runs in New York, say even 50 more, he wouldn't have garnered enough support to cross the threshold of receiving 75% of the vote in a given year. Although Dave Kingman, Foster's boyhood teammate whom he also played with on the Giants and Mets, was not as good an all-around player as George (and neither was Hack Wilson for that matter), Kingman did hit 442 home runs in his career; yet he didn't come close to being elected to the Hall of Fame either.

Foster hit 99 home runs as a New York Met, and it is a fair question to ask, Did playing for the Mets at least suppress the number of homers he hit during those four and a half years? Greg Gajus, a fine baseball analyst who lives in Cincinnati, studied the park effect of Shea Stadium in comparison to

Riverfront Stadium and concluded that, while Shea Stadium was a little worse than Riverfront for home runs and run scoring, Foster's playing half his games at Shea had no detectable effect on his home run output during the 1982–1986 period. In fact, Foster hit more homers at Shea Stadium (53) than he did on the road (46); however, concluding that Shea was not a tougher ballpark to homer in than Riverfront Stadium does not mean that Foster's move from Cincinnati to New York did not negatively affect his performance. In fact, Foster's performance in his first year in New York was such an aberration that it is clear he was deeply affected, for the worse, by the shift from the Reds to the Mets, by the move from sleepy Cincinnati to the craziness of New York. While any number of factors may have played a part in his off-year, the likelihood is greatest that Foster simply tried too hard; despite the fact that he understood the danger of putting too much pressure on himself. Shortly after he'd signed with the Mets in early 1982, he said as much to sportswriter Ira Berkow. "I don't like to set specific goals because sometimes the situations don't lend themselves to great statistics, but you can be doing an equally good job," he said. "The year after I hit 52 homers, I hit 40 homers and I thought I had a better long-ball season. Pitchers weren't challenging me as much. In 1977 they were saying, 'I don't believe this, I'll get him out.' But the next year, they said, 'I believe.' The only thing I can do is stay within my own abilities. And not try to be or do something I'm not. I think Dave Winfield made a mistake in the World Series (of 1981) by trying too hard. He was going hitless, and the outs he was making were pop-ups. He was trying to make his first hit in a World Series a homer. I could tell, I've been in that situation too."

Foster later reiterated the most likely explanation for his decline in New York during a mid-season interview with Cincinnati reporter Jack Moran which appeared in the August 1984 issue of *RedsVue* newspaper. Asked about his .241 batting average in 1983 for the Mets, which was about 50 points below his norm, Foster said, "Maybe I've been trying too hard. True, my average fell quite a bit and I probably wasn't concentrating on getting base hits. I'm expected to knock the ball out of the park and that may have been my problem." Foster basically admitted that he had been doing the same thing he'd noticed Winfield doing, and his response to Moran is a reminder that being aware of the cause of a problem is not enough to make a solution to it; especially when the problem involves a major league batter not swinging the bat as he's capable of doing.

Playing for the Mets, then, probably cost Foster something in the overall numbers he compiled for his career but not enough to have seriously ruined his chances of making the Hall of Fame. On the other hand, his reputation as a player and as a person was sullied by his stay in New York. Mets' fans were

9. Fall 1977 and Beyond

looking for a savior, and given the amount of money it took to get Foster to New York, they practically demanded that he play like one. When Foster didn't risk injury by diving for low line drives or by running into outfield walls in pursuit of fly balls, they accused him of being lazy or not hustling. Hitting only 13 home runs that first year branded him as a flop, and he was never able to overcome that first impression. And, while he improved his communication skills over the years, his honesty and forthrightness were liabilities, not assets, in the unforgiving, sensationalistic Big Apple media arena. In a 2006 piece for *NY Sports Day* Bob Sikes summed up Foster's experience as a New York Met as well as anyone has. "Foster probably wasn't up to the attention that went with his stature as a highly paid player," he wrote. "The jihad over athlete's salaries wasn't yet in full swing and his was one of the first big contracts. He had to carry the load in his early days for the Mets before the arrival of (Keith) Hernandez. He was quietly religious and a devoted family man. George did not have many friends on the club, but was generally a likable sort with a dry sense of humor. He once turned on the dugout heaters at Shea during a 90-degree day game, and also enjoyed doing Sparky Anderson impressions with Howard Johnson. I really do not believe that Foster held any serious racially motivated grudges, but the timing of it all had been bad. A proud sensitive man succumbed to the realization of a fading career and spilled his guts to a media who never embraced him and whom he was never comfortable with."

Even today, more than 30 years after Foster last played for the Mets, his controversial departure from the team is a hot topic; at least on an amazing website called *The Ultimate Mets Database*. In addition to ranking former Mets' players—interestingly, Foster is ranked #41 of 1,060 players—and providing a wealth of information about them, the site allows Mets' fans to post their thoughts and memories about the players. Mets' fans are as passionate as any baseball fans anywhere, and many of the posts about Foster are negative, describing him as a failure and a disappointment. But others focus on his friendliness, kindness, and goodness. Like the one posted by Mudge01, who wrote: "My brother and I were at a game in San Fran in '84. My bro asked George Foster for an autograph. George whipped a card out of his back pocket and handed it over. It was a picture of George with some bats, autographed, with the words, 'What you are is God's gift to you. What you do with what you are is your gift to God.' Yeah, he was a New York bust. But I've got nothing bad to say about Mr. Foster."

New York baseball fans and media members did not get George Foster in his baseball prime. They did not enjoy the thrill of watching come to the plate the ultra-confident and laser-focused Foster who was a threat to hit any pitcher's next offering into the far reaches of any ballpark.

But they did get the essential, truly important Foster, even if their desire to have a winning team to root for blinded them to his presence.

Hal McCoy, the venerable, highly respected Reds' beat writer for the *Dayton Daily News*, covered the Big Red Machine and got to know George Foster as well as anybody. McCoy called Foster "the greatest person in baseball. I mean as a person, not just as a ballplayer. He never raises his voice, no matter how harassed he may be by fans. I asked him once if he'd let me use his name for Building Bridges, an organization for underprivileged kids. He said, 'No, you'll have more than my name. I'll be there too.' "

For someone who has cared far more about the needs and welfare of other people than his own aggrandizement, George Foster created quite a legacy for himself. It's a legacy that the humble Foster has every right to be extremely proud of, and it's a long-lasting legacy.

Author of the CASEY Award-winning book *56: Joe DiMaggio and the Last Magic Number in Sports,* Kostya Kennedy is the reigning expert on baseball streaks and the longevity of baseball records. He knows as well as anyone what George Foster achieved in 1977 with 52 swings of his power-packed black bat. "Leaving aside the 1977 through 2003 seasons, when Steroid Era big leaguers piled up 50-homer seasons with unnatural ease, only 16 players have ever hit more home runs than George Foster did for the Reds in 1977," he says. "That's an illustration of just how rare and precious Foster's accomplishment is (And consider: 14 teams have never had a player hit as many as Foster did that year). Things broke right for Foster who was an excellent all-around hitter in the middle of what was still one of the greatest lineups of all time. Cincinnati is not at all likely to field an offense on par with the Big Red Machine anytime soon, and Foster's home-run record, already entering its fifth decade, could be around for many decades more."

One reason Cincinnati baseball fans have loved Pete Rose so much, despite his shortcoming and foibles, is that they identified with him. A hometown boy through and through, Rose came from the poor side of town and was nothing but rough edges. He was brought up by blue collar, working class parents, graduated (barely) from an average public high school, and never set foot on a college campus. He practically cadged his way into professional baseball with help from a relative owed a favor, and he clawed his way up the minor leagues ladder. He lived and breathed baseball and forced his way onto his first major league roster through hustle, ultra-competitiveness, and constantly-honed skill. In other words, Pete Rose earned his place in the game, his stardom, and its many rewards, every step of the way.

The same thing might be said of George Foster, a man and ball player with little else in common with Rose. Foster grew up without a father in his life; and as a youngster, he was a tongue-tied, extremely shy introvert who had trouble adjusting to an all-white society after his family's move to Hawthorne, California, from Alabama. He was not a highly-recruited prospect; the team that signed him to his original pro contract thought him expendable; and the team that traded for him was finally willing to go down the line with him only after they desperately needed what they thought he had to offer: consistent power hitting. In fact, Foster had his hopes raised and dashed so many times that when Sparky Anderson told him of the Reds' plans to install him as the regular left fielder, he was visibly suspicious of Anderson's sincerity. In an effort to reassure Foster, Anderson said, "George, I haven't done you any favors in the past, and I'm not doing you one now. You're ready."

At least Anderson and the Reds hoped Foster was ready. Of course, he was, and he went on to do far more than play well enough to hold onto his position as a regular. Through perseverance, confidence in his God-given ability, and hard work, he became an All-Star, the most feared slugger in the National League, and a record-setting home run hitter.

After he passed his prime, circumstances conspired to paint the latter years of his career in less glorious colors, yet that period of inevitable decline should cause no one to forget or underestimate the great achievement of his 1977 season.

"Thusly," until another player beats his record, he deserves the title he worked so hard to earn. He is George Foster, Cincinnati Reds Home Run King.

Appendix A

Log of George Foster's 52-Home Run Season in 1977

Appendix A

HR#	Game #	Date	Opp	W/L	Score	Pitcher	Inn	Outs	On	B. Order	Field	H/AB	B. Avg*
1	8	A 15	@SD	W	9–5	Metzger	9	1	1	4th	LF	1-4	.259
2	15	A 25	@ATL	W	23–9	Niekro	1	1	2	6th	LF	4-4	.321
3	15	A 25	@ATL			Beard	5	2	1				
4	24	M 7	@PIT	L	12–10	Kison	1	1	0	5th	LF	2-5	.315
5	39	M 25	@SF	L	6–5	Curtis	2	1	0	5th	LF	2-4	.295
6	39	M 25	@SF			Curtis	4	1	1		LF		
7	41	M 27	@LA	L	10–3	John	4	0	0	5th	LF	1-3	.299
8	42	M 28	@LA	W	6–3	Sutton	2	1	0	6th	LF	2-4	.305
9	42	M 28	@LA			Sutton	3	1	0		LF		
10	43	M 29	@LA	W	8–1	Wall	8	1	0	6th	CF	1-4	.303
11	44	M 30	vs. ATL	W	7–3	Messersmith	6	0	0	6th	LF	1-3	.304
12	52	J 8	@NY	W	5–0	Koosman	1	1	2	4th	LF	1-4	.301
13	53	J 10	vs. MON	W	13–1	Warthen	4	2	1	5th	LF	2-5	.304
14	57	J 13	vs. PHI	W	5–4	Carlton	1	1	2	4th	RF	2-4	.316
15	59	J 15	vs. PHI	W	8–7	Garber	9	2	0	4th	CF	2-5	.313
16	60	J 17	@MON	W	9–4	Rogers	5	2	2	5th	LF	2-5	.315
17	60	J 17	@MON			Atkinson	9	0	0		CF		
18	61	J 18	@MON	W	6–0	Alcala	4	1	0	5th	RF	1-5	.313
19	64	J 21	@PHI	W	10–5	Brusstar	6	0	2	4th	R/CF	2-5	.308
20	65	J 22	@PHI	L	15–9	Christenson	1	2	2	5th	R/CF	3-5	.314
21	74	J 1	@SD	W	2–1	Shirley	3	0	1	4th	R/CF	1-3	.315
22	76	J 3	@SD	L	8–7	Freisleben	1	2	0	5th	LF	2-5	.316
23	78	J 5	@ATL	W	9–3	Capra	5	0	0	4th	L/CF	1-5	.309
24	80	J 8	@HOU	W	8–5	Bannister	7	1	2	4th	LF	2-5	.311
25	85	J 13	vs. ATL	L	4–3	Capra	6	2	1	5th	CF	1-4	.309
26	86	J 14	vs. ATL	W	7–1	Ruthven	4	0	0	4th	LF	3-4	.309
27	86	J 14	vs. ATL			Ruthven	5	2	2		CF		.314

Appendix A   191

28	J 14	vs. ATL	W	8–3	Kline	8	0	0		L/CF	2–3	.317
29	J 15	vs. HOU	L	9–8	Pentz	6	1	1	4th	LF	2–5	.317
30	J 25	@STL			Falcone	3	2	1	4th	RF	2–5	.310
31	J 25	@STL			Eastwick	9	1	0		LF		
32	J 27	@CHI	W	6–2	Broberg	6	0	0	4th	CF	3–4	.315
33	A 1	vs. CHI	W	7–6	Renko	1	2	1	4th	LF	2–3	.317
34	A 1	vs. CHI			Renko	3	2	1		LF		
35	A 2	vs. CHI	L	5–2	Broberg	9	0	0	4th	LF	1–2	.318
36	A 3	vs. CHI	W	5–3	Hernandez	8	0	1	4th	LF	3–5	.322
37	A 5	vs. PIT	L	10–6	O. Jones	3	2	0	4th	LF	3–5	.322
38	A 5	vs. PIT			Jackson	5	1	1	5th	RF		
39	A 17	vs. SD	L	7–4	Shirley	7	1	2	4th	CF	1–5	.311
40	A 19	@NY	W	4–1	Matlack	6	0	0	4th	L/CF	2–4	.313
41	A 19	@NY	W	4–3	Espinosa	1	2	1	5th	L/CF	1–3	.313
42	A 24	vs. NY	W	11–4	Matlack	1	1	0	4th	LF	2–4	.314
43	A 28	vs. PHI	W	9–0	Brusstar	2	1	2	4th	L/CF	2–4	.311
44	A 30	@MON	W	4–3	J. Brown	1	2	1	4th	LF	3–5	.312
45	S 4	@PHI	W	5–2	Kaat	5	1	0	4th	RF	4–5	.315
46	S 7	vs. SF	L	6–3	Halicki	5	1	0	4th	LF	1–4	.313
47	S 13	vs. HOU	L	13–4	Bannister	4	0	0	4th	LF	2–3	.316
48	S 14	@ LA	W	9–8	John	1	2	1	4th	RF	2–5	.317
49	S 20	@ SD	W	4–0	Owchinko	1	2	1	4th	LF	1–3	.319
50	S 23	@ ATL	W	5–1	Capra	9	2	0	4th	LF	4–5	.325
51	S 25	@ ATL	W	4–0	Neikro	7	0	0	4th	LF	1–4	.324
52	S 28	vs. SD	W	8–0	D'Acquisto	5	2	0	4th	CF	2–3	.324

* The figure in this last column represents Foster's batting average after the completion of the game in question.

Appendix B

Statistical Breakdown of the 52 Home Runs Hit by George Foster in 1977

Games homered in: 43.
Reds' record in those 43 games: 31–12.
Multiple home run games: 8; seven 2-home runs games and one 3-home run game. He had 2-home-runs games on April 25 @ ATL, May 25 @ SF, May 28 @ LA, June 17 @ MON, July 25 @ STL, August 1 vs. CHI, and August 5 vs. PIT. His one 3-home-run game came on July 14 vs. ATL.
Multiple hits games in which at least one hit was a home run: 28. Of these 28 games, 19 were 2-hit games, 6 were 3-hit games, and 3 were 4-hit games. In 15 games Foster's only hit was a home run.
By Handedness of pitchers: 32 vs. right handers; 20 vs. left handers.
By Pitcher type: 36 vs. starters; 16 vs. relievers.
By Location: 31 Away; 21 Home.
By Inning: 1st (12); 2nd (3); 3rd (5); 4th (6); 5th (8); 6th (6); 7th (3); 8th (3); 9th (6).
By Outs: 0 Outs (14); 1 Out (20); 2 Outs (18).
By Runners on Base: O on (26); 1 on (16); 2 on (10); bases loaded (0).
By Position in the Batting Order: 4th (31); 5th (15); 6th (6).
By Field: LF (30); CF (8); RF (6); L/CF (5); R/CF (3).
By Day of the Week: Monday (8); Tuesday (6); Wednesday (13); Thursday (3; all 3 came in the same game, July 14 vs. Atlanta). Friday (13); Saturday (4); Sunday (5).
By Month: April (3); May (8); June (9); July (12); August (12); September (8).
By National League Team, Total and Home/Away: 10 Atlanta 5/5; 6 Philadelphia 3/3; 6 San Diego 2/4; 5 Chicago 4/1; 5 Los Angeles 0/5; 5 Montreal 1/4; 4 New York 1/3; 3 Houston 2/1; 3 Pittsburgh 2/1; 3 San Francisco 1/2; 2 St. Louis 0/2.

Pitchers Victimized: 39.

Alcala, Santo, MON
Atkinson, Bill, MON
Bannister, Floyd, HOU (2)
Beard, Mike, ATL
Broberg, Pete, CHI (2)
Brown, Jackie, MON
Brusstar, Warren, PHI (2)
Capra, Buzz, ATL (3)
Carlton, Steve, PHI
Christenson, Larry, PHI
Curtis, John, SF (2)
D'Acquisto, John, SD
Eastwick, Rawly, STL
Espinosa, Nino, NY
Falcone, Pete, STL
Freisleben, Dave, SD
Garber, Gene, ATL
Halicki, Ed, SF
Hernandez, Willie, CHI
Jackson, Grant, PIT
John, Tommy, LA (2)
Jones, Odell, PIT
Kaat, Jim, PHI
Kison, Bruce, PIT
Kline, Steve, ATL
Koosman, Jerry, NY
Matlack, Jon, NY (2)
Messersmith, Andy, LA
Metzer, Butch, STL
Niekro, Phil, ATL
Owchinko, Bob, SD
Pentz, Gene, HOU
Renko, Steve, CHI (2)
Rogers, Steve, MON
Ruthven, Dick (2), PHI
Shirley, Bob, SD (2)
Sutton, Don, LA (2)
Wall, Stan, LA
Warthen, Dan, MON

Foster homered twice against 11 different pitchers and three times against one pitcher (Capra). He homered twice against the same pitcher in the same game four times (Curtis, Renko, Ruthven, and Sutton). Seven of Foster's victims won 20 or more games in a season at least once (Carlton, John, Kaat, Koosman, Messersmith, Neikro, and Sutton). Carlton, Neikro, and Sutton are Hall of Famers; and a strong case can be made that John and Kaat are also worthy of election into the Hall of Fame.

Longest Streak of Home Runs Away: 10, #1 (April 15)–#10 (May 29).

Longest Streak of Home Runs at Home: 7, #33 (August 1)–#39 (August 17).

Longest Streak without a Home Run: 11 days and 12 games, between August 5 and August 17.

Highest Batting Average after a Home Run Game: .325, which is where Foster's average stood after the game of September 23 @ ATL, in which he had gone 4 hits for 5 at-bats.

Appendix C

George Foster's Career Home Runs in Perspective

George Foster Career Home Runs
San Francisco Giants: 4
Cincinnati Reds: 244 (number of home runs Foster hit for Cincinnati Reds before 1977: 75; number of home runs Foster hit for Cincinnati Reds after 1977: 117)
New York Mets: 99
Chicago White Sox: 1
Total: 348

Cincinnati Reds All-Time Home Run Leaders
Johnny Bench, 389
Frank Robinson, 324
Tony Perez, 287
Adam Dunn, 270
Joey Votto, 257*
Ted Kluszewski, 251
George Foster, 244
   *Votto had 257 home runs at the end of the 2017 season. He is the only player on the list who is still active.

Evolution of Cincinnati Reds Single-Season Home Run Record
1900 Sam Crawford, 7
1901 Sam Crawford, 16
1930 Harry Heilmann, 19
1938 Ival Goodman, 30
1948 Hank Sauer, 35
1953 Ted Kluszewski, 40
1954 Ted Kluszewski, 49
1977 George Foster, 52

Appendix C

Number of Red Seat Home Runs Hit in Riverfront Stadium (1970–2002): 35

Most by one player: 6, George Foster
June 14, 1976 vs. Joe Coleman, Chicago, LF
August 3, 1977 vs. Willie Hernandez, Chicago, LF
September 7, 1977 vs. Ed Halicki, San Francisco, LF
July 29, 1978 vs. Jim Lonborg, Philadelphia, LF
September 6, 1979 vs. Tom Griffin, San Francisco, LF
August 14, 1981 vs. Al Ripley, San Francisco, LF

Appendix D

Single-Season Home Run Leaders for Every Major League Franchise

Team	Player	HR	Year
Giants	Barry Bonds	73	2001
Cardinals	Mark McGwire	70	1998
Cubs	Sammy Sosa	66	1998
Yankees	Roger Maris	61	1961
Marlins	Giancarlo Stanton	59	2017
Athletics	Jimmie Foxx	58	1932
Tigers	Hank Greenberg	58	1938
Phillies	Ryan Howard	58	2006
Diamondbacks	Luis Gonzalez	57	2001
Rangers	Alex Rodriguez	57	2002
Mariners	Ken Griffey Jr.	56	1997/1998
Pirates	Ralph Kiner	54	1949
Red Sox	David Ortiz	54	2006
Blue Jays	Jose Bautista	54	2010
Reds	George Foster	52	1977
Indians	Jim Thome	52	2002
Braves	Andruw Jones	51	2005
Orioles	Brady Anderson	50	1996
Padres	Greg Vaughn	50	1998
Brewers	Prince Fielder	50	2007
Twins	Harmon Killebrew	49	1964/1969
Rockies	Larry Walker	49	1997
	Todd Helton	49	2001
White Sox	Albert Belle	49	1998
Dodgers	Shawn Green	49	2001
Angels	Troy Glaus	47	2000
Astros	Jeff Bagwell	47	2000
Rays	Carlos Pena	46	2007
Nationals	Alfonso Soriano	46	2006

Team	Player	HR	Year
Mets	Todd Hundley	41	1996
	Carlos Beltran	41	2006
Royals	Steve Balboni	36	1985

*** *Only five of the team records listed above are older than George Foster's: those held by Jimmie Foxx, Hank Greenberg, Ralph Kiner, Roger Maris, and Harmon Killebrew.*

Bibliography

Books

Adelman, Tom. *The Long Ball: The Summer of '75—Spaceman, Catfish, Charlie Hustle, and the Greatest World Series Ever played.* Boston: Little, Brown, 2003.

Allen, Maury. *Baseball's 100: A Personal Ranking of the Best Players in Baseball History.* New York: A & W Visual Library, 1981.

Armour, Mark, ed. *The Great Eight: The 1975 Cincinnati Reds.* Lincoln: University of Nebraska Press, 2014.

Benson, Michael. *Ballparks of North America: A Comprehensive Historical Reference to Baseball Grounds, Yard and Stadiums, 1845 to Present.* Jefferson, NC: McFarland, 1989.

Bryant, Howard. *Juicing the Game: Drugs, Power, and the Fight for the Soul of Major League Baseball.* New York: Viking, 2005.

Burson, Rusty. *100 Things Rangers Fans Should Know & Do Before They Die.* Chicago: Triumph Books, 2012.

Cohen, Robert W. *MVP: A Controversial Look at Baseball's Greatest Players: Who Won the Award, and Who Should Have.* Las Vegas: Cardoza Publishing, 2010.

Collett, Ritter. *Men of the Machine: An Inside Look at Baseball's Team of the '70s.* Dayton, OH: Landfall Press, 1977.

Deane, Bill. *Award Voting.* Kansas City: Society for American Baseball Research, 1988.

Dickson, Paul. *The Dickson Baseball Dictionary: 5,000 Terms Used by Players, the Press and People Who Love the Game.* New York: Facts on File, 1989.

Dowling, Jerry. *Drawing the Big Red Machine.* Cincinnati: Edgecliff Press, 2010.

Drucker, Malka, with George Foster. *The George Foster Story.* New York: Holiday House, 1979.

Epstein, Dan. *Stars and Strikes: Baseball and America in the Bicentennial Summer of '76.* New York: Thomas Dunne Books, 2014.

Feldman, Doug. *The 1976 Cincinnati Reds: Last Hurrah for the Big Red Machine.* Jefferson, NC: McFarland, 2009.

Frost, Mark. *Game Six: Cincinnati, Boston, and the 1975 World Series: The Triumph of America's Pastime.* New York: Hyperion, 2009.

Garratt, Robert F. *Home Team: The Turbulent History of the San Francisco Giants.* Lincoln: University of Nebraska Press, 2017.

Golenbock, Peter. *The Forever Boys; The Bittersweet World of Major League Baseball as Seen Through the Eyes of the Men Who Played One More Time.* New York: Birch Lane Press, 1991.

Griffey, Ken, and Phil Pepe. *Big Red: Baseball, Fatherhood, and My Life in the Big Red Machine.* Chicago: Triumph Books, 2014.

Gutman, Bill. *Grand Slammers: Rice, Luzinski, Foster, Hisle.* New York: Tempo Books, 1979.

Gutman, Bill. *It's Outta Here! The History of the Home Run from Babe Ruth to Barry Bonds.* Dallas: Taylor Trade, 2005.

Hall, Donald, with Dock Ellis. *Dock Ellis in the Country of Baseball.* New York: Coward, McCann & Geoghegan, 1976.

Johnson, Davey, with Erik Sherman. *Davey Johnson: My Wild Ride in Baseball and Beyond.* New York: Triumph Books, 2018.

Leventhal, Josh. *Take Me Out to the Ballpark: An Illustrated Tour of Baseball Parks Past and Present.* New York: Black Dog & Leventhal, 2011.

Liebman, Glenn. *Baseball Shorts: 1,000 of the Game's Funniest One-Liners.* Chicago: Contemporary Books, 1994.

McCoy, Hal. *The Relentless Reds.* Shelbyville, KY: PressCo, 1976.

McNeil, William F. *The Single-Season Home Run Kings: Ruth, Maris, McGwire, Sosa, and Bonds.* Jefferson, NC: McFarland, 2003.

Nathan, David. H. *Baseball Quotations.* Jefferson, NC: McFarland, 1991.

Neft, David S., Richard M. Cohen, and Michael

L. Neft. *The Sports Encyclopedia: Baseball 2007.* New York: St. Martin's Griffin, 2007.

Posnanski, Joe. *The Machine: A Hot Team, a Legendary Season, and a Heart-Stopping World Series: The Story of the 1975 Cincinnati Reds.* New York: William Morrow, 2009.

Rhodes, Greg, and John Erardi. *Big Red Dynasty: How Bob Howsam & Sparky Anderson Built the Big Red Machine.* Cincinnati: Road West, 1997.

Rhodes, Greg, and John Erardi. *Opening Day: Celebrating Cincinnati's Baseball Holiday.* Cincinnati: Road West, 2004.

Rhodes, Greg, and John Snyder. *Redleg Journal: Year by Year and Day by Day with the Cincinnati Reds Since 1866.* Cincinnati: Road West, 2000.

Rosen, Ira. *Blue Skies, Green Fields: A Celebration of 50 Major League Baseball Stadiums.* New York: Clarkson Potter, 2001.

Shannon, Mike. *Cincinnati Reds Legends.* Illus. Chris Felix, Scott Hannig, and Donnie Pollard. Kent, OH: Kent State University Press, 2015.

Shannon, Mike. *Riverfront Stadium: Home of the Big Red Machine.* Charleston, SC: Arcadia, 2003.

Snyder, John. *Dodgers Journal: Year by Year & Day by Day with the Brooklyn & Los Angeles Dodgers Since 1884.* Cincinnati: Clerisy Press, 2009.

Snyder, John. *White Sox Journal: Year by Year & Day by Day with the Chicago White Sox Since 1901.* Cincinnati: Clerisy Press, 2009.

Staub, Rusty, with Phil Pepe. *Few and Chosen: Defining Mets Greatness Across the Eras.* Chicago: Triumph Books, 2009.

Vincent, David. *Home Run: The Definitive History of Baseball's Ultimate Weapon.* Washington, D.C.: Potomac Books, 2007.

Vincent, David, Lyle Spatz, and David W. Smith. *The Midsummer Classic: The Complete History of Baseball's All-Star Game.* Lincoln: University of Nebraska Press, 2001.

Wheeler, Lonnie, and John Baskin. *The Cincinnati Game.* Wilmington, OH: Orange Frazer Press, 1988.

Wilson, Doug. *The Bird: The Life and Legacy of Mark Fidrych.* New York: St. Martin's Press, 2013.

Zardetto, Ray. *'30: Major League Baseball's Year of the Batter.* Jefferson, NC: McFarland, 2008.

Periodical Articles

Berkow, Ira. "Sports of the Times: The Foster Cloud." *New York Times,* August 12, 1986.

Berkow, Ira. "Up at Bat, George Foster." *New York Times,* February 21, 1982.

Downey, Mike. "White Sox's George Foster Lookin' for Love in All the Wrong Places." *Los Angeles Times,* August 18, 1986.

Durso, Joseph. "Mets to Drop Foster Amid Racial Controversy." *New York Times,* August 7, 1986.

"Franchise Single-Season HR Leaders." *Baseball Digest,* May/June 2010.

Hardin, Marc. "King George: Vaughn's Great 1998 Still Short of Foster's 1977." *Cincinnati Enquirer,* April 3, 1999.

Kuenster, John. "Reds' George Foster, a Deserving Choice as Player of the Year." *Baseball Digest,* December 1977.

Lawson, Earl. "Foster Finds a Home as Reds' No. 1 Wrecker." *The Sporting News,* July 3, 1976.

McDill, Kent. "The Chicago White Sox Friday Signed Veteran George Foster." *UPI,* August 15, 1986.

Rasmussen, Larry F. "George Foster: Will He Win His Fourth RBI Title in a Row?" *Baseball Digest,* March 1979.

Sikes, Bob. "The Last Days of George Foster." *NY Sports Day,* February 14, 2006.

Index

Aaron, Hank 81, 140, 148
Albert, Jeff 39
Alcala, Santo 21, 23, 33, 63, 92, 173
Almon, Bill 36, 37, 139–140, 160
Alphonso, Carlos 77
Alston, Walter 20, 168
Altobelli, Joe 138
Anderson, Dave 117
Anderson, Mike 54, 56
Anderson, Sparky 3, 10, 11, 12, 13, 20, 21, 22, 23, 24, 25, 28, 31, 32, 34, 35, 36, 38, 39, 40, 41, 42, 44, 45, 47, 49, 50, 52, 53, 54, 55, 56, 60, 61, 66, 76, 68, 71, 72, 75, 76, 81, 83, 84, 85, 86, 87, 88, 89, 90, 92, 93, 94, 95, 96, 97, 98, 100, 101, 102, 106, 107, 108, 109, 110, 111, 112, 115, 116, 117, 119, 122, 123, 124, 125, 128–129, 134, 135, 136, 138, 143, 144, 146, 147, 153–154, 156, 159–160, 161, 163, 172, 173, 174, 185, 186
Andrews, Rob 101, 138, 152
Andujar, Joaquin 77, 112, 151
Apodaca, Bob 62
Arbrister, Ed 43, 54, 56, 84, 109, 130
Ashford, Tucker 165
Atkinson, Bill 91
Auerbach, Rick 89, 110, 159, 169

Bailey, Bob 54, 56, 61, 89, 122, 129, 138, 158–159, 160
Baker, Dusty 38, 39, 99, 100, 154, 158, 166
Ballou, George 57
Bamberger, George 178
Bannister, Floyd 111, 155
Barr, Jim 58, 138
Beard, Mike 43
Bench, Johnny 1, 2, 3, 7, 8, 15, 16, 20, 21, 22, 23, 28, 30, 31, 34, 35, 36, 40, 49, 51, 52, 54, 57, 58, 60, 63, 64, 66, 67, 68, 69, 70, 73, 77, 78, 79–80, 83, 87, 89, 91, 94, 96, 98, 99, 100, 101, 102, 103, 105, 106, 107, 110, 112, 113, 115, 116, 121, 125, 127, 128, 132, 133, 134, 135, 138, 139, 146, 147, 150, 151, 153, 154–155, 158, 159, 162, 164, 167, 169, 174, 175, 177, 182
Benson, Vern 59
Berkow, Ira 180, 184

Bescher, Bob 63
Big Red Dynasty: How Bob Howsam and Sparky Anderson Built the Big Red Machine 16–17
Biittner, Larry 45
Billingham, Jack 23, 32, 34, 38, 42, 45, 47, 52, 56, 60, 63, 67, 68, 69, 76, 80, 81, 84, 91, 95, 101, 108–109, 110, 114, 120, 122, 123, 124, 139, 154, 173
Black, Stu 31
Blair, Paul 92
Blue, Vida 118
Bonds, Barry 5
Bonds, Bobby 9
Bonham, Bill 40
Boone, Bob 85, 88
Borbon, Pedro 33, 35, 36, 56, 58, 61, 67, 83, 86, 88, 89, 96, 102, 108, 112, 122, 124, 125, 130, 135, 138, 139, 141, 144, 147
Borgman, Jim 103
Boswell, Tom 28
Bowa, Larry 50, 85, 86, 93, 95
Braucher, Bill 74, 96
Braun, Bob 81
Brennaman, Marty 158
Bristol, Dave 42, 59, 60, 72
Broberg, Pete 123, 127
Brock, Lou 50, 56
Brosnan, Jim 12
Brown, Jackie 84, 147
Bruce, Jay 5
Brusstar, Warren 94, 146
Buckner, Bill 39, 128
Burris, Ray 42, 45
Burroughs, Jeff 57, 78, 91, 110, 115

Cabel, Enos 116, 151
Caen, Herb 65
Caldwell, Mike 26, 33, 42, 56, 60, 63, 89
Camp, Rick 57, 71, 109, 113
Campbell, Dave 169, 170
Candelaria, John 52, 60, 175
Capilla, Doug 89, 102, 109, 111, 113, 116, 120, 123, 125, 131, 135–136, 140, 151, 159, 162
Capra, Buzz 43, 109, 114, 163

201

Carew, Rod 2, 118, 119, 166
Carlton, Steve 85, 86, 145, 171
Carter, Gary 48, 84, 93, 144, 178, 179
Cash, Dave 84
Cashen, Frank 179, 180, 181
Cedeno, Cesar 112, 151, 155
Cey, Ron 38, 39, 47, 49–50, 71, 78, 79–80, 91, 97, 98, 103, 135, 136, 155, 158, 166
Chaney, Darrel 106
Christenson, Larry 95, 150
Cincinnati Enquirer 24, 26, 27, 28, 32–33, 35, 42, 47, 49, 50, 53, 54–55, 58–59, 60, 67, 74, 77, 79, 86–87, 90, 94, 96, 100, 103, 113, 119–120, 124, 130, 131–135, 144, 148, 158, 164, 165, 167, 172–173
Clark, Jack 65, 101, 138
Clarke, Norm 28–29, 135
Clines, Gene 45
Cobb, Ty 2, 121, 150, 165, 174
Collins, Rip 38
Colosi, Nick 21
Concepcion, Dave 19, 21, 25, 30, 32, 34, 36, 37, 42, 56, 64, 73, 78, 81, 84, 94, 98, 100, 106, 109, 110, 112, 114, 115, 116, 125, 128, 130, 135–136, 147, 156, 158, 162, 169, 182
Corbett, Brad 101
Corbett, Jim 179
Crawford, Jerry 103, 119
Crawford, Willie 35
Cromarti, Warren 83, 144, 147
Crosley, Powell, Jr. 59
Cruz, Hector 49, 54
Cruz, Jose 35, 76, 112, 116
Curtis, john 66, 102, 103

D'Acquisto, John 56, 165
Dale, Jerry 126
Darcy, Pat 26
Dark, Alvin 117
Darling, Ron 178
Davey Johnson: My Wild Ride in Baseball and Beyond 180
Davidson, John 69
Davis, Tommy 2
Dawson, Andre 84, 93
Dayton Daily News 186
DeJesus, Ivan 39, 45
Demery, Larry 133
Dempsey, Rick 44
Denny, John 125
Dent, Bucky 79
Detroit News 49–50
Dewitt, Bill 17
DiMaggio, Joe 118
Dock Ellis in the Country of Baseball 52
Doubleday, Abner 107
Dowling, Jerry 49–50, 54–55, 79–80, 96, 103, 113, 130–131, 172–173
Downing, Al 67, 99
Driessen, Dan 7, 17, 20, 25, 34, 40, 42, 44, 51, 52, 56, 58, 63, 73, 80, 83, 86, 91, 93, 94, 99, 100, 102, 103, 109, 119, 122, 125, 127, 129, 130, 137, 138, 143–144, 145, 146, 158, 160, 164, 167, 169
Drucker, Malka 172
Duffy, Frank 9
Dumoulin, Dan 150, 151, 155
Dunn, Adam 5
Durso, Joseph 179, 180
Duvall, Adam 5
Dyer, Duffy 53
Dykstra, Lenny 178, 179, 180

Easterly, Jamie 43
Eastwick, Rawley 30, 32, 35, 36, 37, 44, 45, 56, 58, 67, 76, 84–85, 87, 88, 90, 96, 97, 122, 125, 173
Eckes, Chris 1
Elliott, Randy 58
Ellis, Dock 51–52, 101
Erardi, John 27, 41, 171, 174
Espinosa, Nino 63, 141
Evans, Darrel 65, 66, 101, 138, 140

Falcone, Pete 56, 121
Feeney, Chub 42, 57
Ferguson, Joe 71, 112
Fidrych, Mark 61–62, 118
Fielder, Cecil 4, 5
56: Joe DiMaggio and the Last Magic Number in Sports 186
Figueroa, Ed 7
Fingers, Rollie 32, 36, 109, 162, 165
Fisher, Ray 176
Fisk, Carlton 26
Flynn, Doug 37, 49, 54, 78, 84, 87, 88
Foli, Tim 58
Foote, Barry 146
Ford, Whitey 15
Forsch, Bob 50, 125
Forsch, Ken 34
Forster, Terry 60, 133
Fort Worth Star-Telegram 101
Fosse, Ray 4
Foster, George 1, 2, 3, 4, 5, 6–13, 18, 19, 22, 23, 24, 25, 28, 29, 31, 32, 34, 35, 36, 37, 38, 39, 40, 41, 42, 43, 44, 45, 46, 47, 49, 50, 51, 52, 54, 56, 58, 61, 62, 64, 66, 67, 70, 71, 74–75, 77, 78, 79–80, 81, 83, 84, 86, 88, 91, 92, 93, 94, 95–96, 98, 99, 100, 102, 103, 107, 108, 109, 111, 112, 113, 114, 115, 116, 118, 119, 120, 121–122, 123, 125–126, 127–128, 129–131, 132–133, 134, 135, 137, 138, 140, 141, 143, 144, 145, 146, 147, 148, 150, 152, 153–154, 155, 156–157, 158, 159, 160, 161, 162–163, 164, 165–166, 167, 169, 170, 171–187
Foxx, Jimmie 4, 171
Franks, Herman 40, 45, 93
Frazier, Joe 62, 63, 64, 74
Freisleben, Dave 32, 36, 108
Frisch, Frankie 58, 120
Fryman, Woody 18–19, 21, 23, 26, 30, 32, 42, 44, 45, 50, 51, 62, 65, 66, 76–77, 86, 87, 93, 99, 103, 109–110, 113

Index

Gaedel, Eddie 43
Gajus, Greg 183–184
Garber, Gene 88
Garland, Wayne 37–38
Garman, Mike 39
Garner, Phil 53
Garratt, Robert F. 65
Garrett, Wayne 84
Garvey, Steve 18, 38, 39, 97, 99, 100, 118, 155, 158, 166, 168
Gaston, Cito 110
Genovese, George 12
Geronimo, Cesar 8, 29, 30, 31, 34, 35, 37, 49, 52, 56, 61, 73, 80, 94, 98, 99, 125, 147, 151, 162, 182
Gilbreath, Rod 114
Glavine, Tom 43
Globe-Democrat 90
Gonzalez, Fernando 53
Gooden, Dwight 178–179
Gossage, Goose 52
Grant, Donald M. 79, 86–87, 91
Greenberg, Hank 4
Gregg, Eric 110
Griffey, Ken 10, 18, 19, 22, 25, 26, 29, 34, 37, 38, 44, 52, 54, 56, 67, 70, 71, 72, 73, 81, 83, 86, 94, 98, 100, 102, 110, 112, 114, 119, 132, 134, 138, 141, 145, 153, 156, 157, 160, 167, 177, 182
Griffey, Ken, Jr. 4
Grote, Jerry 62
Gullett, Don 14–16, 19, 22, 28, 35, 44, 96, 137, 173

Halicki, Ed 152
Hall, Donald 52
Hanna, Preston 168–169
Hannig, Scott 105–106
Hardin, Marc 47
Harmon, Terry 50
Harrelson, Bud 62, 143
Harrelson, Ken 181
Harridge, Will 43
Harris, Greg 177
Harvey, Doug 147
Hebner, Richie 88
Heep, Danny 178, 179
Helms, Tommy 53
Henderson, Joe 23, 101, 103, 113
Henderson, Steve 87, 88
Hendrick, George 39
Hendrickson, Craig 89
Herman, Jack 90
Hernandez, Keith 124, 125, 178, 179, 185
Hernandez, Willie 123, 129
Herndon, Larry 58
Hertzel, Bob 19, 20, 21, 25, 43, 67, 77, 79, 81, 84, 85, 86–87, 94, 95, 96, 99, 100, 107, 109, 113–114, 119, 120, 122, 124, 129, 133–134, 144, 148, 150, 153, 155, 157, 160, 162, 164, 165, 167
Herzog, Whitey 8
Hill, Marc 58

Hinds, Bill 58
Hodges, Ron 62
Hoerner, Joe 95, 101, 122, 132
Holdsworth, Fred 146–147
Home Team: The Turbulent History of the San Francisco Giants 65
Hooten, Burt 171
Hornsby, Rogers 2, 174
Hough, Charlie 171
Householder, Paul 1, 2
Howard, Wilbur 111, 116
Howe, Art 78
Howsam, Bob 12, 13, 16, 17, 18, 25, 31, 81, 85
Hoyt, Waite 59
Hrabosky, Al 54, 125–126
Hume, Tom 63, 65–66, 71, 77–78, 88, 93, 95, 150, 154–155, 168
Hunter, Jimmy 159
Hunter, Ryan 101
Hutch: Baseball's Fred Hutchinson and a Legacy of Courage 105
Hutchinson, Fred 59

Irving, Julius 80
Ivie, Mike 32, 108

Jackson, Grant 52, 132
Jackson, Reggie 22, 40, 47, 75, 78, 92, 113, 171
Jarvis, Pat 106
Jenkins, Fergie 159
John, Tommy 67, 97–98, 134, 154, 156, 167, 171
Johnson, Cliff 34
Johnson, Davey 85, 86, 140, 178, 179–180, 181
Johnson, Deron 17
Johnson, Howard 178, 185
Johnstone, Jay 85, 146
Jones, Odell 132
Jones, Rabdy 139, 162
Judge, Aaron 5

Kaplan, Jim 2
Kapstein, Jerry 16, 18, 85
Katt, Jim 150, 159
Katz, Reuven 22, 26
Kennedy, Kostya 186
Kern, Jim 177
Kessinger, Don 57
Kibler, john 128
Kiner, Ralph 6, 157
King, Hal 105–107, 144
Kingman, Dave 23, 29, 64, 75, 79, 108, 183
Kison, Bruce 82, 87
Kline, Ron 115
Kluszewski, Ted 12, 32, 51, 55, 73, 133–134, 140–141, 148, 157, 160–161
Knight, Ray 20, 22, 24, 25, 54, 108, 123, 138
Konieczny, Doug 34
Koosman, Jerry 62, 63, 80, 92, 141, 143
Koufax, Sandy 15, 80
Kranepool, Ed 62

Krukow, Mike 123
Kuhn, Bowie 42

L. A. Times 167
Lang, Jack 90, 172
Lansford, Carney 8
LaRoche, Dave 118
Lasorda, Tommy 20, 32, 39, 55, 67, 72, 88, 117, 156, 167–168
Lavelle, Gary 138, 152
Lawson, Earl 165
LeMaster, Johnnie 58
Lemongello, Mark 116, 150–151
Leon, Max 57
Leonard, Dave 145
Lerch, Barry 146
Lewis, Allen 119–120
Linville, Bud 106
Lockwood, Skip 24, 63, 143
Lonborg, Jim 150
Long Beach Independent 90
Lopes, Dave 38, 88, 90, 97, 99, 100, 136, 137, 158, 167–168
Lucas, Maurice 80
Lucchesi, Frank 101
Lum, Mike 49, 114, 122, 137, 159
Luzinski, Greg 85, 86, 88, 91, 95, 98, 111, 118, 127, 164, 170, 171, 174
Lyle, Sparky 118
Lynn, Fred 118
Lyons, Ruth 59

Maddox, Garry 85, 86
Maddux, Greg 43
Madlock, Bill 29, 58, 59, 60, 65
Mahler, Mickey 169
Major League Baseball's Year of the Batter 183
Mann, David 59
Mantle, Mickey 4, 105, 152, 157, 167
Marichal, Juan 123
Maris, Roger 4, 148, 167
Martin, Billy 8, 22, 40, 92, 112–118
Martin, Fred 48
Martin, Jerry 87, 145
Mason, Jim 8
Mathews, Judge William S. 59
Matlack, Jon 62, 88, 144
May, Carlos 78
Mays, Willie 2, 8, 9, 60, 118, 159, 182
Mazilli, Lee 140, 179
McBride, Bake 150
McCarver, Tim 85, 86
McCormick, Frank 169
McCovey, Willie 60, 65, 101, 152, 153, 159–160
McCoy, Hal 135, 186
McDonald, Joe 87
McEnaney, Will 7, 8, 9, 11, 16, 19, 28
McGraw, Tug 95, 145, 150
McGwire, Mark 4, 5
McKechnie, Bill 143
McNamara, John 174–175

McRae, Hal 145
Medwick, Joe 2, 174
Messersmith, Andy 43, 71
Metzger, Butch 36, 125
Metzger, Roger 34, 111
Milan, Felix 62, 80, 81
Miller, Jeff 58
Miller, Stu 65
Millwood, Kevin 43
Milner, John 62
Minton, Greg 159
Mitchell, Kevin 179, 180
Mitterwald, George 45, 93, 128
Mize, Johnny 2
Moffit, Randy 138, 153
Monday, Rick 29, 39, 97, 99, 155, 158, 160
Money, Don 118
Montanez, Willie 114
Morales, Jerry 128
Moran, Jack 184
Morgan, Joe 2, 3, 7, 11, 13, 16, 18, 19, 22, 25, 29, 32, 33, 36, 38, 42, 44, 47, 51, 52, 53, 54, 56, 57, 62, 63, 65, 67, 69, 70, 71, 72, 73, 81, 86, 87, 91, 96, 97, 98, 99, 100, 101, 102, 103, 106, 110, 112, 113, 116, 118, 120, 123, 125, 127, 128–129, 133, 136, 137, 138, 143, 144, 147, 148, 151, 153, 156, 159–160, 161, 162, 169, 174, 175, 182
Morgana 170
Moskau, Paul 23, 94, 100, 102, 108, 109, 112, 124, 134, 141, 146, 150, 155, 160, 165
Mumphrey, Jerry 125
Munson, Thurman 11, 21, 22, 79, 118
Murcer, Bobby 42, 128
Murphy, Dale 168
Murray, Dale 19, 26, 32, 33, 36, 37, 54, 57, 63, 73, 76, 77, 83, 84, 94, 102, 103, 108, 110, 111, 116, 123, 124, 128, 132, 138, 139, 155, 156, 162
Murtaugh, Danny 52
Myers, Hap 169

Neagle, Denny 43
Nettles, Graig 11
New York Times 117, 177–178, 180–181
Newcomer, Frank 160
Newhan, Ross 167
Niekro, Joe 34, 116
Niekro, Phil 43, 72, 73, 109, 113, 164, 166–167
Nixon, Russ 55
Nolan, Gary 9, 22, 23, 38, 55, 56, 59, 60, 62, 78, 83, 88, 89, 92, 102, 173
Norman, Dan 88
Norman, Fred 23, 32, 39, 44, 51, 53, 58, 61, 70, 77, 83, 87–88, 93, 94, 100, 107, 110, 113, 119, 122, 125, 131, 132, 136, 138, 141, 144, 150, 154, 156, 162, 169, 173
NY Daily News 90
NY Sports Day 185

Oester, Ron 20
Office, Rowland 110, 114
Oh, Sadaharu 148, 174

O'Keefe, Dick 89
Oliver, Al 52, 87, 133
Ontiveros, Steve 42
Opening Day: Celebrating Cincinnati's Baseball Holiday 27
Ott, Mel 2
Owchinko, Bob 108, 160
Ozark, Danny 86
Ozymandias 1

Palmer, Jim 118
Pappas, Milt 16
Parker, Dave 52, 53, 111, 118, 119, 130, 131, 163, 166, 171
Parrish, Lance 181
Parrish, Larry 84
Patterson, Red 152
Pence, Gene 115
Perez, Eduardo 19
Perez, Pituka 19
Perez, Tony 3, 7, 16, 17, 18, 19, 20, 28, 35, 40, 43, 44, 51, 59, 81–84, 106, 112, 129, 133, 143–144, 147, 155, 169, 182
Perez, Victor 19
Perry, Gaylord 159
Phillips, Mike 64
Plummer, Bill 24, 30, 58, 103, 105, 106, 132, 159
Pocoroba, Biff 50
Post, Wally 133
Powell, Boog 99
Pryor, Paul 60, 61
Purdy, Mark 35–36
Pyka, Garry 89

Quick, Jim 153

Ramsay, Jack 80
Rapp, Vern 12, 54, 56, 90
Rasmussen, Eric 121, 124
Rau, Doug 154, 158, 168
Rawley, Shane 63
Redleg Journal 171, 174
RedsVue 184
Reed, Ron 95
Reeves, Jim 101
Renko, Steve 123, 127
Reuschel, Paul 127
Reuschel, Rick 48, 93, 122, 127
Revering, Dave 23, 150
Rhoden, Rick 70, 90, 136, 155
Rhodes, Greg 16, 17, 171, 174
Rhodes, James 59
Riccelli, Frank 41
Rice, Jim 92, 166
Richard, J.R. 34, 78, 113, 116, 155
Rivers, Mickey 10, 11
Roberts, Dave 37, 128
Robinson, Bill 132, 133
Robinson, Brooks 143
Robinson, Frank 16–17, 93, 164
Rodriguez, Alex 4

Rogers, Steve 48, 91, 144
Rooker, Jim 120
Rose, David 25
Rose, Karolyn 19
Rose, Pete 2, 3, 4, 10, 11, 16, 18, 19, 20, 22, 24, 25, 26, 29, 32–33, 34, 35–36, 38, 40, 42, 43, 44, 47, 48, 49, 51, 52, 53, 54, 55, 56, 59, 63, 64, 67, 70, 71, 77, 80, 81, 83, 84, 86, 87, 89, 98, 100, 101, 102, 106, 108, 110, 111, 120–121, 122, 124, 125, 130, 133, 135, 136–137, 139, 144, 147, 150, 151, 153, 156, 159, 162–163, 164, 165, 166, 169, 174, 177, 182, 186
Rose, Pete, Jr. 19, 166
Roush, Edd 11
Royster, Jerry 72
Ruehlmann, Eugene P. 59
Ruess, Jerry 61, 65, 119
Ruhle, Vern 61
Russell, Bill 38, 40, 97, 99, 137, 167
Ruth, Babe 2, 4, 59, 83, 88, 105, 148, 157, 167, 171, 174
Ruthven, Dick 43, 110, 115
Ryan, Connie 101
Ryan, Nolan 117–118, 166
Ryder, Brian 177

Sadek, Mike 58, 102, 103
Sambito, Joe 116, 151
Sanchez, Luis 77
Sarmiento, Manny 23, 119, 123, 168
Scherger, George 42, 55
Schmidt, Mike 2, 23, 29, 75, 85, 86, 88, 91, 93, 95, 96, 107, 146, 157
Schultz, Buddy 56
Scott, Tony 50, 56, 57, 125
Seaver, Tom 21, 24, 62, 77, 79, 80, 86, 88, 89, 90, 91–92, 97, 98, 102, 109, 112, 114, 115, 117, 118, 120, 124, 133, 137, 139, 141–143, 145, 147–148, 150, 154, 158, 160, 164, 166
Shelley, Percy Bysshe 1
Sheppard, Larry 20, 55, 65, 88
Shirley, Bob 33, 107, 165
Sikes, Bob 185
Simmons, Ted 54
Sinatra, Barbara 134
Sinatra, Frank 134
Sizemore, Ted 87, 95
Smith, Reggie 38, 39, 71, 78, 91, 93, 97, 137, 153, 155, 166, 167, 171
Smoltz, John 43
Solomon, Eddie 43
Sosa, Elias 67, 171
Sosa, Sammy 5
Soto, Mario 119, 122–123, 128, 134, 140, 152, 155
Spahn, Warren 15
Sport 31
The Sporting News 23
Sports Illustrated 2
Sports Psyching 35–36
Stanhouse, Dan 93, 147
Stanky, Eddie 101

Stanton, Giancarlo 5
Stargell, Willie 25, 47, 52, 60, 140
Steinbrenner, George 105
Stengel, Casey 65
Stennett, Rennie 53
Stobbs, Chuck 152
Stoneham, Horace 64
Strawberry, Darryl 178, 179, 180
Strom, Brent 32, 36
Sudol, Ed 98
Summers, Champ 22, 26, 34, 89, 107, 113, 132
Sutter, Bruce 40, 48, 118, 127
Sutton, Don 32, 39, 67, 106, 119, 141, 168
Swan, Craig 62

Taft, Charles P. 59
Tanana, Frank 117–118
Tanner, Chuck 60
Tata, Terry 58
Taveras, Frank 53, 119, 132
Templeton, Gary 49, 50, 56
Tenace, Gene 30, 37, 107, 162
Theiss, Duane 167
Thomas, Derrel 65, 101
Thomasson, Gary 32, 65, 101
Thome, Jim 4
Thompson, Jason 44
Tidrow, Dick 7
Todd, Jackson 64
Tolan, Bobby 106, 133
Toliver, Fred 177
Tomlin, Dave 33
Torborg, Jeff 93
Torre, Joe 62, 74, 79
Torres, Angel 63, 150, 155
Travers, Bill 37
Trevino, Alex 177
Trillo, Manny 42, 128
Tuite, Jim 177–178
Turner, Jerry 36, 37
Turner, Ted 42, 57, 101
Tutko, Thomas 35–36
Twitchell, Wayne 86, 93, 144, 147
Tyson, Mike 49, 54, 125

The Ultimate Mets Database 185
Underwood, Tom 24, 25, 87
Unser, Del 48
Urrea, John 49

Valentine, Ellis 83, 93
Veeck, Bill 43
Velez, Otto 8, 9, 10
Verrell, Gordon 90
Votto, Joey 5

Wagner, Dick 16, 22, 25, 26, 30, 85, 89
Wagner, Honus 174
Walker, Dan 84
Wall, Stan 70
Wallace, Joe 45
Wallis, Joe 123
Walsh, Joseph P. 59
Walton, Bill 80
Warthen, Dan 83
The Washington Post 28
Watson, Bob 34, 76, 113, 116, 155
Wegman, Bill 181
Werner, Don 23, 150, 160, 170
Weyer, Lee 72, 135
White, Roy 7, 11
Whitfield, Terry 59, 60, 65
Williams, Art 76, 116
Williams, the Rev. Austin 172
Wilson, Hack 2, 120, 144, 148, 163, 165, 169, 171, 183
Wilson, Mookie 179, 180
Windsor Herald 49
Winfield, Dave 37, 162, 177, 184

Yastrzemski, Carl 25, 118
Yeager, Steve 38, 156
Young, Dick 91
Youngblood, Joel 49

Zachry, Pat 23, 34, 38, 44, 52, 57, 67, 75, 88, 90, 92, 173
Zardetto, Ray 183
Zeber, George 79
Zisk, Richie 118